Death and Money in the Afternoon

Adrian Shubert

DEATH AND MONEY IN THE AFTERNOON

A History
of the Spanish Bullfight

New York   Oxford   Oxford University Press   1999

Oxford University Press

Oxford   New York
Athens   Auckland   Bangkok   Bogotá   Buenos Aires   Calcutta
Cape Town   Chennai   Dar es Salaam   Delhi   Florence   Hong Kong   Istanbul
Karachi   Kuala Lumpur   Madrid   Melbourne   Mexico City   Mumbai
Nairobi   Paris   São Paulo   Singapore   Taipei   Tokyo   Toronto   Warsaw

and associated companies in
Berlin   Ibadan

Published by Oxford University Press, Inc.
198 Madison Avenue, New York, NY 10016

Library of Congress Cataloging-in-Publication Data
Shubert, Adrian, 1953–
Death and money in the afternoon : a history of the Spanish bullfight /
Adrian Shubert
p.   cm.
Includes bibliographical references and index.
ISBN 0–19–509524–3
1. Bullfights—Social aspects—Spain—History—18th century.
2. Bullfights—Social aspects—Spain—History—19th century.
I. Title.
GV1108.5.S58   1999
791.8'2'0946—DC21   98–28292

1 3 5 7 9 8 6 4 2
Printed in the United States of America
on acid-free paper.

To Bill Callahan,
for getting me started

CONTENTS

Research and writing require money and time. A three-year research grant from the Social Science and Humanities Research Council of Canada and two smaller grants from York University permitted me to carry out the research for this book. A fellowship from the John Simon Guggenheim Memorial Foundation allowed me the luxury of spending the 1997–1998 academic year writing it.

I benefited from the work of three excellent research assistants: Milena Kras in Toronto, Teresa Arboledas Márquez in Granada, and Gregorio "Goyo" de la Fuente in Madrid. I am also indebted to the staffs of a number of archives and libraries: in Madrid, the Biblioteca Nacional, the Hemeroteca Municipal, the Archivo Municipal de la Villa, the Archivo Histórico Nacional, the Archivo Histórico de Protocolos, and the Archivo del Palacio Real; in Granada the Archivo de la Cancillería Real; in Sevilla the Real Maestranza, and especially its Hermano Mayor, who granted access to its superb archive; and Manuel Ravina Martín at the Archivo Histórico Provincial in Cádiz. I want to make special mention of Berta Bravo and her exceptionally efficient and attentive staff at the Centro de Archivos de la Comunidad de Madrid.

Many colleagues in the field of Spanish history provided me with references to sources on bullfighting; so, too, did colleagues in French, British, United States, Canadian, and Chinese history. Their contributions made this book richer, and I thank them all. José Alvarez Junco, Renato Barahona, William J. Callahan, Jesús Cruz, Chris Cunningham, Judy Hellman, Richard Hoffmann, Virginia Hunter, Richard Kagan, Kathryn McPherson, Enrique Moradiellos, Viv Nelles, Adele Perry, Pamela Radcliff, David Ringrose, and Nick Rogers all read and commented on parts of this book at various stages in its evolution. Finally, Antonio Cazorla Sánchez read the entire manuscript and was a constant source of helpful criticism and important ideas.

ACKNOWLEDGMENTS

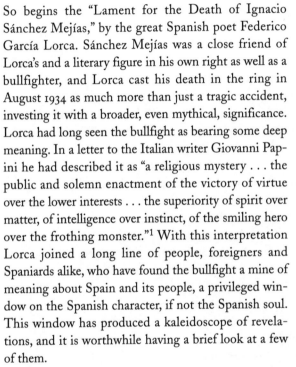

Five in the afternoon,
It was five, sharp, in the afternoon.
Five in the afternoon,
It was five, sharp, in the afternoon.
afternoon.

So begins the "Lament for the Death of Ignacio Sánchez Mejías," by the great Spanish poet Federico García Lorca. Sánchez Mejías was a close friend of Lorca's and a literary figure in his own right as well as a bullfighter, and Lorca cast his death in the ring in August 1934 as much more than just a tragic accident, investing it with a broader, even mythical, significance. Lorca had long seen the bullfight as bearing some deep meaning. In a letter to the Italian writer Giovanni Papini he had described it as "a religious mystery . . . the public and solemn enactment of the victory of virtue over the lower interests . . . the superiority of spirit over matter, of intelligence over instinct, of the smiling hero over the frothing monster."[1] With this interpretation Lorca joined a long line of people, foreigners and Spaniards alike, who have found the bullfight a mine of meaning about Spain and its people, a privileged window on the Spanish character, if not the Spanish soul. This window has produced a kaleidoscope of revelations, and it is worthwhile having a brief look at a few of them.

From the nineteenth century on, the bullfight was taken up by Spanish intellectuals as part of what they saw as the "problem" of their country. César Graña summarized the process in this way: "Spain as a 'problem' is a wounded and traumatized nation speaking through cries and alarms, thirsting for redeeming visions. . . . The critical 'higher spirits' faced with a society in disintegration, the victim of a great historic shipwreck, seek the rediscovery or resurrection of Spanish nationality, looking to their roots or to the

stars for broad guidelines to the foundations of the Spanish character, identity or destiny."[2] Thus Joaquín Costa sought to regenerate Spain, to make it
European, which meant, among many other things, getting rid of the bullfight: "We want to breathe the air of Europe, so that Spain ceases to be
African and becomes European. . . . The bullfights are a great evil that harm
us more than many believe . . . from the perversion of public feeling to lowering us in the eyes of foreigners, there is a dismal series of comparisons that
degrade us."[3]

Many of the eclectic group of writers known as the Generation of 1898
used the *corrida*[4] as evidence for their view of the country and its condition.
The thread that connected the diverse range of ideas of the members of the
Generation was their reflection on the state of Spain following the so-called
Disaster of 1898: Spain's humiliating defeat at the hands of the United States
in the Spanish-American War. For some, the defeat was the result of the
failure to modernize sufficiently; for others it came from having abandoned
tradition in order to modernize. The bullfight could be invoked on either
count, and on balance these writers were "open enemies" of the bullfight.[5]
The poet Antonio Machado saw the corrida as a "sacrifice . . . to an unknown
god" that constituted a part of "Spanishness." And just because it was Spanish, it should not necessarily be "spat upon," since "this type of criticism of
that which is ours will not only prevent us from knowing it but will lead us to
detest ourselves."[6]

Yet others showed precisely this disdain for indigenous institutions. For
Ramiro de Maeztu it was part of the frivolity that had led to the Disaster:
"What to blame! Our idleness, our laziness . . . the bullfight, the national
chick pea, the ground we tread and the water we drink." Pío Baroja saw it as
cowardly and brutal, and Azorín attacked it as a frivolity that perverted the
ideal of valor and belonged to the "España de pandereta," not to the "real"
Spain.[7] Finally, the great philosopher Miguel de Unamuno criticized the
corrida, not for its cruelty but because it distracted Spaniards from more
serious matters: "The bullfight does not make our people braver or more
savage, but it does make them more stupid. . . . All those people who spend
half their lives talking about bulls and bullfighters are people who could not
be bothered to talk about anything else. Everything is reduced to a spectacle
. . . there is a horror of seriousness."[8] (Laments such as this were not limited
to Spain. The great American art historian Charles Eliot Norton
denounced university sports in almost identical terms: "The evils in the

field of sport are all the more dangerous because of the profit which the newspaper press finds in fostering the unhealthy popular excitement concerning these public games. The excessive space devoted to highly colored and extravagant reports of them, totally out of proportion to their real importance, is one of the marked indications of the prevalence of conditions unfavorable to civilization.")[9]

Eugenio Noel (1885–1936) was the most determined and best-known crusader against the corrida in the early twentieth century. He picked up many of the themes of the Generation of 1898, especially that of national decadence. For Noel, the bullfight was the basic cause of Spain's problems, and his list was a long one:

> From the bullrings we get the following characteristics of our race: the majority of crimes committed with a knife . . . pornography without voluptuousness, art nor conscience; political corruption; all, absolutely all, aspects of bossism and godfatherism; the complete lack of respect for a pure idea . . . the cruelty of our feelings; the desire to make war; our ridiculous Don Juanism . . . and in sum, whatever has to do with enthusiasm, grace, arrogance, sumptuousness, everything, everything is made negative, corrupted, bastardized, deteriorated, because of those emanations that come from the bullrings to the city and from here to the countryside.[10]

The most sweeping assessment came from the great Spanish philosopher José Ortega y Gasset. In his *Interpretation of Universal History*, published in 1948, Ortega declared that "not only is the bullfight an important reality in the history of Spain since 1740 . . . but—and I say this in the most express and formal manner—one cannot write the history of Spain from 1650 to our own time without keeping the bullfight clearly in mind." The bullfight was the clearest symptom of what Ortega saw as the prime pathology of Spanish history from the eighteenth century on: "For the first time Spain sealed itself off hermetically from the rest of the world, even from its own hispanic world. I call this the tibetanization of Spain."[11]

Ortega's contention that the bullfight embodied Spain's rejection of the modern world, and especially its rejection of the Enlightenment, has remained alive and influential. Novelist and historian Carmen Martín Gaite made this claim in her much cited study of the eighteenth century, and American literary critic Timothy Mitchell has echoed it in his works on the bullfight: It was "no trivial pastime, but the very mirror of Spain's social and historical traumas in the modern period," and "Spain was to remain, deep down, a very anti-modern country; and the rise of bullfighting on foot gave a new lease on life to a thoroughly primitive cosmovision."[12]

Anthropologists and psychologists have been prolific in uncovering the meaning of the corrida. Garry Marvin sees it as "a confrontation between nature and culture, which is worked out in a controlled environment in a stylized and regulated way."[13] Others find in the bullfight the embodiment of Spanish gender relations: "a comprehensive statement about honour, both male and female . . . in which the treatment of the bull is similar to the treatment of women under the Honour Code;"[14] or about relations between sons and their parents: "the story of a battle between a father and a son . . . after a series of encounters [the son] dominates and defeats the father"; [15] or "the triumph of the mothers: a symbolic reenactment of the fate of Spanish men who flee the control of their mothers for a temporary freedom that is brought to an end by marriage. The bull is the young man whose dream of freedom is destroyed by the bullfighter, who represents Woman, acting as the agent of the Community, which must impose order on disorder";[16] or the symbolic depiction of "the power of the father, the subtle demands of the mother, and the fear of the child" in which the child-matador destroys authority by killing the bull.[17] Still others see the bullfight as a key to Spanish sexuality: a sacrifice in which the killing of the bull is a symbolic rape and "a symbolic violation of the menstrual taboo"[18] or a seduction in which "the audience may then be considered as the witness to the primal scene, and their excitement can be viewed as corresponding to the excitement children have when witnessing parental sexual intercourse."[19] In a study commissioned by the European Parliament in 1992, Julian Pitt-Rivers claimed that the bullfight is "inherent in the Spanish mentality."[20]

The bullfight has also provided less scholarly observers with the "key" to understanding Spain and the Spaniards. A few examples, all from Americans. In the 1870s, in the midst of the Cuban revolt against Spanish rule, writer Kate Field made a ten-day visit to Spain, which was authority enough for her to write: "If Spaniards could only agree as cordially about a government as they do about a bullfight, the world would gaze upon such a happy family as never yet roared in a menagerie. Alas! unanimity among Spaniards means butchery—either horses or bulls, Cuban students or Cuban patriots.

The taste of the Inquisition is still in their mouths."[21] (Little surprise, then, that this book, which was first published in 1875, was reissued in 1898, the year that the United States declared war on Spain over Cuba.) In 1896, Mary F. Lovell, superintendent of the Department of Mercy of the Women's Christian Temperance Union, organized a petition to the pope to protest against the Church's failure to oppose bullfighting. For Lovell and other equally righteous American women, Spain's war against Cuban independence was a direct product of the corrida: "If they had been trained in their youth to be gentle and merciful instead of being amused by witnessing the torture of bulls," they would not be committing "horrors" in Cuba.[22] Four years later Katherine L. Bates described the bullfight as being "in the air, in the soil, in the blood; a national institution, *a hereditary rage*."[23] For social reformer Jane Addams the bullfight proved an epiphany that pushed her toward founding Hull House:

> in the evening the *natural and inevitable* reaction came, and in deep chagrin I felt myself tried and condemned, not only for this disgusting experience, but by the entire moral situation which it revealed. . . . Nothing less than the moral reaction following the experience at a bullfight had been able to reveal to me that so far from following in the wake of a chariot of philanthropic fire, I had been tied to the tail of the veriest ox-cart of self-seeking. I had made up my mind that next day, whatever happened, I would begin to carry out the plan.[24]

Finally, Richard Wright, the African American novelist, was less judgmental but no less convinced that the popularity of bullfighting meant that Spaniards were fundamentally different from Americans, among whom, incidentally, he drew no distinctions between black and white. "As an American, a man from a world that valued and eulogized intelligence, responsibility, industrial processes, social-mindedness, property, etc., it was indeed odd to hear personal bravery extolled so highly. But Spain was another world with other values."[25]

The search for meaning has had the result of obscuring the bullfight's more mundane reality—and its true importance. The corrida is not the timeless marker of some essential and unchanging Spanishness but a social institution created by human beings. Like the society in which it dwells, the bullfight has a history: As time has passed, both have changed, as has their relation to each other.

People have been doing things with bulls in public for many centuries and in many places. Few such activities remain today, at least in Europe and the Americas, and of those that do, the bullfight is undoubtedly the best-known. The contemporary corrida has a relatively brief history, dating only from the early part of the eighteenth century, but the search for its distant origins has been a contentious one.

In the eighteenth and nineteenth centuries, writers debated whether bullfighting had evolved from Roman entertainments or was an indigenous product, created by the Muslims. The "Arab thesis" was first proposed by Nicolás Fernández de Moratín in his *Carta histórica sobre el origen y progreso de la fiesta de toros en España*, published in 1777. It was taken up by Goya and included in many nineteenth-century "histories" of the bullfight: Santiago López Pelegrín's *Filosofía del toreo* (1842), F. G. Bedoya's *Historia del toreo* (1850), and Sicilia de Arenzana's *Las corridas de toros* (1873). The "Roman thesis" was older. It had been used in the sixteenth and seventeenth centuries by opponents of the bullfight, and echoed the arguments of early Christian authors that it was pagan and heretical. Less popular than the "Arab thesis," it still had its proponents in the nineteenth century. [26] And even in the mid-twentieth: In his classic *Homo Ludens*, the great Dutch historian Johan Huizinga wrote that the "bullfight in Spain is a direct continuation of the Roman *ludi* . . . which bears a family resemblance to the gladiatorial combats of ancient times."[27]

The two theories shared an absolute absence of evidence, and in the twentieth century they gave way to other approaches that attributed to the bullfight a prehistoric origin. The new departure came from the count of Navas, who saw the bullfight as an indigenous Iberian activity deriving from the hunting of wild bulls. This theory became very popular in the early twentieth century, although more among historians of the bullfight than among archaeologists. An exhibition held in Madrid in 1918, *El Arte en la Tauromaquia*, concluded that the bullfight originated in "the sacrifices that people offered to their divinities."[28] There were also proponents, mostly French, for the bullfight as part of the cult of Mithras, and Picasso adopted the idea in the 1940s. In the 1930s, influenced by Arthur Evans's work on Crete, an alternative theory emerged that connected the corrida to Minoan bull events. Then, in the 1950s, E. Casas Gaspar proposed that the bullfight was but the Spanish version of a widely practiced agrarian rite.[29]

Whatever its remote origins, by the Middle Ages fighting bulls was an established activity in both elite and popular culture. The elite version, akin to the joust, is much the better known: Mounted nobles fought bulls using long lances. One of the earliest references to such activities comes from the *Poem of the Cid*, when the hero fought a bull at the marriage of the king's daughter around 1040. There are two references to bullfights at royal weddings in the twelfth century, the beginning of a tradition that would last until the twentieth.[30] Most theories of the origins of the the modern bullfight have it derive from this aristocratic tradition. The arrival of the Bourbon dynasty at the beginning of the eighteenth century and the new king's lack of interest made the nobles lose interest, leaving the field open to plebeians who fought on foot. In this vein, one history of the bullfight written at the end of the nineteenth century stated that Philip V communicated his "aversion" to the corrida to his nobles, and "what had earlier been a festival of the nobility became a spectacle accessible to and exploitable by everyone."[31]

By this time the bullfight had been taken up by other elements of the elite. The celebration of religious events, such as the canonization of saints, frequently included bullfights. The rejoicing for the canonization of Saint Theresa in 1622 included thirty corridas in Madrid alone. And the inauguration of a chapel to Saint Tecla in the cathedral of Burgos in 1736 was also accompanied by a bullfight. (That the papacy had frequently expressed its strong opposition to the bullfight clearly had little impact in Spain.)[32]

Bullfights were also integral parts of celebrations at the University of Salamanca. The canonization of Saints Luis Gonzaga and Estanislao Koska was the occasion for students from Navarre to organize a bullfight that was held in the main square of the city. The students dressed up for the occasion, as Don Quijote, Sancho Panza, Dulcinea, as astrologers, fools, and many as women. Eight student bullfighters performed, of whom three were dressed as women. At the end, one young bull was set loose for the spectators to fight. As Padre Isla put it in his description of the occasion, "The bullock was relaxed into the arm of the crowd."[33] (His selection of words was very deliberate: When the Inquisition condemned someone to death, it "relaxed" the victim into the "secular arm" so that the state, not the Church, would be responsible for the execution.)

The taking of a doctorate at the university was also occasion for elaborate festivities, a bullfight among them.

> Members of the bullfight committee betook themselves in coach to the home of the *corregidor* to beseech his authorization for the fight; if they obtained it they presented him with half an *arroba* (about twelve and a half pounds) of bonbons contained in a silver dish covered with silk. Coins and small gifts were tossed to the crowds from the windows of the university library. On the eve of the examination a solemn procession was organized in which all the members of the university rode on horseback. This was followed by a light repast . . . and supper at the home of the future doctor. The bullfight took place on the day of the examination.[34]

When it was over, the new doctor put his symbol on the outer wall of his college, using the dead bull's blood. This tradition remains alive in attenuated form, as bull's blood has given way to red paint.

But bull events were never the monopoly of the elite. For at least as long as the nobility used bulls to help celebrate royal weddings, ordinary Spaniards had incorporated bulls into a number of rituals of their own. Many of these were also related to marriage, with the idea that the bull's believed sexual potency could be transferred to the newlyweds. One such ritual is described in one of the *Cántigas de Santa María*, written by the thirteenth-century king of Castile, Alfonso X, the Wise. A similar ritual was still being practiced in parts of Extremadura in the late nineteenth century: Two days before the wedding, the groom and his friends would take a bull from the slaughterhouse and, its horns tied with a rope, run it through the town taunting it with their jackets until they got to the bride's house, where the groom placed a pair of darts, decorated by his fiancée, in the bull's back.[35]

It is in these popular rituals that a number of writers have located the origins of the bullfight. Alvarez de Miranda has been the most influential. For him, "the rural custom of the nuptial bullfight is not a belated and countrified imitation of the modern bullfight but, quite the contrary, it is an older predecessor . . . The modern bullfight is a deformed, secularized and ludic prolongation of the popular ritual of the nuptial bull."[36] En route, it passed through the hands of the nobility, which added the element of death, changing the bullfight from "rite to struggle."[37] By the time the corrida became a popular entertainment, it had lost its ritual charge: Born from a belief in the "sexual magic of the bull," it—like Greek tragedy—made the transit from "religious rite to a game."[38]

More recently, Araceli Guillaume-Alonso has argued that "bullfighting on foot coexisted with official bullfighting on horseback from long before the eighteenth century."[39] Not only did "plebeians" or "lackeys" have a role in the aristocratic bullfight, but in northern Spain professionals who fought on foot existed by the seventeenth century. This northern corrida, which was centered in Pamplona, did not include the killing of the bull but focused on "taunting or playing" with it. Killing was introduced "as the climax of the spectacle" during the later seventeenth century, imported from Madrid with its "court atmosphere."[40] Rather than an offshoot of the aristocratic spectacle, the modern bullfight was the product of two long-standing, parallel developments with different geographical centers: "Tauromachy evolved and developed simultaneously but with differing characteristics. [Different] cities contributed very different elements to the future spectacle: professionalism and, certainly, a series of moves that had been used since time immemorial from one; the supreme act [of death] from the other . . . although it would not be until the eighteenth century that Seville exported the fruit of its experience to other parts of the country."[41]

The modern bullfight emerged from the confluence of elite and popular cultures. Its precise beginnings are unclear, but it developed very quickly in the first half of the eighteenth century. Francisco Romero is frequently cited as the founder figure. Born in the southern town of Ronda around 1700, he was a shoemaker by trade. He first became involved in bullfighting assisting a nobleman who fought on horseback. At some point he began to give exhibitions of fighting bulls on foot that included the technique of killing the bull from in front with a single sword thrust. By 1726 Romero had become famous, and bullfighting was on the way to becoming a commercialized entertainment. By 1749 Madrid had a bullring, and five years later King Ferdinand VI gave it to the city's hospitals as a source of revenues. In the southern cities of Ronda and Seville, the bullfight was promoted by the Maestranzas de Caballería, aristocratic organizations devoted to horsemanship. By midcentury the corrida was drawing large paying crowds, and leading bullfighters were famous—and very well paid. The bullfight had arrived as a commercialized spectator spectacle.

The bullfight changed with time, as did Spain. And so did their relationship to each other, which frequently made the corrida the cause of controversy. Let us return to the "Lament for the Death of Ignacio Sánchez Mejías" for one example. Lorca's poem draws much of its power from the repetition of the phrase "at five in the afternoon," which appears twenty-eight times in the fifty-two lines of the first section. Yet the resonance of the words does not derive from repetition alone, for to a Spaniard—or to anyone familiar with Spain—the words have a particular meaning: They denote the time at which the bullfight begins. In Lorca's time perhaps, but not always. The "five in the afternoon" that so many people recognize is neither inevitable nor natural; the time at which the bullfight would start, like the days on which it would be held, has been the topic of debate and contention among various groups and institutions, each with its own quite quotidian agenda.

The basic problem has been the conflict between bullfights and work, for in the Spanish organization of daily time five in the afternoon is just after the resumption of work following the siesta. The conflict goes back to the mid-eighteenth century, at least, and arose because of the popularity of the corrida among the laboring classes, especially the artisans. The enlightened government minister Count Pedro de Campomanes recognized that the "innocent recreations" of the people were "an essential part of police and good government," but the custom of holding them during working hours was harming the economy.[42] Campomanes had little success in changing this, but in 1821 a royal decree did limit Monday bullfights to the afternoon, instead of the habitual morning and afternoon. The custom in the eighteenth century was to fight ten bulls in the morning and ten more in the afternoon. The more streamlined event featured eight bulls, but over the second half of the nineteenth century this was further reduced to the six that constitute the corrida today.

In 1846, the weekly *Semanario Pintoresco Español* denounced the disruption of the workweek:

> Is it not necessary to avoid the losses to labor, industry, and commerce by this harmful custom of allowing bullfights on work days? They may be a popular diversion . . . but would it not be useful for the authorities to order them held on Sundays, to the exclusion of all other days, thus avoiding that the workers are distracted and lose six or eight hours EVERY MONDAY?[43]

The problem was still around forty years later. Social reformer Concepción Arenal lamented that workers wasted their limited resources on nonrational recreations such as the bullfight. In 1884, the Madrid City Council approved a motion calling on the provincial deputation, the owner of the bullring, to include a clause in the rental agreement forbidding bullfights on workdays; the next year the mayor briefly floated the idea of banning bullfights on workdays because "the excessive enthusiasm of the working class for this type of spectacle leads them to forget their work, doing harm to their families, who are left without the basic necessities." The deputation reminded him that their goal was to generate maximum revenues for welfare institutions and that this type of restriction would be "counterproductive . . . since anything that impedes the business freedom of the promoter" would reduce those revenues.[44] In 1904, when the government passed a Sunday Rest Law that included a prohibition on Sunday bullfights, it provoked a huge controversy.[45]

Keeping corridas out of work time meant that they would intrude on religious time, and this raised the hackles of ecclesiastical authorities. One eighteenth-century bishop tried unsuccessfully to have the government prohibit Sunday bullfights, although he did achieve a ban for religious holidays. The bishop's concern is not surprising when we know that in 1811, during the French occupation, Madrid city officials had mass rescheduled on those Sundays on which there were morning and afternoon corridas. Officials of the Archdiocese of Seville made a similar request in both 1797 and 1823, condemning the fact that youngsters and "'other thoughtless people' spend the night before a bullfight and the following morning at the roundup and then 'go to sleep and get ready for the corrida' . . . in other words, they sleep instead of going to hear mass in the morning and then go to the bullfight."[46] In 1834 the cardinal archbishop himself wrote to the queen regent to denounce "the moral and canonical unsuitableness" of holding bullfights on religious holidays, days that "were never consecrated to pleasure but to great and sacred objectives."[47]

The bullfight continued to encroach on what once had been religious time. In 1860 the promoter in Madrid sought government permission to hold bullfights during Lent on the grounds that his was "a free industry that can operate with no restriction other than paying the appropriate taxes" and that his contract with the owners of the ring did not specify any blackout dates. He also claimed that it would be much better "if artisans went to the bullfights on Sunday rather than Monday, when they lose their pay for half and even a full day." The Ministry of the Interior consulted with the archbishop of Toledo, who said no, but he approved the request anyway, "however much the Ecclesiastical Authorities might be opposed."[48] The farewell tour of the great Rafael Molina, "Lagartijo," in 1892–1893 generated so much excitement that Church authorities in Madrid, "fearing the competition from the retired colossus of the bullring," changed the time of the Corpus Christi service.[49]

The issue of when to schedule corridas was part of a larger conflict between religious holidays and work routines. The Spanish government went so far as to petition Pius IX to reduce the number of religious holidays, and the pope obliged in May 1867 with his bull *Can Pluries*, which eliminated a number of half holidays and moved the rest to Sundays. Supporters of the change argued that it would serve the economy, in part by by removing opportunities for Spaniards to indulge their "excessive fondness for amusement." They also claimed that reducing the number of days on which people did not work would prevent social unrest: "How often do those meetings produce criminal projects that [workers] would never have imagined when they were at work?"[50]

Both France and England offer examples of similar conflicts over the existence of popular entertainments involving bulls. During the 1880s the French government began to ban leisure activities that it considered socially dangerous, such as billiard playing in cafés and illegal gambling. In 1890 it added bullfighting, which had become popular during the 1889 Paris International Exposition, to the list. The ban was limited to Paris, which led organizations such as the League for the Protection of Horses, the Society for the Protection of Animals and the Anti-Vivisectionist League to campaign for prohibition in the provinces as well. These organizations were "not a marginal group of eccentrics" but embodied "a general liberal intellectual and political movement in favour of the 'emancipation' of so-called 'inferior beings,' whether 'savages' or animals." Raymond Poincaré was a prominent champion of animal rights, and when, as president of France, he made a state visit to Spain in 1913, he refused to attend a bullfight with King Alfonso XIII.[51] The French campaign included bringing charges against bullfighters—376 in 1896 alone—under the 1852 Grammont Law, which prohibited the maltreatment of domestic animals. The matter ended up in the Supreme Court, which ruled that bullfighting would be prohibited in the north but permitted in the south because of an indigenous tradition of bull events.[52]

In England, the victory over bull events was more complete, but also more violent. This was part of a widespread attack on animal sports during the first decades of the nineteenth century, of which bull running proved the most resistant. In Stamford (Lincolnshire), the running of the bulls was "a major festive occasion for the town and its surrounding countryside which attracted each year hundreds of spectators and participants. It seems to have been much like some of the bull runnings recently (or still) found in parts of France and Spain." The Stamford bull running was suppressed, but only after a long campaign that lasted from 1788 to 1840 and was brought to a successful conclusion only after "the dragoons had been called in to protect the police."[53] This outcome would appear to be a victory for civilized values, but it was also part of the assault launched by one class against the values and activities of another. The critique of animal sports was, as Keith Thomas puts it, "the orthodoxy of the educated middle class . . . a combination of religious piety and bourgeois sensibility."[54] The famous British "love of animals" is not a transcendent feature of English character and society but historically contingent and class specific. It also required the repressive force of the police to sustain it. On March 28, 1870, a Spanish bullfight was underway at the Agricultural Hall in London when "the secretary of the Royal Society for the Prevention of Cruelty to Animals jumped over the barrier into the arena followed by . . . Mr. Superintendant Green and officers of the police . . . Upon the secretary . . . indicating that no further performance would be tolerated, yells and execrations filled the hall from hundreds of roughs present and a general rush was made into the arena. Many efforts were made to 'mob' the officers and take from them the arrows seized, apparently for evidence; but the officers fought their way gallantly out of the hall . . . The performance, after this event, collapsed, and the occupants of the boxes made a hasty retreat from the hall."[55]

Bullfighting was also illegal in the United States, but that did not mean that Americans were universally hostile to it, as the authorities in St. Louis discovered during the 1904 World's Fair. On June 4, a crowd of eight thousand sat through a Wild West show impatiently waiting for the beginning of the bullfight, the first of a summer-long series. Just before it began, the sheriff, acting on orders from the governor of Missouri, arrested the promoter and the bullfighters. When a spokesman for the Norris Amusement Company announced that there would be no refunds, the crowd rioted and burned the bullring to the ground.[56]

By placing the bullfight in history, we escape from the idea that it is a peculiarly Iberian activity and can begin to compare it to similar spectacles elsewhere. There are numerous comparisons available in the many other entertainments for which large numbers of people pay money to get into special buildings to watch the performances of highly paid professionals, who are also the objects of great popular adulation. That is, bullfighting is a form of commercialized mass leisure, a cultural industry. Seen this way, the bullfight loses its singularity; it also ceases to be the symbol of national failure and the unfortunate remnant of the past and turns into something very different.

These forms of commercialized mass leisure are relatively new and constitute one of the most characteristic features of the modern world. With the exception of the theater and the music hall, they emerged in the last thirty or so years of the nineteenth century, and first appeared in Britain and the United States, the most economically advanced nations of the time. These developments are nicely summarized by two historians of cricket: "Commercialized sport was one of the growth points of the late Victorian economy. A substantial rise in working-class spending power, growing urbanization, and a concentration of free-time into Saturday afternoons all encouraged the marketing of spectator sport and, in response, throughout Britain sports promoters and sports club executives enclosed grounds, erected stadia and charged gate-money."[57] David Nasaw invokes similar explanations for the rise in the United States, after about 1870, of what he calls the "era of public amusements," a wide range of activities that included baseball but also movies, vaudeville, dance halls, amusement parks, and world's fairs.[58]

This chronology has some relevance to the corrida. The period beginning around 1870 was one of dramatic expansion: The number of bullfights increased, and the price of fighting bulls and the fees bullfighters commanded both skyrocketed. But this was expansion from a solid and long-standing base: The corrida had existed as a commercialized, spectator entertainment at least a full century before the period that these authors and others identify as the beginnings of commercialized leisure. In this sense, the bullfight that had emerged in the eighteenth century was not archaic and atavistic but fully modern. From the late eighteenth century to the end of the nineteenth, the bullfight was one of the most modern things in Spain and a herald of the future for a wider world.

one Before and beyond all else, the bullfight was a business. Its purpose, from its inception, was to make money: for private institutions and public purposes as well as for the growing myriad of individuals for whom it was a source of income, sometimes the sole source of income. The bullfight was a cultural industry, and as in any industry, it brought together a number of groups with divergent interests whose relations were complex and conflictual. Bullfighters, breeders, promoters, critics, and fans presented a kaleidoscope of competing interests and fought among themselves for power and profit.

The corrida was well established by the end of the eighteenth century, but it experienced a major takeoff in the second half of the nineteenth century, and especially during the 1880s and 1890s. The number of bullfights increased, from some four hundred per year in the 1860s to more than seven hundred by 1895 and more than eight hundred by 1912.[1] This growth led to the construction of more bullrings, the creation of more ranches, and the production of more bulls, which sold at ever higher prices. The number of bullfighters increased significantly, as did the size of the fees they commanded. This burgeoning business had its own specialized press that grew with it and gave voice to its internal conflicts.

Fund-raising

The corrida's potential as a money spinner was realized almost immediately, especially by religious and welfare institutions and cash-strapped local authorities who deluged the Crown with their requests to hold bullfights. For their part, royal officials were almost always prepared to accede, even when they felt that the bullfight was not a desirable custom. Much like government lotteries today, bullfights constituted a comfortable alternative to taxation that usually trumped any qualms officials had about their nonmonetary value.[2]

The first to request bullfights as fund-raisers were corporate institutions that served a public purpose: the Royal Maestranzas, welfare institutions, and the Church.

In many cities, the professional bullfight was intimately connected to a specific public institution. In southern Spain, the corrida was synonymous with the Maestranza. The Reales Maestranzas de Caballería, to give them their full name, were privileged corporations of aristocrats that had been created in the sixteenth and seventeenth centuries with the specific mission of stimulating fine horsemanship. (The Sevillian Maestranza was created in 1573; that in Ronda in 1572, and in Granada in 1686.) This involved them in spectacles such as *juegos de cañas,* a kind of jousting, and military-style skirmishes as well as the aristocratic style of fighting bulls on horseback. The move from this role to that of sponsor and promoter of professional bullfighting was a small one. In the eighteenth century Philip V granted them local monopolies on bullfights—Seville in 1729, Ronda in 1739—to help with their finances. The Ronda Maestranza received "the privilege of holding four bullfights per year . . . with the purpose of using the income to attend to the necessary expenses of the association . . . only the Maestranza may use a fixed ring and no other Body, Cabildo, or Community may use it without permission of His Majesty or the Hermano Mayor. It will have the same prerogative in any portable ring it might construct."[3]

By the time the Seville Maestranza obtained its bullfight monopoly it had to deal with a protest by Carlos Torreli, a local businessman who had already received permission from municipal authorities to stage three bullfights and build the ring to accommodate them. Torreli had held only one of the three bullfights, but he lost his case and had to dismantle the wooden ring he and his partners had built.[4]

In other cities, especially Madrid and Valencia, the bullfight became the province of hospitals and other welfare institutions. In November 1747 the Royal Hospitals of the capital petitioned Ferdinand VI for "the grace of some bullfights" to raise funds in light of "the large number of sick and suffering due to the increase which began in the early summer when the usual experience of other years has been for it to begin at the end and in the fall." Two years later he gave the Madrid bullring to the city's Hospital Commission. In 1739 he had granted the Provincial Hospital of Valencia "all the bullfights to be held in the city, in the squares of the outskirts and in places with many crowds within half a league."[5]

These monopolies quickly became an integral and lucrative part of the finances of these institutions, and they guarded their privileges zealously. In 1793 the count of la Cañada, president of the Madrid Hospital Commission (Junta de Hospitales), found himself with only two bullfighters and wrote to the Maestranza of Seville asking it to release Francisco Garcés from his contract so he could fight in the capital. The count also reminded the Maestranza of the "privilege of the Court," which gave Madrid "the right to count on the services of those subjects who are employed elsewhere."[6] In August 1835 the owner of the Cipolo pleasure garden in Madrid sought permission to stage horse races and *novilladas* fights featuring younger bulls than usual, to bolster his business, which had been badly weakened by a recent outbreak of cholera. The government acceded to his request, which brought a protest from the city's Hospital Commission, which owned the municipal bullring: "Bullfights are one of our principal sources of income . . . although [the pleasure garden] will be unable to compete with them in the quality and comfort of the ring, nor in the quality of the animals nor in the number or skill of the bullfighters . . . we are worried that the attraction of the novelty . . . of such small-scale spectacles and the advantage of the gardens' other attractions will . . . diminish the crowds that currently attend the ordinary bullfights."[7]

The connection between the corrida and Catholicism is an old one, and one that the condemnations of the highest Church authorities were unable to break.[8] A bull event of some sort frequently formed part of local religious celebrations and pilgrimages, perhaps as the survival of pre-Christian practices that became associated with the cult of the Virgin. Some of the earliest bullrings were attached to hermitages: At Belén in Puebla de Sancho Pérez (Badajoz) the bullring was built in the fourteenth century; at Nuestra Señora de las Virtudes in Santa Cruz de Mudela (Ciudad Real) and Castañar de Béjar (Salamanca) in the seventeenth. [9]

By the end of the eighteenth century many religious institutions were turning to the bullfight as a source of cash. The connection to hermitages continued: Vera Cruz de Consuegra (Toledo) requested bullfights "to attend to the structure of the hermitage,"[10] but other branches of the Church also became involved. In 1744 the curate of Madrid's San Andrés parish needed bullfights to pay off debts from "unavoidable repairs to the tabernacle, seating, and floor [of his church], which were in an indecent condition."[11] In Alazar (Huelva) money was needed to complete the altarpiece, and in Chozas (Albacete) the priest wanted to build a new church.[12] So, too, in

Chiclana (Cádiz) in 1813, when the parish building committee requested ten bullfights per year over six years, a request that was supported by the civil governor on the grounds that "it does not burden the public nor, in my opinion, does it harm agriculture in any way and finally because this class of truly national festivals greatly contributes to sustaining in the Spanish people that firmness of character which has made them superior to all the other nations of the world."[13]

Religious orders also made use of the bullfight. Sometimes they needed cash to rebuild their facilities, as was the case with one monastery in Andújar, which had found that the twelve bullfights it had already held were insufficient and in 1807 asked for thirty-two or more.[14] Many of the novilladas held in Madrid in the 1780s and 1790s were to help rebuild the monastery of the Padres Agonizantes.[15] Other orders were in more desperate straits, needing money to pay off debts or, as happened to the Congregation of Nuestra Señora de los Dolores, even "attend to our needy brothers."[16]

Municipal authorities were a little slower to get on the bullfight bandwagon to support local public works. There were some requests in the eighteenth century: In 1756 Ocaña was granted bullfights to raise money "to repair the buildings in the square, which are threatening to collapse,"[17] while Salamanca paid the debt incurred on the construction of its grandiose Plaza Mayor with the income from selling balcony seats for bullfights held in that same square.[18] In the 1790s both Cartagena (Murcia) and Villacarrillo (Jaén) sought to use bullfights to pay for fixing the streets[19]; in 1800 Utrera (Sevilla) wanted to "cover a creek . . . which during the summer produces vapors that cause epidemics which kill many residents,"[20] and two years later Caravaca (Murcia) wanted to provide drinking water for the town. In this case the Council of Castile gave its permission only reluctantly: "This spectacle is little suited to the softness of customs of a cultured nation [but] one must find some use in it when the money it generates is invested in projects of public utility."[21]

The economic appeal of the bullfight even crossed the Atlantic. In 1759 the Viceroy of Peru proposed to build a hospice to incarcerate Lima's vagabonds and saw the corridas as the way to finance this project and others. Building a bullring would leave the capital with a "secure and permanent resource with which to confront promptly any novelty."[22]

The disruption and destruction of the war against Napoleon and its effects on state finances pushed town governments and local welfare institutions to make greater use of the bullfight to pay for basic infrastructure and services.

When the baron of Casa Davalillo took up his post as governor of Córdoba late in 1813, he was shocked by the masses of beggars he found there:

> The multitude of beggars of all classes who inundated the town, capable of softening even the most stonelike heart urgently caught my attention. I immediately determined whether there was a hospice or a workhouse where they could be housed and made useful to the state, but unfortunately, this populous city lacks such necessary establishments. To partially fill this need I formed a patriotic association and invited the residents to contribute what their piety dictated . . .
>
> But the result has not lived up to my hopes, as the charitable impulse is quite dampened and as there are no funds to spend on an object of so much interest, especially when the most important thing was to prevent the prostitution of young women, so opposed to Christian morality, and to prevent soldiers from being disabled by this.

The baron was left with no choice but to turn to bullfights to carry out his plans.[23]

In Madrid and Valencia the hospitals continued to control the bullrings, but hospitals in smaller centers also became involved. In 1826 the Crown granted corridas to the Charity Hospital of Cartagena (Murcia) in recognition of the "the deplorable state to which it has been reduced"; two years later the organization in charge of the General Hospital of Toro (Zamora) requested permission to hold six bullfights per year for eight years "to excite zeal for welfare."[24] Hospitals were not the only public institutions that sought to use the bullfight to support their inmates. During the 1830s the Committee of Ladies-in-Waiting (Junta de Damas de Honor) used bullfights to help finance the foundling hospital (Inclusa) and the Colegio de Niños de la Paz, which it oversaw, and authorities in both Valverde del Camino and Almería requested corridas "to attend to the subsistence of prisoners in the jail."[25]

For impoverished local governments, the bullfight took on even greater importance in the aftermath of the war against the French. Valdepeñas (Ciudad Real) and Astorga (León) needed the money to repair the roads; Roda (Cuenca) for "repairs to the town hall, the school, and the meat market, which were ruined during the recent war," and Talavera (Toledo) to complete work on a water system that had been undertaken through a public subscription.[26] Val de Santo Domingo had to rebuild the jail, the meat market, the tavern, and the wells; Burgos, to "pay off the debts incurred during the war"; and Zamora, to fix the cavalry barracks.[27] A few years later, in 1820, the civil governor of Zamora supported city officials in their quest for a school:

> The Civil Governor states that: he has been much concerned to improve education, which is very backward in this province, and in agreement with the Provincial Deputation and City Hall considered creating a Normal School, but they knew that such a plan could not be carried out due to the total lack of funds. To overcome this difficulty City Hall proposed requesting permission to hold three bullfights, the profit from which would serve to establish the school and finish an aqueduct.[28]

In both 1826 and 1831, Alcalá de Henares requested bullfights to clean the sewers and fix the fountains.[29]

The corrida's contribution to welfare was so significant and, by the 1830s and 1840s so well established, that private entrepreneurs frequently made it part of their requests for permission to build bullrings. Thus, Antonio María Alvarez began his petition for a bullring in Málaga by describing the "tremendous decadence" of the province's welfare institutions and the benefits of having a bullring: "Taxes on luxury goods, especially when they match individual interest with the common good, are the most useful and the least burdensome, as they do not weigh on the needy classes like the *consumos* [consumption tax]." If the government also granted him the right to hold ten bullfights per year he would give 800 reales to welfare institutions.[30] Pablo Espinosa Serrano, who wanted to build a bullring in Palencia in 1847, offered 10 percent of the receipts to local welfare institutions, while the representative of the limited company pushing for a bullring in Ecija (Seville) promised the profits of one bullfight per year to the local orphanage.[31]

Both the fiscal demands and the political instability triggered by the Napoleonic invasion in 1808 put the bullfight at the service of political causes. Perhaps the first such instance, and one that makes glaringly clear the calamitous state of government finances, emerged in Cádiz in 1813. Francisco Laiglesia had requested and been granted the right to hold eighty-four bullfights because the government was unable to pay him the 842,000 reales he was owed for supplying saddles to the army, which was fighting against Napoleon. Laiglesia, who was also director of the Military Riding Academy, described himself, undoubtedly with some exaggeration, as "afflicted with and persecuted for debts before the courts . . . persecuted in the streets, hounded by those unfortunate artisans whom I owe money for commissions they took from me."[32]

In November 1815 the city of Jerez de la Frontera requested corridas "to supply the troops who will form part of the expeditions [to reconquer] America with arms, munitions, and other materiel and to repair the barracks designated for them."[33] And in August 1820, only months after that same army had rebelled against the absolute monarchy of Ferdinand VII in the name of the liberal Constitution of 1812, the leader of the revolution, Colonel Rafael de Riego, requested permission to hold bullfights in Seville and Córdoba:

> Aware of the impossibility of the National Treasury providing, with the speed which necessity demands, for the replacement of the clothing of the army that I command, and unable to look with indifference upon the poor condition and discomforts that are being endured by the valiant defenders of our liberties . . . I have resorted to the expedient of describing their situation to the citizens worthy of the name and invited them to contribute their own resources to such a praiseworthy object. It has not been in vain, and many good Spaniards have provided amounts proportionate with their abilities, but as this was insufficient and as I have been assured that holding some bullfights in the city of Córdoba will produce a considerable amount . . . [34]

As the political pendulum swung between liberalism and reaction during the 1820s and 1830s, each side made use of the bullfight to fit out its supporters. Thus in 1821 the local authorities of Lucena, "desiring to organize and arm the National Militia so that it will be capable of realizing its goals, so beneficial to the fatherland . . . and having had insuperable difficulties in raising funds for this most important service," requested twenty bullfights.[35] In December 1835 members of the Madrid National Guard needed a bullfight to raise money, and a few months later the commander of the National Guard in Granada argued that eight bullfights would allow him to meet his needs without raising taxes.[36] On the other side, in 1826 the captain of the Royalist Volunteers of Badajoz asked for bullfights to equip his troops, and the next year Bilbao requested them to finance its Royalist Volunteers and the hospital.[37]

By the 1870s, the profile of the fund-raising bullfight had changed significantly from earlier in the century. Welfare institutions, especially the provincial hospitals in cities such as Madrid and Valencia, remained important, but religion, local public works, and politics had yielded to disaster relief and voluntary organizations as the other leading beneficiaries.[38]

The hospitals of Madrid continued to benefit from the annual leasing of the bullring, but in 1856 the provincial diputation, which had responsibility for those institutions, inaugurated a tradition that continues to the present day. Realizing that the lease agreement gave it the "authority to hold an extraordinary bullfight," the diputation decided that this would be used to raise additional funds for welfare institutions. The annual Corrida Extraordinaria de Beneficencia quickly became an important social event and a profitable one for the hospitals.[39]

The first bullfight to provide relief to the victims of accidents and natural disasters was held in Aranjuez in 1829 to raise money for the victims of the earthquakes that had hit Murcia and Orihuela (Alicante),[40] but it was only later in the century, in the 1880s and 1890s, that this became at all common. In July 1884 the officers of the Cuenca Regiment held a *becerrada*, a fight using bulls less than one year old, at the Pardo, outside Madrid, to benefit the families of "the victims of the disaster in Alcudia." (The meat from the dead animals was given to "the Asilo, the poor of the town and the soldiers."[41]) Similar events were held in Madrid and Seville in 1879 to help the provinces of Alicante, Almería, and Murcia deal with floods; in 1885 for the families of cholera victims in Aranjuez; in 1891 for the victims of the floods in Toledo and Almería; in 1895 for the Red Cross sanatorium and for the victims of the sinking of the naval vessel the *Reina Regente,* and in 1896 to benefit sick and wounded soldiers returning from Cuba and the Philippines.[42] In Málaga, in 1886, a bullfight formed part of a larger program that included a flower show, a concert, a dance, a military display, and a raffle organized by the Liceo to benefit victims of flooding in the province.

The initiative for the 1879 corrida in Madrid came from the editor of the bullfight paper *El Toreo,* who proposed the idea to the president of the provincial diputation of Madrid. As bullfighters' fees and the purchase of bulls constituted by far the greatest expenses involved, the success of such an event depended on "stimulating the generosity of bullfighters and breeders." In this instance, "a number of bullfighters"—Frascuelo, Gonzalo Mora, and Angel Pastor—had "already come to our offices offering to fight for free." Others were approached: Francisco Arjona, "Cúchares," replied to the president of the diputation that he would fight for free: "I would not be a good

Spaniard nor a good citizen if I did not respond to the impulses of my heart with my small strength to the urgent call that has been made to all social classes in Spain," while Lagartijo excused himself on the grounds of sickness but did donate 500 pesetas. Some breeders, such as the duke of Veragua, the count of La Patilla, and the marquis of Salas, were prepared to donate bulls. A fourth breeder, Félix Gómez, was less generous: He was prepared to take 30 percent off the price of one bull and donate another "that has one defective horn," and a number of others replied that they had no bulls available.[43]

These bullfights were for worthy causes, but that did not mean that key figures were always easy to deal with, as the preparations for the July 1885 corrida for cholera victims shows. The idea was the civil governor's; it was taken up by the provincial diputation on July 8, and an organizing committee was struck the next day. This committee got to work immediately: On July 11 it set ticket prices and on the thirteenth it wrote to accept the offer by two breeders who had each volunteered to donate a bull. At its meeting on the fourteenth, the president of the diputation announced that "some other breeders had generously offered to donate one bull each" and urged the committee to accept, "since this would reduce costs and increase the profit from the bullfight." At this point the leaseholder of the Madrid bullring informed the committee that "he had been authorized by *Lagartijo*, *Frascuelo*, *El Gallo*, and *Mazzantini* to state that with each ranch providing a single bull without charge, they withdrew their offer to work for free, since they had made this offer on the understanding that all the bulls would come from a single ranch, or two at most." The committee concluded that it had no alternative but "to accede to the demands of the bullfighters, that the bulls before which they were going to risk their lives without any material reward not come from so many different ranches." The result was to accept one free bull from the duke of Veragua and buy two more from him and buy three from the Muruve ranch. In addition "all the other breeders who had offered bulls would be thanked on the poster . . . expressing the Committee's regrets that insuperable obstacles independent of the Committee's will had prevented them accepting their gift." This decision certainly made economic sense: The five bulls cost 9,625 pesetas, more than half the total expenses, but these bullfighters normally commanded 4,000 pesetas each.[44]

Things went more smoothly from then on. By the seventeenth the poster had been drawn up and received the civil governor's approval, and tickets went on sale two days later. (There was a minor scare when a telegram arrived from Mazzantini on the twenty-first to say that he had been held up in Barcelona, but later that day the civil governor of Barcelona sent a telegram announcing that Mazzantini had left on the night train. On his arrival Mazzantini presented the committee with a bill for expenses: 200 pesetas for a round-trip ticket in first class for him, 868 pesetas for second-class tickets for his assistants, and 132 pesetas for "excess baggage and various other things.") At the end of the day, the corrida produced a profit of 24,256 pesetas.[45]

Not everyone applauded these charity events. In 1890 one critic expressed his concern that organizers were taking advantage of bullfighters' "humanitarian sentiments and even their self-respect" in getting them to participate for free and that this was becoming an easy way out: "It would be more worthy of applause if [organizers] themselves resorted to other means that affect them directly and personally to raise the funds they seek." Imposing on bullfighters was particularly problematic: "Singers and actors can accede to these requests, since they give only their talent . . . and one day's pay, whereas bullfighters also risk their lives." If bullfighters had been paid for their services, in the critic's view, they would probably have made a donation to the cause at hand; after all, their "charity was undeniable," but "keep in mind that the glory of this virtue would always fall to those who, without risking anything, came up with the idea and realized it on the backs of others."[46]

By the turn of the century, private organizations, and especially workers' mutual aid societies, regularly used bullfights as fund-raisers to raise money for themselves. Generally these were novilladas and becerradas, fights that used bulls younger than those in regular corridas and that often did not have picadors. This was particularly common in Madrid, where the smaller, suburban Tetuán ring was frequently used. There were becerradas in July 1907 organized by the tram workers, the barbers, and "the shoemakers to benefit their friendly society,"[47] and in September it was the turn of the Republican Workers' Center of the Buenavista district.[48] In August 1908 alone such events were held by the Employees' Organization of the Wine, Spirits, and Liquor Sellers Guild, the Federal Republican Center of southern Madrid on behalf of its schools, the General Association of Shop Assistants "with the profits to be used to spread knowledge among its members," and the "Juventud" Society of Grocery Store Clerks.[49] These events were less serious than regular, full-scale bullfights and often included other activities. Thus the becerrada organized by the Mutual Aid Society of the Inn, Restaurant, and Café Workers in September 1906 featured "rabbit hunting on bicycles" and the "children's batallion of the Santa Cristina home, which executed tactical maneuvers as if they were veteran soldiers."[50] The first Corrida de la Prensa, to benefit the Madrid Press Association, was held in the main Madrid ring in 1900, and it quickly became an annual tradition that remains to this day.

Women had a special role in these charitable corridas, as this type of caring was consonant with the ideas about female nature that were dominant at the time, especially among the middle and upper classes.[51] They were encouraged to attend: "The ring will seem a bouquet of flowers if all the young ladies who have tickets attend, which also has the attraction of benefiting such a noble cause as the education of the disinherited classes."[52] The organizers of Madrid's annual Charity Bullfight invited "distinguished women" to donate *moñas* (ribbons to be placed on the bulls), which were auctioned off to raise more money. In 1873, those invited included the daughter of Emilio Castelar and the wife of Francisco Pi y Margall, both men presidents of the short-lived First Republic (1873-1874). The women refused to give the ribbon, preferring to make a cash donation instead. Petra de Pi replied to the invitation that the bullfight was "not in harmony with my sentiments, but as it assists Welfare, I will give one thousand reales for such a philanthropic purpose."[53] Two years later, with the monarchy back in place, the princess of Asturias and "various distinguished ladies"—all but one nobles—donated ribbons. (At 560 reales, the princess's turned out to be the most valuable by far.)[54] These bullfights were even occasions at which women could preside over and direct the proceedings, advised, of course, by knowledgeable men.[55]

Builders and Promoters

All bullfights, from the riotous village *capea* to the highly formalized aristocratic affair, originally took place in public spaces, in the streets or squares of cities, towns, and villages. As the corrida became more commercialized and better established as a regular event, especially in large cities such as Madrid and Seville, the organizers built specialized structures, the *plazas de toros,* or bullrings. Such buildings were without recent precedent in Spain or anywhere else in Europe. Not since the time of the Romans had anyone built permanent arenas for public spectacles of this sort, and even then Roman gladiatorial games and other competitions were not commercial operations that people paid to attend. Writing on soccer, Martyn Bowden notes that other than bullrings, "no stadiums had existed anywhere in Europe since Greek and Roman times," while Brian Neilson observed that the baseball stadiums that were being built in the United States in the 1870s were, "except for horse racing courses, the first large structures dedicated to commercial recreation."[56] Well before football grounds and baseball stadiums made their appearance, bullrings had become a standard feature of the Spanish urban landscape, and not just in cities such as Madrid, Barcelona, and Seville, which could claim major-league status.

The first formal bullrings were rectangular in shape, copies of the public squares in which bullfights had previously taken place. The original building commissioned by the Real Maestranza in Seville was a rectangle, as were the plans for a new one drawn up in 1733 but never executed. Around the middle of the eighteenth century, however, the rectangle gave way to the circle. A temporary circular ring was built by the Archicofradía Sacramental de San Isidro of Madrid to house the three bullfights it was granted by Philip V in 1737. Also circular was the ring that Ferdinand VI had built for the capital's charity hospitals in 1749, and this exercised a strong influence on the design of the permanent ring built by the Seville Maestranza beginning in 1759.

The reasons for this change in shape are not clear, but at least two suggestions have been proposed. Fátima Halcón Alvarez Ossario argues that the circular bullring emerged more or less spontaneously as the form that "the people and the bullfight required." Experience had shown that in rectangular rings the bull often fled to the corners, while in village bullfights people automatically arranged themselves in a circle,[57] much like children around a schoolyard fight. For his part, Pedro Romero de Solís finds a more concrete model for the circular bullring in the classical amphitheater, and especially the recently discovered ruins of Pompeii and Herculaneum, in an eighteenth century in which the baroque gave way to the neoclassical in architectural tastes.[58] The circle as a form also enjoyed considerable prestige among architects in the second half of the eighteenth century: In his *Principi di architettura civile,* F. Malizia described the circle as "the most grandiose of . . . shapes, because the smallest size has the greatest capacity and because it has the appearance of greater strength."[59]

Specially built bullrings began to appear in large numbers in the second half of the eighteenth century: in Zaragoza in 1764, Ronda in 1785, and Aranjuez in 1797, as well as in Madrid and Seville, but Napoleon's invasion of Spain in 1808, the subsequent political crisis, and the First Carlist War (1833–1840) put the brakes on such projects. These rings were built by or, as in the case of Madrid, for the organization to which the Crown had granted local monopoly privileges over the bullfight. In both Ronda and Seville this monopoly and the bullring belonged to the Real Maestranza. In Madrid, the bullring was built by King Ferdinand VI and given to the city's hospitals as a fund-raising vehicle. Similar institutions owned the bullrings in other major cities such as Zaragoza, Valencia, and Barcelona. In Valencia, the Provincial Hospital had a permanent bullring built in 1803, but it was torn down a few years later to help with the barricades against the French invaders. For the next fifty years the city had to make do with a series of temporary wooden rings.[60]

The real takeoff in bullring construction came in the half century following the restoration of relative political and economic stability in 1840. A survey done by the Ministry of the Interior in 1862 came up with 101 plazas de toros; by 1880 there were at least 105 permanent bullrings in the country, ranging in seating capacity from 2,500 to 12,500, with many more to follow.[61]

In this period, bullrings were built primarily by local businessmen, either as an end in themselves or as an investment in the urban infrastructure that would bring benefits to the local economy and in particular to their own businesses. Mayors and local councils generally offered strong support for this second type of project. Ecija, a town of some 24,000 people fifty miles from Seville, is an excellent early example. In 1845 José María López wrote to the civil governor of the province on behalf of a limited company that sought permission to build a bullring and hold eight corridas per year for a period of eight years. This request carried the enthusiastic support of mayor Antonio Díaz, clearly a forward-looking fellow with an eye on what today we would call tourism and economic spin-offs:

> An establishment of this sort will directly add to the revenues of the population; artisans and laborers will be actively involved in building the bullring; commerce will prosper selling its goods; the arrival of outsiders attracted by the entertainment means that money will circulate in profusion. . . . With the improvements that are being made to its public facilities, and with the resources it enjoys to undertake reforms that will later be valuable to all social classes, this city will be able to consider itself and be considered a capital.[62]

This combination of economics and local pride was present in the support of the city government of Cádiz for a private company that wanted to build a bullring there in 1861. The city fathers refused to debate "the pros and cons of the bullfight, a much debated question," and addressed only more practical matters: "The movement of travelers and the subsequent circulation of money to which the bullfight gives rise is well known. Cádiz has seen itself reduced to a mere tributary of all the nearby centers that have those powerful elements of attraction and stimulus for the most numerous fans of that spectacle."[63] The original bullring in Calatayud (Zaragoza) had been built by the Hospicio in 1830, but it was torn down in 1875 so that an extension could be added to the institution. A new ring was built almost immediately, this time "at the urging of various merchants" who took out shares and convinced the municipal government to provide a generous subsidy.[64]

By the 1880s, both the importance of tourism to the local economy and the role of a bullring in promoting it were well appreciated. And perhaps nowhere more than in Gijón, a city on the north coast that found itself competing with Bilbao, Santander, and San Sebastián as the summer destination of choice for Spanish vacationers. In August 1886, a group of local businessmen, "merchants, owners of cafés, and inns" got together

> to try to raise funds for the purpose of building a bullring. . . . San Sebastián, Bilbao, and Santander, like Gijón, possess superb beaches, but they understood that to attract the largest number of visitors it was necessary to include the bullfight among their attractions. . . . If this summer twelve thousand people visit Gijón, then next year, if we have the attraction of the bullfight, there will be twenty thousand. . . . The bullring is another of the powerful attractions that will direct a strong current of summer vacation migration to our beaches.[65]

In Bilbao, the summer season ran for two months from the middle of July, and reached its climax during August's Semana Grande. Bullfights were a central part of this week, which was drawing some ten thousand visitors as early as the 1880s.[66]

The benefits of such a development, the businessmen argued, would be spread widely:

> Much of the capital invested would pass to the poor laborers and artisans whose labor supports their families. The landowner, the merchant, the industrialist, etc., who buys a share may not derive any direct benefit, but he will see indirect ones because with the increased number of people, consumption will

be greater, and rents will be greater. The larger number of vacationers that this spectacle will draw, as has happened in San Sebastián and Bilbao, will give greater vitality to their establishments. The benefits will reach even the long-suffering local farmers, who will get better prices for the crops they harvest.[67]

Something similar was taking place in Almería, at the other end of the country, at precisely the same time. A group that included Caralampio Ayuso, "a rich landowner"; deputy mayor Francisco Jover y Tovar, a "capitalist" and member of parliament; José González Canet, a banker and senator; Emilio Pérez Ibáñez, member of parliament and local head of the ruling Conservative Party; and Felipe Vilches Gómez, a "rich landowner," formed a private company to build a bullring. This, they sensed, was a "great business opportunity," not in itself but for its contribution to local economic development and municipal improvement, both of which could only benefit men with money, land, and political influence.

> The great influx of outsiders in search of our ideal climate, the construction of the railroad and our wonderful port, and the opening of the offices of the foreign mining companies exploiting our rich mineral resources led local municipalities to promote projects for parks, wide avenues, spas, etc., all elements of a future prosperity . . . which led to the idea to build a new bullring.[68]

Gijón was an industrial city, a major port, and a budding tourist destination; Almería, a provincial capital with an expanding economy based on mining and the export of grapes, but the importance of the bullring was not limited to places of such relative economic vitality. Smaller, more out-of-the-way centers with sluggish economies might also benefit from a plaza de toros. So thought a group of local leaders, what Spaniards call *fuerzas vivas*—literally "vital forces"—in Guijuelo, an agricultural town of 4,900 people near the provincial capital, Salamanca. Motivated by "the urgent need to give more vitality to the fairs and have worthy lodging for the numerous dealers and salesmen who travel to Guijuelo," in 1908 they created a limited company called La Recreativa to build a bullring as well as an inn, a café, and a theater. The group included a pharmacist, a merchant, a retired army officer, two landowners, a tax collector, an administrator of the tobacco monopoly, and Abdón Rodilla Maldonado, a veterinarian and merchant. The following year the company's shares were purchased by the town government; by then Rodilla Maldonado was mayor, and one wonders how much profit he and his fellow shareholders made on the deal.[69]

Salamanca itself was an administrative center and a cathedral and university town, but here, too, the connection between the bullring and local business interests was a close one. The city got its first bullring in 1840, but by 1861 it had been sold and dismantled. With the prospect of no bullfights during the annual festival, the business community decided to organize them itself, for which the local newspaper extended its "congratulations for having finally overcome the difficulties in the way of there being bullfights this year."[70] The solution was only temporary. Two years later Bernabé Vilches petitioned the government for permission to use the Plaza Mayor for three corridas during the fair. There had been no bullfights the previous year, and Vilches wanted to restore "the former animation that was so beneficial." The city council supported him, as did the civil governor, who noted "the great advantage that would accrue to commerce and business in general from the crowds who come to the city for this reason."[71]

In 1864 the Martínez family, a widow and her four sons who ran a wholesale business, built a new bullring with a capacity of seven thousand. It lasted until 1892 when a group of merchants, small manufacturers, and artisans "for whom the bullfight was not a passion but a way of improving their incomes" created a limited company that built a new eleven-thousand-seat ring.[72] Fernando Araujo, who visited Salamanca in 1892 after a three-year absence, was impressed by the changes he saw, and above all by the new bullring:

> It reveals the awakening of . . . individual initiative, the vigorous affirmation of the real life of the tax-paying public entirely independent of official stimulus.
>
> It is nothing short of a revelation, a complete revolution. Those shopkeepers, manufacturers, and ranchers who organized themselves into a limited company, breaking away from musty old concerns, understood that in the times in which we live life presents urgent demands. . . . It matters little whether it was a bullring, a theater, a market, or a tram line that has moved them to act; what matters is the very existence of this individual initiative, that today it is understood that a good bullring is essential to get crowds to come to the fair.[73]

Even when they did not themselves own the bullring, local economic elites took an active interest in its construction. In Valencia, only in the 1850s did the Provincial Hospital undertake the construction of a new permanent ring to replace the one that had been destroyed in 1808. The project was initially financed through the sale of shares that gave holders the right to a "preferred seat" for all fights, but when this proved insufficient, the Sociedad de Crédito Valenciano, a local financial institution, provided an interest-free loan. The civil governor also pitched in, providing "large squads of prisoners to help lay the foundation."[74]

In Valencia bullfights were an integral part of the festival of Saint James (San Jaume) in July, and they drew large numbers of people to the city, especially after the construction of the railroad. "For three days the city was literally overwhelmed, the cafes, drink stands *[orxateries]*, squares, and streets packed, the inns and hostels unable to take in the numerous contingent of bullfight fans who arrived from both the nearby towns and Palma or Madrid."[75] The popularity of the corrida was at the heart of the transformation of the traditional festival into a more modern and business-oriented fair. Although the first fair was not held until 1871, the *Diario Mercantil* had launched the idea more than ten years earlier: "If we agreed to hold an exposition and if this were combined with the annual bullfight season, would the number of outsiders who would come to pass a few days in our beautiful city for either of these events, or both, not be much greater?"[76] This new fair became a major tourist attraction, and more days and additional events were added over the years.

By the beginning of the twentieth century bullrings had become synonymous with urban improvement and profit making. In 1908 the Vista Alegre ring opened in the poor Madrid suburb of Carabanchel Bajo, much to the joy of local businessmen. According to *El País*:

Few were the shopkeepers, manufacturers and others . . . who did not dream of a better future once the bullring opened. . . . The greatest and the least of these shopkeepers and manufacturers rushed to reform and beautify their establishments, to stock them to extravagant levels, to extend their contracts and commitments so as not to lose any of the opportunity from the influx of crowds on bullfight days. . . .

Certain profits led a number of businessmen to pay elevated prices for land around the bullring in order to build pleasant and comfortable restaurants, or use poles and cotton cloth to create modest yet suggestive snack bars or improvise salons artistically decorated with lanterns, streamers, and garlands where cold drinks and other refreshments were served shielded from the summer sun until the bullfight began.[77]

The connection between the bullring and business could even have an international dimension. Part of the Spanish contribution to the 1889 Paris International Exposition, held to celebrate the centenary of the French Revolution, was a bullring with a retractable roof and electric lights. This ring, which featured "an unusual degree of comfort, comparable only to a theater," was financed by a group led by the duke of Veragua, one of the most important breeders of fighting bulls, who saw the world's fair as an opportunity "to internationalize the bullfight and develop an export market for fighting bulls."[78] And for a while this initiative bore fruit: The corrida became fashionable in Paris and other parts of northern France "and outlasted the Exposition as commercial entertainment."[79] This popularity was cut short due to the opposition of animal protection societies and the Anti-Vivisectionist League: In 1896 alone they brought 376 actions against bullfighters under an 1852 law against the maltreatment of domestic animals, and achieved a ban on the bullfight in Paris and a parliamentary inquiry, which "was shocked by the foul language of the crowd in the cheaper seats. Around the same time a few Socialists began to worry that the popularity of the corrida would corrupt and brutalize the proletariat."[80] The legislature eventually passed a bill banning bullfighting altogether, but this was challenged until the Supreme Court ruled that the corrida would be allowed in the southern part of the country, where there was an indigenous bullfighting tradition.

Whether bullrings were owned by public institutions or by private entrepreneurs, the first choice an owner had to make was whether to organize the bullfights directly or lease the plaza to a promoter. Businessmen, whether as individuals or as limited companies, generally served as their own promoters; institutions such as the hospitals of Madrid and the Maestranza of Seville usually preferred to lease their rings, realizing a secure income and not bothering with the work—and risk—of putting on corridas themselves.

Leases were put out to public tender. The owners would publicize the terms and conditions (in Madrid in 1760 this was done through "edicts and town criers" [*pregones*]; in the 1840s by edicts and newspaper ads) and then invite interested parties to submit a bid. In Seville this was sometimes done through an auction: In 1796 the bidding began at 17,000 reales; Manuel Burgos offeed 17,200, Agustín de Soto bid 17,500, and a third party bid 18,000 when the auctioned was called off without explanation.[81] In Madrid, potential tenants submitted their offers in sealed envelopes: The lease for 1886-1892 drew forty-one bids, ranging from 110,000 pesetas to the winning bid of 188,885. Wily aspirants occasionally tried to pull a fast one: Ramón Menéndez de la Vega once submitted two separate bids, and when the higher one proved the winner, he claimed that it did not meet the specifications set out by the deputation and that the other, lower bid should be accepted.[82]

The bullfight may have been the *fiesta nacional*, but like any other business it had its ups and downs. Madrid certainly had its problems. On a number of occasions—from 1814 to 1823, from 1830 to 1834, in 1855, and in 1870—there were no bidders, and the Hospital Commission and its successors were forced to run it themselves. These were all years of political uncertainty, even revolution, but the return of political stability in 1875 helped make the business more attractive.

We can see these difficulties in the severe fluctuations in the amount paid to lease the Seville ring. The late eighteenth century was a golden age: The Maestranza received 190,500 reales in 1762, 222,000 in 1776, and 546,373 in 1795. That was the peak: Income had fallen to 438,694 reales in 1800, but much worse was to come, as graph 1 in Appendix A shows. The decade from 1825 to 1835 was a particularly difficult one. Rents had to be continually lowered, and produced only eighteen thousand or nineteen thousand reales. In 1832 there were no bidders at all. A modest recovery around 1840 was followed by record low returns.[83] The fluctuations in Seville did not always correspond so closely to political events as in Madrid. The collapse after 1800 was probably connected to the independence of the American colonies between 1810 and 1820, a development that would have seriously disrupted a local economy long connected to colonial trade. There is no apparent political cause for the severe drop between 1846 and 1850.

Who were the promoters? Occasionally they were bullfighters: José León and Lucas Blanco took on the Seville ring in 1836, and Luis Mazzantini tried his hand in Madrid in 1887, managing to lose considerable popularity, as well as 350,000 pesetas, in two years. Other promoters in Madrid came from the ranks of small business rather than from the economic elite: Casiano Hernández and Julián Javier were dealers in meats; Joaquín Verdier, a lithographer and paper wholsealer; and Pedro Niembro, a wine dealer. Eulogio Antón, who ran the suburban Tetuán ring in 1907, owned a tavern.

Breeders

The most serious task facing promoters was to sign up bullfighters and buy bulls so that they could put together and advertise their programs (*carteles*).

Bullfighters were undoubtedly the headliners, but it takes two to *torear,* and the bulls they fought were also important. Not all ranches were equal in the eyes of the fans, and featuring bulls from a breeder with a good reputation could make a fight much more attractive. Indeed, until well into the nineteenth century posters gave breeders pride of place over bullfighters: Their names came first and appeared in larger print.[84]

Provenance mattered because the bull that shared the limelight was a human creation that had been carefully distilled over time to produce the characteristics considered most suitable for the corrida. The naturally occurring wild bull could not be relied upon to offer a suitable performance. The demands of—and the demand for—the commercial bullfight led to the creation of another animal, the product of human manipulation. The fighting bull was "a cultural product" contemporaneous with, and analogous to, the "invention of the thoroughbred horse" for the specialized functions of hunting and steeplechasing.[85]

The most important characteristic is *bravura,* what the author of the highly influential *Diccionario enciclopédico de agricultura, ganadería e industrias rurales* defined as "aggressiveness . . . the more consistently a [bull] responds aggressively to provocation, the braver it is." This sort of aggressiveness was sufficient to distinguish the fighting bull (*toro bravo*) from other types of bull and make it, literally, a race apart. And this meant that "*bravura* is not something fortuitous that randomly appears or disappears but is something the rancher can direct according to his will . . . obeying the rules that science sets out so precisely."[86]

As early as the second half of the eighteenth century Spanish ranchers were carefully using unnatural selection to weed out animals that were not adequately aggressive. This was done through the *tienta*: Cows were tested in the corral, where they were observed charging a picador and then a bullfighter. This constituted a kind of trial by ordeal intended to reveal the participants' "moral qualities": "The punishment was carried to the limit, not only with the cows, with which it is always advisable and can never be excessive, but also with the bulls. . . . The cows were pushed to the edge and punished as if they were being fought in the ring; only those that successfully passed the test were destined to carry on the race." The duke of Veragua, the most successful of the eighteenth-century ranchers, also practiced crossbreeding, what the *Diccionario* calls "miscegenation." He acquired bulls from various ranches, and when he had put each group through the tienta, he bred them with each other to produce bulls "with the three qualities he sought to give them: bravery, nobility, and appearance."[87]

Members of the nobility quickly took an important role in the early days of breeding fighting bulls, at least in Seville. The Maestranza, which owned the bullring, was an association of noblemen, and it was only a small step for some of them to provide bulls for the corrida. By 1732 the Maestranza was acquiring bulls from titled ranchers, and animals from the ranches of the count of Vistahermosa and the marquis of Casa Ulloa became the foundation of the Andalusian fighting bull. Practices of selective breeding came naturally to men of the nobility, although they would have used the language of lineage or family rather than that of race. After all, as Pedro Romero de Solís writes, they only had "to project the logic of the nobility onto the logic of the rancher, basing both on consanguinity and selection" of mates.[88]

Noblemen came to be overshadowed as ranchers by men without titles, or whose titles came later. (Of the 150 breeders who supplied bulls to the Madrid bullring in the eighteenth century only six were titled.[89]) These non-noble ranchers were men with money, some already involved in agriculture, others, who saw the breeding of bulls as promising good returns, both economically and socially. In this they were typical of the social elite that emerged from the liberal revolution of the first four decades of the nineteenth century.[90] Even the famous Veragua ranch was created by a commoner. The founder, Vicente José Vázquez, was a tax farmer, collecting tithes for the cathedral chapter of Seville. He acquired his first cows when the count of Vistahermosa agreed to make them part of his tithe payment.[91] The herd was eventually sold to King Ferdinand VII, who later sold it to the duke of Veraguas, a descendant of Christopher Columbus.

The Miuras, who became some of the most famous breeders, originated in the Basque provinces but moved to Seville, where they became wealthy hatmakers. By the 1830s they had done some work for the Maestranza and were also leasing land from the duke of Andrá. It was only in 1842, apparently at the urging of his son, that Juan Rodríguez Miura first purchased some cows; over the next decade these were crossed with animals from a number of different ranches to produce the bull that soon came to be considered more dangerous than any other.[92]

Juan José Fuentes, son of a permanent alderman of Madrid, started his ranch in Colmenar Viejo, near Madrid in 1797. In 1852 the ranch was sold for 275,000 pesetas to Vicente Martínez, the embodiment of the successful

Madrid businessman and revolutionary described by Jesús Cruz.[93] A native of Valle de Soba in the northern province of Santander, Martínez began his career in the capital as a clerk (probably in a business owned by a relative). From there he managed to build a fortune, in part through government contracts, selling granite from Colmenar to the city of Madrid for use as paving stones. He became a landowner during the disentailment of 1836, when the state auctioned off the lands of the Church. Politically Martínez was a liberal and was even elected to the provincial deputation.[94]

The prices fetched by fighting bulls increased significantly in the long term, although there were some fluctuations. Bulls that fought in Seville generally sold for less than 500 reales in the 1730s and 1740s but underwent "a considerable price increase" in the 1760s, when they went for between 600 and 800 reales. By the end of the century they cost a minimum of 1,200 reales and went as high as 1,750.[95] Madrid promoters began the nineteenth century paying 1,300 reales per bull. The price jumped to between 2,500 and 3,300 in 1814 and 1817 before dropping during the 1820s and 1830s. Then prices began to climb and did not stop for the rest of the century; by 1870, 3,000 reales was the minimum, and by 1889 bulls that fought in Madrid cost between 7,000 and 8,000 reales.[96] Promoters in other cities paid similar prices: from 3,750 to 5,125 per bull in Málaga in 1876 and from 6,800 to 7,166 in Valencia in 1884.[97] Indeed, a nationally structured market for bulls appeared very early: By the 1790s Madrid was buying its bulls from all the major breeding areas, including Andalusia, and by the 1840s—at the latest— other major rings did likewise.[98]

A composite picture of the prices paid by a number of major rings reveals a decline in the 1820s, which corresponds to the decline in rental revenues for ring owners, followed by a steady rise in prices that became explosive in the 1870s and 1880s. As graph 2 in Appendix A shows, the price of bulls rose well beyond that of general wholesale prices, but the most striking feature of this price history is the sharp divergence after about 1875. This stands out all the more in the context of the general deflation caused by the great depression of 1873-1896, a deflation that hit the prices of agricultural products most severely. The composite price index of wheat, barley, olive oil, and wine collapsed in the decade 1884-1893, from a near record high of 135—with 1864-1872 as the base—to a horrendously low 79, and while there was some recovery after that date, the index was back at only 100 in 1900 and had fallen again to 93 in 1905.[99]

In Spain, this collapse is known as the great end-of-the-century agrarian crisis. The market for fighting bulls not only resisted the crisis but throve during it. But if the overall impact of the depression was to raise real wages through price deflation, an industry such as the bullfight, which depended on people having discretionary income to spend, should thrive. More bull-fights required more bulls, which, in turn, drove prices up. In addition, breeders exported bulls to Latin America, especially Mexico.[100]

This perverse price behavior made raising fighting bulls appear a particu-larly lucrative activity, especially when livestock prices fell after 1880 and hit bottom in the mid-1890s, and it undoubtedly contributed to the creation of a number of new ranches. Of the sixty-eight still-existing ranches whose bulls had fought in Madrid by 1894, fourteen had done so since 1885, and another twelve between 1880 and 1884.[101]

The long-term rise in prices for fighting bulls led to the appearance of new ranches and, it appears, a decline in quality. The author of a book on the history of bull ranches published in 1876 charged that ranchers were putting the drive for profits ahead of any concern for the quality of the animals they were selling. "Thus we see four-year-old bulls in the ring when all those who fight should be five or six. Naturally the ranchers do not want to have thirty or forty bulls on their hands for another year or two; that would be dead cap-ital. . . . In addition, there are very few [ranchers] who take care to refine the breeds they have, and those who get rid of animals who do not display the necessary qualities are few indeed."[102] In 1893, an editorial in *El Toreo* charged that "the ranches are a speculative business, and most of the people who own fighting bulls care only for the business aspect and ignore the repu-tation of their herds."[103]

Support for this complaint came from a dispute over the use of dogs in the Madrid bullring. In March 1868 a fan complained about the end of the prohi-bition against the setting of dogs on timid bulls and put the blame on igno-rant fans. The man who had spent sixteen years in charge of security there found different villains: ranchers and promoters. Initially, setting the dogs on an unacceptable bull was "an affront to the ranch," but as the demand for bulls increased and the prices rose, "many [ranchers] who never believed that their animals could ever serve for the bullring saw the fabulous price that each ani-mal brought and crossed their cows with pure-bred bulls and sold the offspring to be fought. This produced bulls that were no good for bullfight-ing, but the promoters accept them because their owners sell them cheaply."

This situation could be resolved without using dogs by "imposing the maximum fine possible on the promoters" for each inadequate bull.[104]

Some ranchers were concerned about the quality and performance of their animals. Pride played a part, but the bottom line was that a rancher whose bulls developed a reputation for fighting well got a better price. The duke of Veragua was probably the extreme case: In the 1870s his bulls were so popular that they pushed up the demand for tickets so that "the promoters pay Veragua 1,000 reales more for each animal than they do to other ranches." But even a small and unknown ranch could benefit if its bulls caught the fans' attention. Félix Gómez of Colmenar Viejo (Madrid) started his ranch in 1829, and it was still insignificant when, on June 23, 1844, his bulls did so well in Madrid that prices for them rose from 900 to 4,500 reales.[105]

A ranch's reputation could easily fluctuate over time. As in the case of Félix Gómez, a little-known brand might earn a big reputation, but once-reputable ranches could also lose their cache. This had happened to the marquis of Saltillo after 1890: His herd had enjoyed "a truly celebrated epoch in which it had great renown and was included in all the bullfights of the highest category [but] it has been losing *bravura* . . . and in general today its bulls are meek and timid. A ranch that was so famous between 1856 and 1890 could recover the lost ground but only if it works with determination." For others, such as the Muruve, the decline was more severe: "The huge descent that this herd has suffered is so painful that one can almost say that it is not the equal of other herds." Or even fatal: The Repamilán ranch "was a name the promoters trusted, and they bought its bulls certain that they would meet the demands of the fans. Then things changed, they lost so much of their former *bravura* that no one remembers them anymore."[106]

We can catch a rare glimpse of how a concerned rancher could respond to a declining reputation in the case of Luis Gutiérrez, the head of the Martínez ranch at the beginning of the twentieth century. By 1900 the ranch was "in a bad way," and Gutiérrez laid the blame on slack grazing and selection practices, especially the habit of the ranch's founder of sending his bulls to graze on a property bordering two ranches that raised ordinary cattle. As a result, "the beasts of the ranches mixed constantly without any order, with the loss of purity of bloodlines that this supposed; in addition, the absence of well-kept fences meant that tame animals from Segovia habitually got into the meadows."[107] In 1903, Gutiérrez wrote to his nephews, who would inherit the ranch: "With the hope that our ranch will once again achieve brilliant successes gone; convinced of my impotence to remedy the evil, and considering that we must have recourse to radical solutions if we want to avoid the ruin of the ranch, I have studied the matter with great care . . . and I am going to propose to you two methods. First, the selection of the cows, testing [*tentando*] and retesting them with the greatest care and, second, breeding them with a stud chosen from the ranch that agrees."[108]

The nephews initially agreed to only the first of their uncle's proposals. He found their resistance extremely frustrating: "I cannot understand my nephews' behavior in this matter, as the imperious necessity of introducing my reforms has been proven and I am totally convinced that, given the state of our ranch, there is no alternative other than regenerating it through cross-breeding or selling the animals to the slaughterhouse." The nephews eventually gave in and agreed to the cross, although arranging this was far from straightforward. Pedro Niembro, who ran the Madrid ring, brought Gutiérrez together with Eduardo Ibarra, who asked 10,000 pesetas for one animal, but this offer was withdrawn when his brother objected. Negotiations with other Andalusian ranches also fell through, "because the owners refused to sell or asked prohibitive prices." In the end, Ibarra decided to sell his entire herd, and Gutiérrez got the animal he wanted. The experiment succeeded in restoring the ranch's reputation, but Luis Gutiérrez died two years before its first products debuted in Madrid in 1909.[109]

The bravery and desirability of bulls was often a subjective matter, but there were two objective measures available: the number of picks a bull took from the picador and the number of horses it killed in doing so. (Until 1926, the picadors' horses wore no padding to protect them from the bull's horns, and this vulnerability was very often fatal. Promoters had to ensure that they had an adequate supply of horses on hand: In the 1884 season, more than 2,000 horses died, compared to 1,244 bulls. Horse dealers were another group who participated in the business of the bullfight.)

On the afternoon on which Félix Gómez's ranch made its name, its first bull took twelve picks and killed eleven horses.[110] The first bullfight review to appear in the Madrid press made a point of mentioning the number of picks and *banderillas* (darts) each bull took as well as the number of horses it killed: "The sixth bull . . . took fourteen picks and seven banderillas; it killed three horses and seriously wounded another."[111] These numbers were an integral part of the statistical summaries that were so common after 1850. Thus Fausto Pontes's review of the 1851 season in Madrid included a table on "ranchers, number of bulls picked, number of picks they took, number of picadors knocked down, and number of horses they have killed," as did a similar review published in 1865.[112] By the 1880s, bullfight magazines such as *El Toreo* were publishing such league tables at the end of every season.

Such statistics were not merely debating points for the fans; they mattered to ranchers, some of whom even worked out averages for their bulls. Thus, in 1897, the marquis of Saltillo's animals had the highest average number of picks (7.25), followed by Campos Varela (7.17), Ibarra (6.58), Miura (5.50), Veragua (5.34), and Muruve (5.33). They also led in knockdowns of picadors (4.12), and were second in numbers of horses killed (2.12).[113]

There were even informal "halls of fame" for unusually outstanding bulls. One consisted of those bulls that, by taking at least sixteen picks, left a "vibrant memory of the fight" and earned themselves the title of *toros de bandera*. Some 202 animals had earned this title in Madrid between 1851 and 1910, of which 24 belonged to the duke of Veragua, 22 to the García Puente ranch, 14 to the Miura ranch, and 13 to that of Vicente Martínez.[114] Another comprised those bulls whose exploits a bullfight chronicler thought worthy of note. Thus Leopoldo Vázquez y Rodríguez included a chapter entitled "Famous Bulls" in his book *Curiosidades tauromacas* and Cossío's encyclopedia had a section on "celebrated bulls." Among them was Cucharero, from the Anastasio Martín ranch, who fought in Málaga on June 3, 1877.

> He took ten picks, but the picadors were unable to draw blood. One of them was tossed and broke his collarbone, the other thrown head first while Cucharero balanced his horse on his horns as if it were a feather. The banderilleros managed to place half a pair each . . . Lagartijo had to face him and . . . in spite of his great abilities, he could not dominate his fear. The time came to kill . . . and only after half an hour of running around at a distance from the bull . . . was Lagartijo able to do so. The great bullfighter ordered Cucharero's head cut off . . . and hung it in his house in Córdoba. When he came home after a night on the town and in his cups, he would grab a cane and unleash his alcoholic frenzy at the inoffensive head as he recalled the panic of that afternoon in Málaga.[115]

Conflicts

Relations between the various interest groups involved in the corrida were complex and changing. Each sought to assert its power within the industry so as to protect, or improve, its economic position. Circumstances were fluid, and so were the alignments they produced: Allies and antagonists could quickly change identities. Moreover, interest groups were not monolithic. Just as the evolution of their profession brought something approaching class conflict to bullfighters,[116] breeders experienced differing degrees of success and prosperity and were moved to defend their interests in different ways. For their part, promoters were concerned to keep costs down and profits up, which meant that they had to deal simultaneously not only with breeders and bullfighters but also with consumers and the critics who frequently voiced their frustrations.

Breeders alternated between fighting with bullfighters and cooperating with them. Some even tried to do both at once. Thus in March 1851, seven breeders from Navarre signed an agreement to fix prices for their bulls (at 1,500 reales each) and to present a united front against the pretensions of the bullfighters, especially their practice of demanding money to fight a breeder's bulls: "Having dealt with the evil and damaging custom, which the bullfighters introduced, of demanding money from us . . . and having observed the ill effects of paying them, even when it has been in agreement with other breeders, we undertake that neither alone nor together will we pay them, and only if they do especially well will they be given refreshments or cigars, etc., and only by all the breeders whose bulls were in the ring."[117] That the "fault" originated with the bullfighters is far from clear. In July 1868, Vicente Pérez de Laborda, one of the breeders who had signed the agreement, learned from a friend that Nazario Carniquire, his leading rival, "gives good tips to the bullfighters, as is well known. . . . A very good friend of the duke of Veraguas [the top breeder of all] told me that Sr. Carniquire became friendly with all the bullfighters so that they would speak well of his bulls."[118] Nor was this an isolated example: the renowned Joselito liked the bulls from the Martínez ranch in Colmenar Viejo (Madrid), and this "opened not a few doors and contributed greatly to the fame of the herd."[119]

This was not a one-way street. Until the end of the nineteenth century a breeder had the right to choose the order in which the bulls from his ranch were fought, and since the bullfighters appeared in strict order of seniority breeders could do a friendly matador a favor by ensuring that he faced bulls that would give him the best opportunity to look good. Not all bullfighters were happy with this arrangement. In his contracts, Mazzantini insisted that the bulls be drawn by lot, which led Rafael Guerra, "Guerrita," who was alleged to have benfited from the favoritism of the other system, to veto his fighting in Madrid. The charge was substantiated by a critic who was a strong supporter of Guerrita's: The breeders gave him "the most manageable animals because the lucid death that this colossus gave them . . . would add to the prestige of their herd. . . . [They] were perfectly within their rights and they acted correctly." Mazzantini's approach was adopted in 1899.[120]

Bullfighters could use their power to damage a ranch as well. The head of the Martínez ranch claimed in 1903 that "the bullfighters prefer . . . bulls that arrive at the last third [of the fight] worn out and without power . . . and as we have arrived at the point at which the bullfighters impose on the promoters, we may find that they boycott our bulls."[121]

The biggest target for this sort of pressure was the Miura ranch, whose bulls had developed a reputation for being particularly deadly. Frascuelo was reputed to have insisted on a "no Miuras" clause in his contracts after having a couple of bad experiences; in February 1874, he certainly did write to one promoter: "This letter is only to inform you that you should not buy bulls from the Miura ranch if you expect me to fight in the corridas because I will not fight them . . . and this has to appear in the contract." And in 1890, Guerrita was publicly criticized for his refusal to fight Miuras.[122]

Eduardo Miura did not accept this sort of thing passively; he was the moving spirit behind the Union of Breeders of Fighting Bulls (Unión de Criadores de Toros de Lidia) which was founded in June 1905 to defend members' interests "in all that relates to sale, purchase, and fighting of our bulls." In practice, the Union sought to act as a cartel and impose its members' bulls, on its own terms, on promoters and bullfighters. Promoters who bought bulls from breeders who were not members were subject to a fine of 1,000 pesetas, and until it was paid, Union members would not sell them any animals. Promoters were also forbidden from signing any bullfighter who tried to include in his contract a veto against facing bulls from Union ranches, and bullfighters who tried this were threatened with retaliation.[123]

The Union had an immediate impact. In the 1908 edition of his annual review of the bullfight season, M. Serrano García-Vao noted that "ranches that had been dead revived [and] their bulls are fighting, to the great disgust of the bullfighters and even more to that of the public." Anastasio Martín was one down-on-his-luck breeder who benefited from the new power relations. In 1908 his bulls were described as having had "a truly celebrated epoch . . . included in all the bullfights of the highest category . . . but today its bulls are generally meek as mice and timid." Yet that same season, when Ricardo Torres, "Bombita," a major star, refused to face Martín's bulls, he was forced to yield because "the Union of Breeders has said so, and not to fight them would mean he would have had to give up being a bullfighter."[124]

Inferior bulls were a problem, but they were not at the forefront of the bullfighters' concerns. What really bothered them was a significant increase in the number of Miura bulls bought by promoters. Miuras had earned a fearsome reputation by having killed a number of important matadors, but some critics felt that the owner of the ranch was trying to cash in on the "tragic legend" of his bulls by pushing inferior ones into the ring. Miuras might very well be "difficult to kill, have the biggest horns, and be the most powerful," but of the 102 that fought in 1907 "more than forty should have been rejected, some for being timid, others for their poor appearance, others for physical defects, and still others for various reasons."[125]

The bullfighters responded with a collective action of their own: A group of fifteen demanded double fees to fight Miura bulls. Their position was set out in a letter from Bombita and Machaquito that appeared in the Madrid daily *El Imparcial* on November 14, 1908. Since the breeders had formed their association the number of Miuras had almost doubled, from 57 in 1904 to 105 in 1907, and there were more to come: "Recently . . . more than three hundred Miura calves have been branded, which assures a truly astonishing number of corridas. If production were to continue in this fashion, the Miura ranch would exercise a monopoly in all the rings, not for the bravery of their animals but based on the tragic legend, which is a great draw." If Miura was using this legend to get up to 13,000 pesetas per bull for animals "that generally make it impossible for us to shine or even gratify the public, it is perfectly legitimate for us bullfighters to exploit this." The extra money was not for them personally, however; after paying their assistants double their usual wage, they would donate the remainder to colleagues who had been disabled and to the families of those who had been killed.[126] In the end, the bullfighters had to yield, and in 1909 they were fighting Miuras for their normal fees.[127]

Ranchers had their problems with promoters as well. In June 1852 six leading ranchers, the duke of Veraguas among them, sent a petition to Isabel II in which they requested permission to build a bullring of their own in Madrid. Using the language of classic economic liberalism they expressed their desire to escape from "the shadow of the exclusive and prohibitive privileges" enjoyed by the Hospital Commisson so as to further their own economic interests.

Economic freedom has been proclaimed as a dogma, and public wealth and population have increased in direct proportion to the extent it has been respected. . . . This has had, as a natural consequence, a greater inclination to enjoyments, and with the means to provide them has come the natural demand for variety and novelty in public spectacles and for all possible comfort in viewing them. . . . Competition is a necessity, and only competition can overcome the problems that always accompany monopolies.

Subject to a baneful monopoly [breeders] are at the mercy of the promoter who . . . imposes his will on most of them, and can even cause the ruin of some by refusing to take their bulls, even when the most reasonable conditions are offered. . . . Right now the promoter of the ring beyond the Alcalá Gate is taking advantage of the economic freedom proclaimed by the laws and has announced that he will introduce Portuguese bulls into that ring. There is no way of stopping this, nor the subsequent damage to the country's ranches, but one way to defend against it . . . would be to balance freedom against freedom, recognizing one while guaranteeing the other against the consequences of the bad old habit of monopolies.

Ministry of the Interior officials did not agree. The financial health of the city's welfare establishments took precedence over the interests of the ranchers; granting their request would cause "grave harm," since the income from the bullring "is absolutely indispensable for the fulfilment of these sacred services, and one can act against this only for the most just and powerful reason, which fortunately does not exist."[128]

Promoters needed the best bullfighters to draw fans into the stadium, but this did not leave them defenseless. Indeed, promoters controlled work, and this gave them considerable control over a bullfighter's professional life. Young bullfighters without established reputations were the most vulnerable. Newly minted full matador Jacinto Machío told Ignacio la Cuadra of Valencia, "[You] need not concern yourself with the question of money; I will work for any amount." And Diego Prieto, a few months beyond his *alternativa* (confirmation as a matador) in September 1882, wrote to the Hospital Commission in Valencia: "Desiring to become known in all the rings of Spain, and especially in this one that is so important, I take the liberty of requesting that you keep me in mind and I remind you that it is not a question of money; *my only desire is to become known.*"[129] Bullfighters on the downside of their careers were also vulnerable. In the 1860s Manuel Arjona was almost pleading with promoters in Valencia to let him work: To one he wrote, "It is well known that your influence is the only thing that will get me work in that ring"; to another, "Let's not fight over money . . . since what I want is for them to see me fight."[130]

Nor were big names exempt. In the spring of 1875, Casiano Hernández canceled his contract with Antonio Carmona, "El Gordito," because of protests from the fans. Carmona did not go quietly and even took the promoter to court.[131] Hernández also promoted a rather mediocre matador by the name of Felipe García, and to give him work he did not sign Frascuelo.[132]

Promoters also sought to strengthen their position against the matadors. From the 1840s, if not earlier, bullfighters enjoyed the customary contractual privilege of naming their own substitute should they be unable to perform. Even when their contract stipulated that the replacement bullfighter had to be "equal in category" or "one of the well-known ones," this was a serious limitation on the promoter's ability to design the program as he wished.[133] It also provided bullfighters with the opportunity to "abuse their power by sending a replacement of lesser category and much lower price to replace them, with the subsequent damage to the interests of the promoter, the quality of the programs, and the enjoyment of the public."[134] By the end of the nineteenth century promoters tried to fight back: In 1899 Vicente Sarcella, the promoter in charge of the Valencia ring, called a meeting of his colleagues to discuss eliminating the bullfighters' power to name substitutes.[135] This initiative was a failure, and it was only in 1910, taking advantage of the bullfighters' defeat in the Miura affair, that the Madrid promoter was able to strip this power from them. He had a strong immediate motivation to do so: During the 1909 season he had paid Bombita for thirteen corridas he didn't fight, and Machaquito for nineteen; neither of them signed for Madrid in 1910.[136]

The promoters' most cherished objective was to limit bullfighters' earnings. In 1916 they sought to impose a "model contract"; this failed, but in 1924 they attempted to impose a cap of 7,000 pesetas per fight. The following year their united front was broken by Eduardo Pagés, who took on the Madrid ring and signed Juan Belmonte, who had been in South America, to an exclusive contract at 30,000 pesetas per corrida.[137] Belmonte and Pagés subsequently found themselves the targets of both breeders and promoters: Belmonte came out of retirement in 1933 because the breeders had put a ban on sales to Pagés. That same year Belmonte, who had become a rancher of some significance, was banned from the ranchers' Union, but with Pagés's help he created a breakaway organization.[138]

The Press

Whatever their difficulties with one another, bullfighters, breeders, and, above all, promoters shared the experience of being attacked by the critics in the press, who frequently claimed to speak on behalf of the fans. The development of widespread press coverage of the corrida, and especially of a plentiful specialized press, is another aspect of the business of the bullfight. And of its modernity, since the spread of the press as a medium of information and opinion "in itself symbolized the new era" in Spain and Europe.[139] (When Spain got radio in the 1920s, the corrida quickly found a home there. A bullfight was first broadcast on October 8, 1925; the first boxing match seven months later, and the first soccer game a year after that.)[140]

The Madrid press regularly announced upcoming bullfights and published financial summaries as early as the 1760s, and the first review seems to have been published in the *Diario de Madrid* on June 20, 1793. The review began: "Your papers will describe a machine, summarize the plot of a new play, describe an unusual spectacle such as those involving the Lunardi balloons, but I have never seen a description of a bullfight. I think the public would appreciate one."[141] The first publication dedicated exclusively to the bullfight, *Estado que manifiesta las particularidades ocurridas en esta corrida,* appeared in 1819, the first of what would turn out to be a never-ending list of specialized newspapers and magazines. Luis Carmena y Millán counted more than three hundred during the nineteenth century.[142] Not surprisingly, Madrid and Seville were the most important centers, followed by Barcelona (which did not get its first such publication until 1852) and Cádiz, but the bullfight press was far from limited to these main centers.

A few papers, such as *El Enano* and *La Lidia,* had long lives; most were ephemeral in the extreme, but the rate of failure did little to dissuade new publishers. Almost forty publications appeared in the 1870s, more than one hundred in the 1880s and again in the 1890s. The rhythm at which new periodicals increased as the century went on reflected both the more general development of the Spanish press and the growth of the bullfight itself. Beyond the plethora of specialized publications, by the last quarter of the nineteenth century a bullfight column was a standard feature of the main Madrid dailies. Together they made possible the emergence of a new figure, the professional critic.

This financial precariousness and the relatively face-to-face nature of the bullfight business combined to make the relationship between the press and the spectacle it covered more intimate than some thought proper. It was widely believed that both promoters and bullfighters—especially the latter—used money and other methods to manipulate the press on their behalf. According to César Jalón, a bullfight critic turned politician, matadors gave critics free tickets in order to "create obligations," and he claimed to have known only one critic who refused to take these tickets.[143] By the turn of the century, the corrupt bullfight critic had made it to the Madrid stage: Early in Antonio Viérgol's comedy *La matadora* (The Bullfighter's Wife), which opened on May 1, 1903, the bullfight critic tells his friend the matador, who is about to leave for an engagement in San Sebastián, "If it goes badly for you, I'll send a telegram to the magazine and you'll see how well it comes out."[144]

In 1874 *El Toreo* claimed that its editor had been viciously assaulted in the street by Frascuelo for having published a table that showed his statistics to be worse than those of other bullfighters. This was an attempt "to intimidate journalists," but such was the risk of remaining aloof from "the bullfighters and their circles" in order "to be always impartial and just in our judgments."[145] In 1888, *La Lidia* proclaimed its intention to "say what we think . . . not to be heralds for bullfighters or promoters, or a mailbox for novice matadors; to be free and independent." *El Toreo Chico* denounced many of its colleagues: "It is sad to say, but the truth is that only rarely does a bullfight paper have its own life. Dependent on promoters and bullfighters, they have no opinions of their own and cannot reflect popular opinion if it contradicts the interests of their protectors."[146] The paper paid for its own outspokenness in June 1904 when the promoter of the Barcelona ring responded to the charge that he had "deceived the public, giving them oxen to pull carts" by banning the sale of the paper in the bullring.[147]

It was bullfighters' agents who received the most blistering criticism. In an article entitled "Agents . . . the Bastards," *El Toreo Chico* denounced them as "that plague that has invaded the most sacred Spanish spectacle . . . Their only objective is to protect and advance their clients, using all imaginable means, from the most ordinary and inoffensive to the vilest and most astute; [they are] true *Jesuits* of the art." One of their tricks was to send "telegrams and reviews to all the newspapers in the country, some of which publish them and become, either knowingly or not, propagators of this terrible plague." It called on promoters not to sign any bullfighter they had not actually seen and on the press "not to publish telegrams or reviews written by these agents or sent by unknown people since some of these *agents* . . . hide beneath the cloak of anonymity. . . . Sensible newspapers and bullfight magazines that do not take money from anyone, either directly or indirectly, should launch a campaign to wipe out this plague as soon as possible."[148]

An extreme, albeit more transparent, example of such conflict of interest was provided by Ferderico Mínguez, the bullfight critic for *El Globo,* who also took on the job of agent for Mazzantini. This earned him two stern open letters in *La Lidia* from Carmena y Millán:

> Your situation is a true conflict between two duties: On the one hand you will want to loyally serve the newspaper for which you write . . . but on the other you will find that the truth this requires will on occasion harm the interests of the friend who has placed his trust in you. . . . If you compared some of your published judgments on the work of Mazzantini during this season with those of the other bullfight critics, you better believe that this would make you uncomfortable, as there would be an enormous difference between the two.[149]

Charges such as this held bullfight journalists and publishers to an ethical standard far beyond that attained by the general press of the late nineteenth and early twentieth centuries. In Madrid as many as thirty or forty dailies competed in a "mean-spirited and harsh atmosphere, businesses without budgets or reasonable financial viability." As a result, journalists and editors made ends meet by blackmailing politicians with threats to publish scandalous news or by taking payoffs from ministers' reserved funds, known popularly as the "reptiles' funds." Some even got government jobs for which they had to do little more than collect their paycheck; Manuel Bueno, who was put on the payroll of the foundling hospital as a wet nurse, certainly could not do anything more.[150]

What most drew the wrath of the critics was the inadequate quality of the product itself, and as promoters were the ones who put the product together and who sold it to the fans, they were the most frequent targets. Beyond general denunciations of their greed, critiques of promoters focused on dishonesty regarding bulls and ticket sales.

One such question was that of having a replacement bull in the "bull pen" should one of the six animals scheduled to fight turn out to be injured or below standard. The Seville weekly *El Alabardero* raised this in 1879, emphasizing that the relationship between the promoter and the ticket buyer took the form of a business contract: "A butcher who gives false weight is punished . . . and a promoter who gives five bulls for six . . . is in violation of a contract in which one party (the promoter) is obliged to do certain things in exchange for the price paid by the other party (the public)."[151] Another was not providing bulls from the ranches that appeared on the posters. In 1905, *Don Jacinto* denounced Pedro Niembro for "announcing the ranches that *in case of circumstances beyond our control* can be changed for others. And as *uncontrollable circumstances* can arise at any time it suits him, he can laugh at what has apparently been offered."[152]

Some promoters used a bait and switch with the bullfighters as a way of selling tickets, especially season tickets, which were sold in Madrid beginning in 1815. The bullfighters who were to perform in the corridas included in the package were signed and announced in advance, and the bigger the names that appeared, the more attractive the season would be. But the bullfighters whose names were used to sell the tickets did not always fight, and not because they were injured and exercising their right to name a substitute. According to José Sánchez de Neira, Rafael Menéndez de la Vega had done just this in 1885:

> The posters announcing the opening of season ticket sales presented Lagartijo, Frascuelo, and El Gallo, and as substitutes Bocanegra, Hermosilla, and Lagartija, and stated that any fight in which any two of them took part would be considered part of the season package. That is, using the names of Lagartijo and Frascuelo as the excuse to raise ticket prices, and as the basis for selling more season tickets ... subscribers were being forced to attend fights in which neither appeared. And it would even be possible ... [to] have as part of the season package fights in which none of the three bullfighters under contract took part.[153]

Twenty-five years later, another critic voiced the same complaint: The promoter "advertises a number of bullfighters and brings them when he feels like it, or not at all."[154]

Some critics had greater sympathy for promoters, whom they saw as at the mercy of greedy breeders and bullfighters. As early as 1880, *El Tío Jindama* worried that the never-ending increases in the price of bulls and bullfighters' fees "would end up killing the corrida," and two decades later *El Toreo Chico* made an almost identical complaint: "We all know the principal causes: demands by breeders and bullfighters that leave promoters no choice but to either lose money or to increase ticket prices by scandalous amounts that, keeping in mind the absolute lack of self-respect of breeders and bullfighters, produce deplorable effects." High ticket prices, combined with "the disappointment that the fan so frequently experiences" were "chilling the fans' enthusiasm and slowly driving them away from their favorite spectacle."[155] After the 1897 season, *El Enano* went on the warpath against breeders and promoters, accusing them both of "swindling" the fans. Of the two, the breeders were much the guiltier party, and the paper proposed that the price paid for bulls appear on the posters announcing the fights. It also singled out for praise José Arana, the promoter in San Sebastián. Having paid the marquis of Saltillo prime prices for bulls that turned out to be "underage and unpresentable," he issued a press release announcing the cost of the animals and revealing "the breeder's indescribable conduct."[156]

One critic urged fans to form a union; another became so exasperated that he called for a consumer revolt.

> The excessive benevolence and consideration we have always shown promoters, breeders, and bullfighters has contributed notably to consolidating their unjustified power and conceit. . . . Our duty consists in taking energetic action to prevent things from continuing as they are now . . .
>
> When a promoter cheats or defrauds us by not fulfilling what he announces on the posters . . . we should not go to three or four consecutive corridas. . . . By using passive resistance, we will control the promoters and stop them from cheating us because they have shown us that scandals and outrage do not bother them . . . Once the ring is full and the cash is in the promoter's strong-box, he couldn't care less about anything else. . . . So, let's go on strike for a couple of Sundays. . . . Let's stop going to the bullring, and the guilty one will pay the consequences.[157]

The strike never happened, and the fans kept on going. For all the variety and intensity of the complaints, the bullfight had already endured—and survived—much worse. The promising beginning of the later eighteenth century had been threatened by the national political crisis of the early nineteenth, but the restoration of relative stability after the civil war of 1833-1840 allowed the corrida to recover lost ground and develop further. The last three decades of the century were a period of explosive growth: more bullrings, more publications, more—and more expensive—bulls, more—and better paid bullfighters. In short, more bullfights and more money, confirming the prediction made by the compiler of the agricultural census of 1865 that, when it came to the corrida, "the curses of the humanitarians will be silenced by the proofs of the economists."[158]

Bullfighters

two The corrida quickly became a star-driven spectacle with the bullfighter at its center. Fighting bulls offered the possibility of wealth and an unprecedented popularity. Successful bullfighters became celebrities, public figures of a new sort. The possibility of vast earnings and intense adulation lured thousands of young men, most of them from the lower classes, into the ring. But the profession was never a stable one; not only did individual figures rise and fall in public esteem, the relationship among the varying categories of bullfighter changed over time. Nor was their status as popular idols uncontested. At times, and especially after about 1890, they were criticized for no longer living up to the expectations the public had invested in them.

Evolution of the Profession

The English word *bullfighter* obscures the fact that the profession contains a number of different categories and that these are arranged hierarchically. Not surprisingly, Spanish is much more specific. Bullfighters work in a team (*cuadrilla*), which is headed by the matador, the one who kills, also called *espada* (sword) and *diestro* (expert). The rest of the cuadrilla consists of the picador who, mounted on a horse, uses a lance to weaken the bull's neck muscles, and the *banderilleros*, who then place the darts that further enrage the bull. (Today there are usually two picadors and three *banderilleros*, but at times during the nineteenth century, the cuadrilla was as large as eleven or twelve. In 1893 the critic Sánchez de Neira denounced the "numerous phalanx" of the time.)[1] The matador is the star of the show and very much the boss; the members of the cuadrilla are employees, totally dependent on the matador for their professional life. But it was not always this way.

Men have made money fighting bulls for hundreds of years. The thirteenth-century law code, the Siete Partidas, proclaimed that "as there are people who receive pay for fighting with a beast . . . those who fight with brave beasts for money are vile," and in the mid-seventeenth century Pamplona had "authentic professionals," some of whom performed as far away as Madrid.[2] Even so, until the eighteenth century, the key figure of the bullfight was the nobleman on horseback: As late as 1727 the *Diccionario de autoridades* defined *toreador* as "he who fights bulls on horseback." These noblemen were assisted by unmounted plebeians, "practiced in inciting the animals and distracting them."[3] The plebeians would often kill the bull as well. Mounted noblemen retained a central role in *funciones reales*, bullfights held to celebrate events such as the accession to the throne of a new monarch or the birth of a royal baby, well into the nineteenth century, but outside these special occasions, they yielded the bullfight to unmounted plebeians early in the eighteenth century.[4]

The reasons for this withdrawal of the nobility are not clear, but it is usually ascribed to the lack of interest in the corrida of the Bourbons, who came to the Spanish throne in 1700. Equally unclear is the precise process through which the modern bullfight emerged. Francisco Romero is frequently cited as the founder figure. Born in the town of Ronda (Málaga) around 1700, he was a shoemaker by trade. He first became involved in bullfighting assisting noblemen. At some point he began to give exhibitions of fighting bulls on foot that included the technique of killing the bull from in front with a single sword thrust. By the late 1720s Romero's activities had generated considerable enthusiasm and launched the corrida on its career as a commercialized entertainment.

Despite Romero's popularity, the unmounted matador did not immediately become the bullfight's star figure. For much of the eighteenth century this position was held by *varilargueros*, horsemen—although now commoners—who fought bulls with a lance. The monopoly granted to the Maestranza of Seville in 1739 specified "bullfights with *vara larga*" (long lance), and until the 1790s it marked the varilargueros' primacy by putting them before the other bullfighters—but behind the bulls—on the posters. This was underlined in the clothing that the Maestranza gave the participants: Varilargueros got silver braid; unmounted bullfighters, white.[5]

The different qualities of clothing disappeared in 1793 when Joaquín Rodriguez Costillares successfully demanded that matadors also receive silver braid on their outfits. This external recognition lagged well behind reality, for by this time the matador was definitively established as the corrida's undisputed focus. As the matadors and their cape work became more important, the picadors became increasingly marginalized. Unredeemed by skilled riding, over the course of the nineteenth century the picador's performance "degenerated" into what the chronicler of the Seville bullring called a "repugnant spectacle" that was barely tolerated by the fans.[6]

The changing fortunes of the two figures can be tracked in their earnings. Through the 1740s the Seville bullring paid the horsemen almost twice the amount it paid matadors. (To underline the point, the accounts rarely mentioned matadors by name.) Thus in 1745, two picadors, as the varilargueros were also called, earned 850 reales, while the third, the famous José Daza, got 1,200; the matadors received only 450. By the 1760s this had changed. In 1763 the picadors were paid 600 reales per day, about the same as two of the matadors and considerably less than the star, Costillares, who got 1680. By the time he demanded silver braid, Costillares was making 3,000 reales a day and the picadors only 1,375.[7] In Zaragoza the differential was even wider. Until 1800, picadors generally earned around 1,000 reales per fight, and in 1799 one got as much as 1,800, while bullfighters' earnings ranged from Juan Conde's 3,600 in 1779 and 5,250 in 1789, to Francisco Garcés's 9,750 in 1790, to Pedro Romero's 11,000 from 1791 to 1798, to Pepe Illo's 15,000 in 1800.[8]

Those who fought on foot were not all equal, and the matador very quickly differentiated himself from the lesser figures. The accounts of the Seville bullring distinguished between matadors and banderilleros as early as 1744, when the earnings of the former were double those of the latter. This gap grew quickly: In 1771 Cándido signed for 4,000 reales, an amount equal to the total paid to the four banderilleros, and in 1793 Pepe Illo was paid 12,000 reales for four days' work compared to 2,045 for each banderillero.[9]

Many matadors came, as we shall see, from artisan backgrounds, and they brought this experience with them. Bullfighters never enjoyed the formal legal privileges that characterized the artisan guilds (until they were abolished in 1834), but they soon applied the organizational structure of that milieu to this new trade. This took the form of the cuadrilla. As with much else in the origins of the bullfight, it is unclear when this structure originated, but it was in use by the third quarter of the eighteenth century. One nineteenth-century history credits Juan Romero with inventing the cuadrilla, bringing together "the most notable or most promising, establishing rules and mutual obligations"; Costillares, who was active in the 1760s and 1770s, certainly had one.[10]

The matador occupied the position of master craftsman, while the other members were his apprentices and journeymen. As in the guilds, these assistants were very much subordinates, a status recognized in the habitual use of the term *subalternos* to describe them. As was the case for artisans, the master was not just an employer; he was their protector and was responsible for teaching his subordinates the secrets of the craft. Apprentices worked as banderilleros and as *media espadas*, whom the matador occasionally allowed to kill a bull. Artisans had their mastery recognized through the production of a "masterpiece"; for bullfighters this took the form of the *alternativa*, a formal ceremony during a bullfight in which the lead matador, known as the *padrino* (godfather), sponsors the aspirant, presents him with a sword and cape, and yields the right to kill the first bull of the afternoon. And there was the strong expectation that after proving their mastery, former apprentices would eventually become masters in their own right.

Picadors retained a vestige of their former glory and continued as independent contractors into the second half of the nineteenth century. They also did their best to prevent promoters from forcing their earnings down, as the agent for the Valencia Provincial Hospital found in 1853. "I have tried to economize but I have not been able to. . . . I have been in contact with two or three picadors, but all had heard what Castañitas was making and none of them was prepared to accept less."[11] By the late 1860s however, Valencia was hiring picadors as part of a cuadrilla.[12]

Not all full matadors were equal. Seniority, as determined by the date of the alternativa, mattered greatly. Order of march in the procession that opened the bullfight was determined by seniority: The most senior matador was on the right, the most junior was in the middle, and their respective cuadrillas followed behind. So was the order of performance, with the senior matador fighting first. The system appears a simple one, but that did not prevent controversies. Occasionally a matador would claim that his prestige trumped strict chronology, as happened in the 1770s when Pedro Romero disputed the undoubted seniority of Costillares. The issue was resolved only with the intervention of the governor of the Council of Castile, who ordered that the mayor of Madrid settle the matter by means of a draw. In 1846 Francisco Aronja, "Cúchares," and José Redondo, "El Chiclanero," caused a "scandal" when they both went out to fight the first bull and came to blows.[13]

This status also had to be protected from misunderstandings. In July 1858 Angel López, "Regatero," complained to the president of the Valencia hospital committee that advertisements for the upcoming corridas announced him as "placing banderillas in one bull each afternoon," with the implication that he was merely a banderillero. In order to "avoid the interpretations and comments that the malicious ones in this business will make," he wanted the poster to state that his appearance as a banderillero was "to please this worthy and deferential public." To allay any doubts that he was a full matador, Regatero included a poster that showed he had taken his alternativa.[14] On one occasion, the promoter in Jérez de la Frontera had to put out a special poster, explaining, "Due to a printing error the posters for today's corrida show the name of the matador Manuel Lara, "el Jerezano," before that of Francisco Carrillo, when it should have been the reverse, as the latter is senior to the former."[15]

In the second half of the nineteenth century, the question of seniority was further complicated by the question of the ring in which the alternativa was taken. Traditional practice measured seniority from alternativas taken in "Madrid, Seville, or cities with a Maestranza, such as Granada or Ronda" so that matadors who took theirs in a "second-class ring" had to confirm it in a "first-class" one. A dispute between Gallito and Lagartija in 1881 compelled four leading bullfighters—Manuel Domínguez, Antonio Carmona, Antonio Sánchez, and Rafael Molina, "Lagartijo"—to send an open letter to one of the principal Madrid dailies: "We the undersigned, bullfighters recognized in almost all the rings of Spain . . . state on our word of honor and as an undeniable truth that there is no bullring that enjoys the right of seniority or primacy with regard to the alternativa." This provoked a response from another group, Frascuelo among them, that it was the alternativa taken in Madrid that counted.[16] Rafael Guerra, "Guerrita," felt so strongly about this that he had a clause inserted into his contracts for the 1888 and 1889 seasons in Madrid that he could not be required to appear with "matadors who have not taken their alternativa in this ring." [17] In 1885 a dispute between two bullfighters who had taken their alternativa on the same day, one in Madrid and the other in Sevilla, put the prestige of Spain's two most important rings in competition. Antonio Ortega, "el Marinero," who was made a matador in Sevilla, won out, in Cossío's words, because "he had a bigger name."[18] Subsequently the custom has been for all matadors to confirm their alternativa in Madrid.

Into the second half of the nineteenth century, bullfighters' actual career patterns followed the artisanal pattern as aspirants learned their trade in a cuadrilla under the orders of a matador before taking their alternativa and setting out on their own. Beginning in the 1850s, however, this pattern was increasingly disrupted. The first change was an assault on the practice of letting the media espada kill bulls. Francisco Montes denounced this as an "abuse": "Killing is the most difficult and lucid act and it should be performed only by full matadors, who do not have the right to yield it to anyone else. . . . This abuse is so frequent that I have seen corridas in which the first matador . . . was to kill four bulls, the second three, and the media espada one, but then the lead matador killed only one, the second only two, and the rest were left to the media espada, two assistants, and a guy who was not even part of the cuadrilla." (Montes's attitude may be due in part to his own unusual apprenticeship: After studying at the Royal Bullfight School created by King Ferdinand VII, he took his alternativa without ever having been another matador's subordinate.) When Melchor Ordóñez issued the first set of government regulations in 1852, he banned the practice altogether.[19]

By the 1870s the artisanal approach to training was breaking down. The increasing prominence of promoters, and their struggle to wrest control of the bullfight from the matadors, turned them into alternative gatekeepers to the profession. Instead of spending many years closely observing a master, aspirants moved as quickly as possible into the role of *novillero*, the lead figure in what we might call the minor league: corridas that featured bulls between two and four years old, compared to the five-year-olds used in full corridas. Luis Mazzantini, who burst onto the scene in 1882, is the classic case of this new pattern. Mazzantini began fighting bulls in *becerradas*, where the bulls were less than two years old, in and around Madrid in 1879, and he fought his first *novillada* the next year without ever having worked in anyone's cuadrilla. He spent the 1881 season touring in a cuadrilla of novilleros before working in France and Uruguay in 1882, and back in Spain in 1883. In 1884 he took his alternativa and immediately established himself as a star.[20] As one critic described it, "He came out of nowhere. . . . He needed only three fights in a fifteen-day period to make all the promoters want to sign him to contracts for many thousands of pesetas."[21] His contemporary, Manuel García, "El Espartero," spent only two years as a banderillero before becoming a matador.

Mazzantini may never have spent time in anyone else's cuadrilla, but he had enjoyed the support and patronage of the great Frascuelo. By the early twentieth century even this was unnecessary, as the career of Juan Belmonte makes clear. Belmonte was a child of the slums of Seville, but his father had a friend who had been a banderillero and who put his contacts at Belmonte's disposal. He secured him an invitation to a tentadero, where the bravery of a ranch's animals were tested, and Belmonte was able to "produce a good impression on the small group of select aficionados." (An invitation was necessary because "these events were then held with great secrecy in the hope of eluding the would-be fighters who invariably descended on them in swarms.") His father's friend talked Belmonte up in "the little world of managers and small impresarios," and this led to his first contract.[22] This engagement speaks volumes of the underside of the bullfight business, and Belmonte's account deserves to be quoted in full:

> It came through a man in Sevilla who earned a precarious living as a bullfighter's manager—his chief claim to the title was that he had it printed on his notepaper, but he wasn't the only one. His method was to send out circular letters to the managements of small bullrings, offering them the incomparable attractions of cuadrillas that didn't exist and famous matadors that nobody had ever heard of. With one of these letters he had managed to make an impression on the impresario of a small Portuguese village, Elvas, where he had contracted for a bullfight in which two famous cuadrillas . . . were to exhibit their skill. He had already given the names of the performers, the posters had been printed, and the people of Elvas were waiting expectantly to see the achievements of these celebrated gladiators; but at the last moment the chief of [one] cuadrilla—a certain Valdivieso who fought under the name of Montes II— refused to go. Finding himself in this dilemma, the manager set out to find a substitute, and having heard rumors that there was a boy called Belmonte . . . who fought with much style, he got hold of me and offered me the job. I call it a "job"; although the conditions were that I should fight according to Portuguese rules, that I should pay for the hire of my costume out of my own pocket, that I should also provide a banderillero on the same terms, that I should receive no payment, and finally that I should have to perform . . . under the name of Montes II, since the posters had already been issued.[23]

Through his father's friend, Belmonte was introduced to "some of the good aficionados who used to meet and talk about bulls at a cab stand" who took him to the Café de la Perla, "the meeting place of many influential aficionados." These included some landowners from the town of El Arahal who had just built a bullring and invited Belmonte to fight in the inaugural corrida in July 1910. After a bad performance lost Belmonte his patrons in Seville, his father's friend convinced a promoter he knew in Valencia to offer Belmonte a contract. For one fight there the only outfit he could find was in the props department of a theater; Belmonte then spent hours with needle and thread fixing it up himself. Valencia was his breakthrough: Despite a goring that put him in the hospital for a month, Belmonte's valor had made him "a torero of some standing" and earned him contracts for Seville. Within two years he was a superstar.[24]

Angel Carmona, "Camisero," was never much more than a marginal matador, but his early career shared a number of features with Belmonte's. He benefited from contacts and patrons who argued his case before the promoter of the Seville bullring at his hangout in the Café de Emperadores and who invited him to tentaderos at their ranches. Before this he had needed the good fortune to overhear conversations in the shirt shop in which he worked to learn about upcoming tentaderos. "Afraid that they would throw me out, I hid myself until three or four animals had been chased down before slipping through the corridor . . . and fighting one with my cape . . . 'Where did this kid come from? Get the hell out of here' the foreman shouted in an ill-tempered and threatening manner." His "friends and partisans" also arranged his first paid fight as a novillero in the village of Fuentes de León (Badajoz), where he did well enough to get "a regular contract for the bullfights during the fiestas the following year."[25]

The corollary to these developments was to turn membership in a cuadrilla into a dead-end job. Some examples: Manuel Martínez Diterlet, "Manene," worked in a team of child bullfighters from Córdoba and then in the cuadrillas of Manuel Molina and Lagartijo. He had aspirations to become a matador but failed to do so and returned to work for Lagartijo. In December 1888, at the age of twenty-eight, he was killed in the ring. Rafael Rodríguez, "El Mojino," started in the same children's cuadrilla as Menene, then worked for Bocanegra, Manuel Molina, Gallo, and Lagartijo before joining the cuadrilla of his childhood friend, Guerrita, for whom he worked until he died of tuberculosis at the age of thirty-seven. José Moyano worked for Cara Ancha and then spent twenty years with Bombita before retiring in 1915.[26]

By the end of the century there could be no doubt that the relations among the different categories of bullfighters were radically different from what they had been a hundred, or even fifty, years before. The matador was the boss, and the members of his team were his dependents, lacking any prospects for professional advance. They were often referred to as peons, and the name was an apt one. An activity that had formerly been artisanal had become industrial; subordinates who once held reasonable hopes of becoming masters now found themselves with little or no prospect of professional advancement. At its best, the relationship could be marked by the kind of patriarchal benevolence with which Frascuelo replied to an invitation to take part in a charity fight in 1883: He was happy to perform "without any kind of payment for myself," but he had to take his full cuadrilla of three banderilleros and two picadors, and they had to be paid, "since I cannot leave any of them without employment."[27] At virtually the same moment, however, in an article entitled "The Social Question," *La Lidia* was denouncing the extreme inequality of income between matadors and *subordinates,* which it claimed was on the order of fifteen to one. The bullfight tolerated "differences more unjust and disproportionate than in any other profession . . . we mean the workplace relations that exist between the bullfighter and the members, both picadors and peons, of his team." To improve this relationship was between "capital" (the bullfighter) and "labor" (the peons), *La Lidia* proposed that bullfighters pay their employees a set percentage of their earnings or, in addition to their pay, contribute 50 pesetas per fight into a special trust fund for "each of their *workers*"; that bullfighters establish "certain humanitarian relations in the contracts" so that sick or injured peons and the families of subordinates killed in the ring would receive some support; and that leading matadors do three benefit corridas each year to raise money for old or indigent peons.[28]

The language of the social question and class conflict soon gave way to their more tangible expressions. In May 1901, the Association of Picadors went on strike, and after intensive negotiations, which involved the civil governor of Madrid, the matadors agreed to a wage scale. First-class matadors would pay their picadors 325 pesetas per fight; second-class ones, 250; and third-class ones, 175. As this dispute was ending, the picadors began to organize. Their demands included a three-tiered pay scale, pensions, and a prohibition on first- and second-class bullfighters making their picadors travel in third class on the trains.[29]

By 1919 banderilleros and picadors had created another union. According to its president, Juan de Lucas, the "subalterns" of the corrida faced three different bourgeoisies: the promoters, the breeders, and the matadors, many of whom supported the promoters. "We were exploited and we wanted to improve our situation. . . . To dignify our class; to improve our wages; to distribute work among our colleagues who, unfortunately, did not have any; to have better traveling conditions; to eliminate the scandalous speculation of scalpers and renters of bullfighting suits." The union also sought to create more employment by increasing the number of banderilleros working each bullfight, a move that the matadors opposed.[30]

There were other equally telling manifestations of these "class" distinctions. Top matadors traveled in first class; their subordinates in second. Seville's Centro Taurino, a social club founded in 1899, admitted bullfighters as members, but only "matadors with alternativa." And according to critic César Jalón, during the second decade of the twentieth century, Madrid's bullfight world socialized in different cafés, "in accordance with their hierarchical rank." Jalón also recalled that around 1900, in the Logroño of his childhood, visiting matadors stayed at one hotel and their "subordinates in a more modest one on the outskirts."[31]

Whatever their category, all bullfighters faced the possibility of being killed in the ring. Even some of the best, at the height of their careers, died

Bullfighters Killed in the Ring, 1740–1920

Date	Matadors	Novilleros	Picadors	Banderilleros
pre-1800	3		4	
1801-1820	6		6	2
1821-1830	1		3	1
1831-1840	0		1	1
1841-1850	3	3	2	3
1851-1860	3	2	3	4
1861-1870	2	2	6	2
1871-1880	2	0	5	5
1881-1890	4	2	8	11
1891-1900	5	14	7	20
1901-1910	6	15	5	25
1911-1920	6	27	8	21

Source: J. de Bonifaz, *Víctimas de la fiesta* (Madrid, 1991).

this way: José Cándido in 1771; Pepe Illo in 1801; Manuel García, "El Espartero," in 1894; Joselito in 1920; and Manolete in 1947. Yet despite these spectacular examples, through the eighteenth and nineteenth centuries bullfighting was a much less lethal occupation than many others. The most comprehensive accounting of the "victims of the fiesta" comes up with a total of 259 deaths between 1771 and 1920.[32]

All four categories experienced an increase in the number of deaths after 1890, novilleros and banderilleros above all. In part this was due to the greater number of bullfights, which meant that there were more opportunities for these tragedies to occur. There were also more bullfighters, and as this expansion took place, there was undoubtedly also a decline in the quality, or at least preparation, especially among the matadors and novilleros, who no longer went through lengthy apprenticeships. The young aspirant had once had in the matador "a true mentor and master who could give him instructions, correct his mistakes, and relieve his ignorance," but the novillero was thrown back on "his instincts and the example of his comrades as well as the practice of watching good matadors and the advice they might have received from learned fans."[33] Finally, the second decade of the twentieth century saw a new—and more dangerous—style of bullfighting, popularized by Belmonte, in which the matador stood much closer to the bull than had been true in the past.[34]

Origins

Who were the bullfighters? Where did they come from: from what parts of the country, from what social backgrounds?

The geographic origins of bullfighters born during the eighteenth and nineteenth centuries reveal one striking continuity: the ongoing predominance of Andalusia as the cradle of matadors. Of those born before 1815, the eight provinces of the south produced 83.2 percent of all bullfighters whose province of birth is known.[35] And even though Andalusia's share declined continually, it still accounted for almost half, 46.3 percent, of those born between 1875 and 1895. Seville remained the unchallenged champion among individual provinces: It was home to 37.8 percent of all bullfighters born in the first period and a full quarter of them in the last.

There were also some striking changes, as graph 3 in Appendix A reveals. The relative decline of Andalusia was matched by the emergence of other regions as significant sources of bullfighters. Madrid was the most productive, although its share peaked in the period 1815–1844. By the end of the nineteenth century Aragon (9 percent), Levante (8.7 percent), Old Castile (7.1 percent), and the Basque provinces (4.9 percent) had all taken on a new importance.

There had also been notable changes at the provincial level. Cádiz and Córdoba, which had been the second and third most important producers of bullfighters born before 1815, with 24.3 percent of the total, were producing only 6.9 and 5.4 percent, respectively, by the end of the nineteenth century. On the other hand, Zaragoza and Valencia had jumped from having no bullfighters in the first period into third and fourth place, with 9.1 and 6.9 percent, respectively.

The prominence of these two provinces points to the most significant change that had taken place: the extension of the bullfight and its popularity across the country, a process we can call the nationalization of the corrida. The vast majority, 88.4 percent, of bullfighters born before 1815 came from only a handful of provinces, all but one of them in the south: Cádiz, Córdoba, Madrid, Málaga, and Seville. (The writers of the early nineteenth century who created the stereotype of the Andalusian bullfighter did so with considerable justification.)[36] Only sixteen of the forty-four provincial or regional units could claim any bullfighters at all, and twenty-eight produced none. For bullfighters born between 1875 and 1895 the picture was very different, with bullfighters totally absent from only seven provinces.

Bullfighters were also heavily urban in origin. Of the 1,940 in our sample, 198 (10.2 percent) came from the city of Seville and 116 (6 percent) from Madrid. The city of Zaragoza produced 57 (2.9 percent) and Valencia 55 (2.8 percent), and between them the Basque capitals of Bilbao and San Sebastián were home to another 39 (2 percent). Barcelona, the country's industrial capital and its largest city, was something of an exception with only 17 bullfighters (0.9 percent). These seven cities produced 24.8 percent of the matadors; given that in 1900 these cities held only 9.8 percent of the national population, bullfighters' urban provenance is truly striking.

Their social origins are more difficult to determine. Some bullfighters came from relatively well-off backgrounds. Matías Lara Merina's (b. 1885) father was an affluent cattle dealer who sent him to study at the seminary, and Juan Gómez de Lesaca y García was the son of an army general.[37] They were very much the exception. An examination of the social origins of sixty-eight

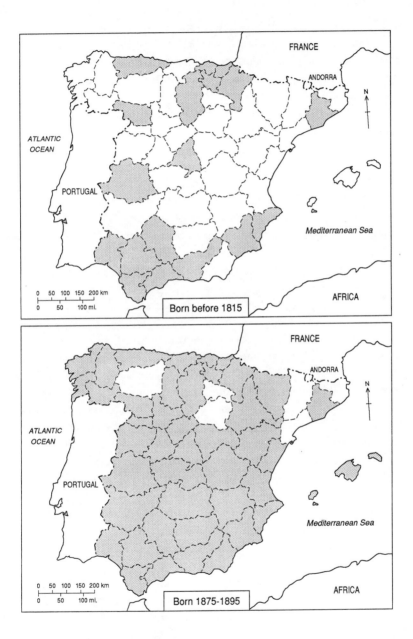

Born before 1815

Born 1875-1895

bullfighters who were active before 1880 revealed that they came from the lower strata of Spanish society.[38] But bullfighters did not generally come from the most marginal groups; they were not the Spanish equivalent of the Jewish and Irish boxers in nineteenth-century Britain or the basketball players produced in the urban ghetto in the United States in the late twentieth century. Few were children of landless laborers, as was El Cordobés, the idol of the 1960s, or of the urban slums, as was Juan Belmonte, the star of the 1920s. This is a twentieth-century pattern. Thirty came from the artisan class, with seventeen different trades represented. The importance of the artisan ambience is apparent from the many who fought under their trade names, as it were: El Confitero (dessert maker), El Relojero (watchmaker), El Panadero (baker), El Sombrerero (hatmaker), and El Sastre (tailor), to mention but a few. Of those who came from the rural world, four were sons of *labradores* (which usually denotes well-off farmers)—one the son of a cattle trader, one the son of a wagoneer, one the son of an employee of a large estate, and one a shepherd.

The frequent use of nicknames further attests to bullfighters' predominantly lower-class origins. Nicknames are ubiquitous among lower-class Spaniards, both rural and urban. These often derive from an occupation, physical characteristics or defects, or place of birth, precisely the types of nicknames most often borne by bullfighters. By the late nineteenth century, however, bullfighters were choosing their own nicknames arbitrarily, frequently ones that referred back to greats of an earlier time such as Costillares or Pepe Illo, with whom they had no connection, least of all in terms of ability. For a bullfighter concerned with distancing himself from the practice, and the background it denoted, the use of nicknames could be demeaning. Thus, Juan Conde asked, "Why do you not use the nicknames of my colleagues with greater prudence . . . ? Would it not be better if people forgot them and began to treat us with greater respect, calling us by the names that we received from our parents?"[39]

There was a considerable element of endogamy, of sons following fathers, among bullfighters. In some cases this extended to entire clans covering three generations. Some families produced a number of outstanding matadors and are referred to as dynasties. The Romeros, who spanned the eighteenth century, were undoubtedly the first family of bullfighting, in every sense of the word. Francisco Romero is widely considered to be the founder of modern bullfighting, and his son Juan is credited with formalizing the cuadrilla structure. Juan Romero's four sons followed in the footsteps of their father and grandfather. The second half of the nineteenth century saw the rise of the Gallo dynasty. This began with José Gómez, "Gallo," a career ban-derillero, and his younger brother Fernando (1847–1897). Fernando's three sons, Rafael Gómez Ortega (b. 1882), Fernando Gómez Ortega (b. 1889), and José Gómez Ortega (b. 1895), all became matadors; the youngest, known as Joselito el Gallo, was one of the most famous of all time. More prolific but much less eminent was the Bejarano clan from Córdoba. It produced at least twelve bullfighters in the half century after 1860, but only one of them, Antonio Bejarano y Millán, "Pegote," achieved any significant success.

This endogamy also involved the women of the family. The Gómez Ortega brothers inherited bullfighting blood from their mother as well as their father. Gabriela Ortega came from a famous bullfighting clan in Cádiz and counted upward of a dozen members of the profession among her rela-tives. Two of the Gómez Ortega sisters married bullfighters; one married Ignacio Sánchez Mejías, whose death in 1934 provoked García Lorca's famous poem. Both had sons who became matadors.[40]

Earnings

Young men and women were drawn to the bullfight as a career for many motives. For some it was glamour and adventure: Angel Carmona, "Camis-ero," was drawn to bullfighting as a young child, and his *afición* (attraction) was stimulated by seeing, in the shirt shop where he worked, bullfighters, "with their majestic attire, their irreproachable dress of BULLFIGHTERS, showing off their graceful figures . . . their tight-fitting trousers 'showing everything God gave them' . . . and their necklaces from which hung monu-mental lockets covered in innumerable and luminous gems, and in which I imagined myself decked out, clothes that were so stylish and so very bull-fighterish."[41] For others it was to escape from an unpromising and unattrac-tive alternative. Martina García came to bullfighting after having worked as a servant and cook in a bar. At a low point in his career, Belmonte worked as a laborer on the construction of a canal on the Guadalquivir River, an experi-ence that convinced him that "I was ready to gamble my life cheerfully. Any-thing was better than being a laborer again."[42] Luis Mazzantini was better off: He had a middle-class job as a white-collar worker for a railroad but was dissatisfied with the genteel poverty it brought. According to his biographers, "One night he had to send off a train and discovered that it was carrying the cuadrilla of one of the most famous bullfighters of the day. He saw that the matador was profoundly asleep in *one of the first-class wagons.* [The rest of the cuadrilla was presumably in second class.] The impression this made on him that cold, damp, and unpleasant early morning . . . decided him to become a bullfighter."[43]

The prospect of otherwise unattainable riches was undoubtedly present in all their minds. From the first days of the professional corrida, bullfighters earned sums that people of lower-class backgrounds could scarcely have dreamed of. Take Pepe Illo as an example. In 1773 he was at the beginning of his career and was one of the most poorly paid matadors signed for the season in Madrid, receiving 4,500 reales for fifteen corridas. What did this mean? His earnings in this fortnight alone were equal to the average for the 381 surgeon-barbers in the capital and not far behind the 5,900 average for its 182 lawyers. As an *annual* income it would have been sufficient for a "family of four or five . . . to achieve a measure of bourgeois comfort," such as employing a maidservant. By 1790, Illo was an established star and was paid as such; that year he fought fourteen times in Madrid for which he earned 28,000 reales. And in 1800, the year before his death, his eleven days' work brought him 30,800 reales plus a tip of 3,000 more. His daily rate of 2,800 reales was two or three times the annual income of an unskilled laborer and half that of many guild masters who owned their own shops. This level of income put him in elevated company: The prosperous merchants of the powerful Five Great Guilds had annual incomes ranging from 17,500 to 37,500 reales, and the 120 titled noblemen who lived in Madrid "averaged 44,000 reales in city-derived income." Those 31,000 reales, earned in eleven days, gave him an annual income among the top 5 percent in the capital. He fought in other cities as well, earning some 23,000 reales for an eight-day season in Seville in 1796. His annual income at the height of his career could well have reached 70,000 reales, three quarters that of a royal councilor.[44] Costillares and Pedro Romero, other stars of the 1780s and 1790s, earned similar amounts; in fact, during the 1790 season in Madrid, Costillares earned more.[45]

Of course, few bullfighters ever achieved this kind of earning power. How did more humble figures do? By the last decade of the eighteenth century banderilleros made between 320 and 610 reales per day. Given that some 70 percent of the population of Madrid earned less than 2,000 reales per year and that annual incomes for unskilled workers ranged from 720 for construction workers to 1,000 for a carpenter's assistant, these were most attractive wages. Cristóbal Díaz placed banderillas in sixteen corridas in 1790 and took home 5,120 reales, enough for a life of modest bourgeois comfort.[46]

Top matadors continued to earn close to 3,000 reales per fight during the first two decades of the nineteenth century, as Gerónimo José Cándido did in Madrid in 1817 and 1819, although by 1822 he had dropped to 2,600 per fight. Banderilleros continued to earn 500 reales per fight.[47] By 1841 the fee had risen to 4,000, and by the following decade, to 4,500. Beginning in the 1840s contracts generally stated a single fee for the matador and his cuadrilla, which makes it difficult to continue the comparison. Moreover, only a small and random sample of contracts are available, and these reveal the earning power of a number of leading matadors at different stages of their careers, which renders any comparisons even less reliable. Yet, some comparison over time should be attempted, and Graph 4 (in Appendix A), which is based on the *highest* per-fight fee available for each year, does so. The result is clear: Fees remained essentially flat between 1850 and 1870 before experiencing a sharp increase over the following two decades.[48]

This graph is based on contracts for fights in a number of different cities, yet another complicating factor. This can be eliminated by analyzing the per-fight fee earned by bullfighters who signed season-long contracts for Madrid, as appears in Graph 5 (in Appendix A). This shows a gradual increase between 1850 and 1865, and a very much steeper one between 1880 and 1890.[49] The strong upward trend in both graphs echoes that for the prices of fighting bulls and confirms that the last quarter of the nineteenth century was a period of immense prosperity for the industry.

The incompleteness of the sources prevents any determination of the actual annual income of individual matadors, but even these fragments leave no doubt that they continued to be hugely well paid. If we move ahead to the end of the nineteenth century, we find Lagartijo's contract for the 1888 Madrid season paying him 22,500 reales per fight plus a tip (*gratificación*) of 12,600.[50] For a season that consisted of twenty-three corridas, this amounted to 517,500 reales. And on top of that he would have fought at least twenty-five times in other cities at a fee of at least 15,000 reales per fight. He was paid 44,000 for two fights in Almería that season.[51] A very conservative estimate would put his earnings for the year at 892,500 reales, in line with the 800,000 reales *El Tendido* estimated that he had made for the 1882 season.[52] (Lagartijo did not fight as often as some of his contemporaries: Guerrita averaged 71 corridas per season betwen 1888 and 1895.) If we, generously, assume that one third of that amount went to pay his subordinates, Lagartijo still would have retained some 600,000 reales. Just three years later Mazzantini would earn 800,000 reales from his contract for twenty corridas in Paris alone![53]

What do these numbers mean? A glance at the annual salaries of public sector employees tells us that bullfighters' earnings were incomparably greater than those of even figures of great prestige and responsibility. In the late 1880s, the 5,000 pesetas Frascuelo, Lagartijo, and Mazzantini commanded for a *single fight* was more than the annual salary of a high school teacher, half the annual salary of the best-paid university professor or mining engineer, and equal to what a captain general and the president of the Supreme Court earned in two months.

Of course, these fees included the salaries of the matadors' subordinates. If we return to our estimate of 150,000 pesetas (600,000 reales) of personal income for Lagartijo in 1882, we find that it equaled what the best-paid judge earned in seventeen years and surpassed fifteen years' salary for a top mining engineer and five years' salary for the president of the Supreme Court. These amounts dwarfed the salaries shown below.

Bullfighters' earnings also dwarfed those of top professional athletes elsewhere. At the end of the nineteenth century, the best cricketers in Britain earned 275 pounds per year; the top soccer players, 208. These annual salaries amounted to 6,875 and 5,200 pesetas, respectively, only marginally more than a leading matador was earning for a single corrida. Jockeys were much better paid than soccer players or cricketers, but even their incomes of 5,000 pounds (125,000 pesetas) were but a fraction of the 600,000 we calculated for Lagartijo.[54] In the United States, Babe Ruth was "the highest-paid player ever" through the 1920s. He earned $52,000 (338,000 pesetas) in 1922, and his annual salary peaked in 1930-1931 at the scandalously high sum of $80,000 (640,000 pesetas). Lagartijo and others had been earning this much and more thirty years earlier. Ruth's contemporary Juan Belmonte earned 30,000 pesetas ($4,300) per fight, and in 1925 he signed a contract worth "millions of pesetas." In 1924, a seven-fight appearance in Lima alone brought him $63,500.[55]

These sums represent single season earnings and tell us nothing of how lucrative an entire career could be. Bullfighting was not just a young person's

Annual Salaries of Public Sector Employees: 1876–1916
(In pesetas)

	1876	1900	1916-22
Postal worker (average)	1,450	1,804	4,353
Teacher (elementary)		3,000	8,000
Teacher (secondary)		4,000	12,500
University professor	10,000	10,000	15,000
Mining engineer	10,000	10,000	18,000
Judge	8,500	8,500	12,800
Supreme Court President	30,000	30,000	50,000
Army:			
Captain			3,500
Colonel			8,000
Brigadier General			10,000
Lieutenant General			25,000
Captain General			30,000

Source: F. Villacorta Baños, *Profesionales y burócratas*, (Madrid, 1989), pp. 210–229; C. Boyd, *Praetorian Politics in Liberal Spain* (Chapel Hill, 1979), p. 33.

profession: The matador who escaped serious injury or death could continue performing to an age unthinkable in almost any other athletic endeavor. Juan León retired in 1847, at the age of fifty-nine. Frascuelo was a full matador for twenty-three years and continued fighting until he was forty-eight. Lagartijo took his alternativa when he was twenty-four and retired twenty-eight years later, at the age of fifty-two.

Careers of this length meant that a successful matador could become quite wealthy. When he was killed in the ring in Madrid in 1801, Pepe Illo left three houses in Seville, three acres of land (including vineyards), personal belongings, six silver place settings among them, and accumulated debts of 127,000 reales. With the debts covered by the sale of one of the houses, the estate retained 185,339 reales in cash. Just the *cash* portion of the estate exceeded the overall wealth of the three Madrid physicians and six of the middle-ranking bureaucrats who formed part of the Madrid elite studied by

Jesús Cruz.[56] The career of Francisco Montes (1805–1851) lasted less than twenty years, but he still managed to build up considerable personal wealth. When he died, at forty-six, he left his two-year-old son, Juan Ramón, three houses, one of which was used as a warehouse for wine, and nine hectares (about twenty acres) of land, including vineyards, valued at 568,101 reales. (Whether he left anything to his wife is not clear, but the son's inheritance did not include any cash or personal belongings, so the actual estate was probably greater.)[57] An estate of this magnitude was larger than those of six of twenty-six leading Madrid merchants of the first half of the nineteenth century. It also equaled or surpassed the personal fortunes of two of the four members of the council of Castile and three of the six members of other royal Councils whose estates Cruz analyzed. Montes's accumulated wealth was greater than that of eight of the nine physicians, four of the five apothecaries, and two of the six lawyers.[58] At his death in 1898, the reported value of Frascuelo's fortune was greater still: two houses in central Madrid worth 300,000 pesetas; an estate in nearby Torrelodones worth 250,000 pesetas; 275,000 pesetas in treasury bonds, and 40,000 pesetas in jewelry. This total of 865,000 pesetas was about half the net worth of Antonio Maura, one of the country's leading lawyers and a major political figure in 1901.[59]

Not all bullfighters were so fortunate. Many had to take other jobs when they retired from the ring, and some ended their lives in abject misery. Francisco González, "Pachón," who was active in the first two decades of the nineteenth century, was seriously injured in 1830. A favorite of King Ferdinand VII because of his strong royalist sentiments, he was given a job driving the mail coach to Andalusia, but lost it for political reasons in 1836. This forced him to return to the ring, but with much less success than before; he died in 1843 from a goring sustained the previous year.[60] Antonio Herrera, "Anillo," a career banderillero active in the 1850s and 1860s, opened a small tavern in Sevilla. Juan Jiménez, who had been senior matador in the bullfight held to celebrate the marriage of Isabella II in 1846, took a job as a bread salesman "to support himself with the meager income it provided," and El Tato, whose career was ended when a goring led to his leg being amputated, got a job in the Seville slaughterhouse. Sadder still was the fate of Juan Lucas Blanco, who slid into alcoholism at the peak of his career and died at the age of forty-three in the Seville charity hospital, or Antonio Ruiz, "El Sombrerero," who lived his retirement in poverty in Seville and died in the charity hospital at the age of seventy-seven.[61] Antonio Suárez Cortés, el Peregrino '(the Pilgrim)', became a beggar when he was unable to make a living as a banderillero. "To stimulate the charity of the public" he dressed as a pilgrim from past times and sold rosaries. Perhaps the most extreme case of all was Juan Castro López, a twenty-two-year-old who was driven to attempt suicide when a novillada in which he was to fight was canceled, robbing him of the opportunity to relieve "the agonizing situation of his mother and sisters."[62]

America

America loomed large in the careers of many Spanish bullfighters, and did so from very early on. Coinciding almost exactly with Spain's reluctant recognition of the independence of its colonies in the 1840s, Spanish bullfighters turned to "the Indies" for professional opportunities, and promoters in Mexico, Cuba, Chile, Brazil, Ecuador, Uruguay, Venezuela, Peru, Colombia, Panama, and Guatemala were eager to sign them. Perhaps the first Spanish bullfighter to work in these newly independent countries was Bernardo Gaviño. Born in the province of Cádiz in 1813, Gaviño went to Cuba in 1831; he was signed there in 1835 by Mexico's consul general in New Orleans. Gaviño spent the rest of his career, and his life, in Mexico and became the founder of Mexican bullfighting.[63]

America served Spanish bullfighters in differing ways, depending on their status and the stage of their career. For the stars it provided lucrative contracts in the Spanish off-season, between November and February. Big names such as Frascuelo, Mazzantini, and Belmonte cost American promoters big money. Frascuelo reportedly received 13,000 "duros libres" for twelve corridas in Lima in 1879, and Mazzantini received 150,000 pesetas for fourteen corridas in Havana in 1886. In 1924 Belmonte earned 500,000 pesetas for seven fights in Lima, almost two and a half times what he earned for a corrida in Spain.[64]

America also offered additional adulation. Mazzantini fought in Mexico and Juan Belmonte fought there, as well as in Peru and Venezuela between 1913 and 1924. In both cases they were the toast of the town, at least for the elite. Mazzantini was taken up by the social elite of Mexico City even though it had turned its back on the bullfight for more "modern," U.S.-inspired entertainments. For his part, Belmonte met many leading political figures: He became a friend of Venezuela's president Juan Vicente Gómez, and in Mexico President Victoriano Huerta invited him to dinner.[65]

Such celebrity tours were much less common than the presence of young bullfighters attempting to make a name for themselves and bullfighters who had taken their alternativa but who had been unable to develop much of a career in Spain itself. An early example was Francisco Sánchez Povedano, the older brother of the great Frascuelo. He had worked in America with Pedro Aixela, "Peroy," but replaced him after he was gored, and this led to a contract for twelve fights in Lima. He returned to Spain for four years as a banderillero, then spent the 1875 and 1876 seasons in Uruguay and Brazil. He took his alternativa in Spain in 1877, but he worked in Montevideo between 1881 and 1884. He later fought in Peru, Panama, and Paris before retiring in 1900 to run a bullfight school.[66]

For aspiring young bullfighters America served as a kind of "minor league," especially through the 1860s. In 1836 Manuel Domínguez y Campos, perhaps the first Spanish bullfighter to cross the Atlantic, led his cuadrilla to Uruguay after having worked with a number of leading matadors in Spain, and in 1840 he performed in the corrida held to celebrate the coronation of Pedro II as emperor of Brazil. Manuel Hermosilla went to Cuba in 1867 where he became known as a banderillero and was invited to join the team of José Ponce; when Ponce returned to Spain, Hermosilla set up his own cuadrilla and fought across Mexico and in Peru before returning to Spain in 1873 to take his alternativa. He split his subsequent career between Spain and Montevideo.[67] Peroy worked as a banderillero and second matador in Spain through the 1850s, but he was able to take his alternativa only after having spent a season in Havana. Finally, José Lara, "Chicorro," spent more than four years in Lima and Havana working for Manuel Díaz, "Lavi," before returning to Spain, where he worked for Gordito for three years before becoming a matador himself.[68]

America also provided a haven for the lesser lights of Spain's bullfighting world. There was the occasional has-been, such as Francisco Arjona Herrera, "Cúchares." He had been a star, but in 1868, at fifty years old, well past his prime and short of money, he signed a contract to fight in Cuba. It was a desperate move that turned out badly; in Cuba he contracted yellow fever and died.[69] Manuel Díaz, "Lavi," who was active in the 1850s, spent much time in America because he enjoyed little respect in Spain, where he was considered the "clown of bullfighting."[70] Enrique Vargas González, "Minuto," had some strong seasons in Spain: forty corridas in 1897 and forty-eight in 1898, before retiring in 1902. He made a comeback three years later but spent almost all of it in Mexico and Uruguay.[71]

Much more numerous were the marginal matadors who were never able to make a living back home. The two or three decades after 1890 saw a flood of Spanish matadors descend on America as the supply of matadors greatly exceeded the amount of work available in Spain itself. In 1905 one critic complained about this oversupply: Many bullfighters "fight no more than once or twice a year and others not at all; some end up offering themselves for some bread and a sausage."[72] Some wound up living abroad for years at a time. These bullfighters formed part of the massive wave of migration, both temporary and permanent, from Europe to South and North America between 1880 and the First World War.

After 1890 there were many bullfighters who worked more in America than in Spain, and not by choice. José Centeno took his alternativa in 1887 (he had already spent a year in Montevideo as a novillero) but "with next to no contracts in our country his bullfight career took place in Havana and Mexico." He retired to Spain in 1906.[73] Manuel Lara Reyes, "Jerezano," fought only 49 corridas in Spain in twelve years but worked continuously in Mexico between 1904 and 1910; Joaquín Hernández managed only 103 fights in Spain over fifteen years but fought regularly in Mexico; and Angel García Padilla fought in Spain only 78 times between 1897 and 1910 and spent most of his career in America. (In comparison, a superstar such as Bombita had 596 corridas between 1899 and 1911.) Francisco Bonal y Casado, "Bonarillo," managed a modest career in Spain—287 fights in eighteen years—but fought widely across America, including less-visited locales such as Brazil, Ecuador, and Guatemala.[74] Francisco González Ruiz, "Faíco," began his career in Spain in 1893 but after 1897 was more and more out of the country. His last season in Spain was 1901, and he made the rest of his career in America, including a stint as advisor to the Lima bullring.[75]

Angel Carmona, "Camisero," is an outstanding example of such a marginal matador. He decided to take his alternativa in 1904 because "the promoter in Mexico City had made me a highly profitable proposition." In the years that followed, his career in Spain went badly, and he was "forced to have recourse to Mexico in the winters." By 1914 he had spent "a number of seasons . . . fighting very little, too little to earning a living," and he set off for Lima. Back in Spain he set up a taxi business but it failed, and he was "forcibly obliged to make another trip to America." By the time he finally retired in April 1918, he had fought in Uruguay, Panama, and Venezuela as well as in Mexico and Peru.[76]

His sojourns in America also allowed Camisero to discover a certain talent for business. Stranded in Mexico in 1910 in the midst of the revolution, he helped set up a currency exchange agency. From 1912 on, he used his American expeditions to buy and sell silk, a sideline that quickly became more lucrative than bullfighting. In retirement, he worked as agent for a number of businesses, including one owned by his brother. He also worked as a bullfighters' agent, a common postretirement activity, and then, much more unusually, put together an annual bullfight guidebook, the *Consultor indicador taurino universal.*[77]

Some bullfighters left Spain permanently. Leandro Sánchez, "Cacheta," had an undistinguished career in Spain before setting definitively in Bogotá, where he died in 1914 at the age of fifty-three. Tomás Parrondo, "Manchao," was a highly successful novillero in Spain before a couple of gorings caused him to lose popularity, a setback that led him to Mexico. He returned to Spain to take his alternativa but left almost immediately and spent the rest of his career in Venezuela and Mexico, where he died in 1900. *La Lidia* described Parrondo as "one novillero among many; when he did not display exceptional qualities . . . we judged it would be difficult for him to reach the same relative level as a full matador and that he would become just another member of the numerous contingent," a classic example of the run-of-the-mill matador for whom the prestige of having qualified in Spain was the key to having a career in the former colonies.[78] The corollary was that few Latin American bullfighters worked in Spain. Ponciano Díaz, the Mexican idol, made one brief trip to Spain in 1889, when he took his alternativa in Madrid; only Rodolfo Gaona, also from Mexico, was able to make a career there.

Celebrity

When the Italian writer Edmondo de Amicis visited Spain in the 1880s he found the cult of celebrity surrounding bullfighters in full flower. "Their names, their faces, and their deeds are even better known to the people than the deeds, faces, and names of their commanders and statesmen. Toreros in comedies, toreros in song, toreros in pictures, toreros in the windows of printshops, statues of toreros, fans painted with toreros, handkerchiefs with figures of toreros—these one sees again and again on evey occasion and in every place."[79] If anything, De Amicis understated the bullfighters' omnipresence, neglecting to mention that they had already achieved the climactic form of celebrity in a capitalist society: the authority to sell products by endorsing them. As early as 1879 Antonio Carmona was gracing the label of a brand of sherry that, he assured potential buyers, made him a better bullfighter. And when Luis Mazzantini burst onto the scene in the 1880s, "Mazzantini hats, Mazzantini ties, Mazzantini collars, and Mazzantini canes" quickly followed. De Amicis wrote before the advent of moving pictures, when "the most famous bullfights and the big name bullfighters were . . . plentifully represented in the films of the era [before 1914]."[80]

Bullfighters knew how to promote their popularity and take advantage of it. We have already mentioned the practice of buying favorable reviews from bullfight critics.[81] Joselito, one of the superstars of the early twentieth century, convinced photographer Juan José Serrano to move to Sevilla, where he "kept him under contract as his personal photographer." (Serrano also shot movies of bullfights.)[82] Lagartijo used his immense popularity to turn his "farewell tour" of 1893 into a hugely profitable enterprise. His fees were unprecedented: from 25,000 to 30,000 pesetas for fights in Valencia, Barcelona, Bilbao, and Zaragoza, and 50,000 for his Madrid appearance. The corridas sold out immediately, and scalpers asked "fabulous prices." In Madrid, Church authorities rescheduled the Corpus Christi procession so that it would not conflict with the corrida.[83] According to one chronicler of Lagartijo's career, however, the rescheduling came about because Lagartijo used "high-level contacts to get Rome to grant permission to move the Corpus Christi procession from the afternoon to the morning to further assure the financial success of the fight." This same chronicler found the whole operation too cynical to bear: "He wanted to make millions out of five corridas that were going to stun the bullfight world. . . . He alone was the sole creator, picking the rings and acquiring the right bulls, and there was advertising in the press and on the street to shake people up and prepare his success beforehand. Lagartijo's farewell was a business deal and nothing more, least of all a show of gratitude to the fans who had . . . filled his pockets with gold and bank notes."[84]

On occasion the cult of celebrity became one of an almost religious devotion that drew directly on Catholicism's reverence for relics. In June 1869, El Tato was gored during a bullfight held to celebrate the proclamation of the new democratic constitution; in the days that followed, the Madrid press carried regular reports on the matador's condition. For example, on June 11, *La Correspondencia de España* reported that:

Yesterday the leading surgeons in Madrid met to consider Tato's condition. . . .
The meeting lasted from three in the afternoon until 6:30, and they agreed to
make large and numerous incisions to the leg and muscle to prevent as much
as possible the extension of the gangrene that has already extended considerably from the leg to above the knee. . . .

  After the operation the patient slept a lot, and today, in the first inspection,
they found the wounds and the leg in a satisfactory condition. . . .

  The Count of Reus [the Prime Minister], and many more important people
in Madrid went yesterday to ask about the condition of the popular matador.[85]

In the end El Tato's leg had to be amputated. The appendage was placed in a
container with alcohol and displayed in a pharmacy in central Madrid. Years
later, the pharmacy caught fire, and "many of his fans threw themselves into
the building to try and save the relic."[86]

This kind of attention was not unique to El Tato. Manuel Domínguez
was gravely wounded in 1857, and "telegrams detailing his medical condition
were posted twice each day in the Iberia Café." The goring of Frascuelo in
Madrid in 1877 "produced an enormous uproar. The street . . . where he lived
swarmed with people anxious to read the medical bulletins that were posted
on the door three times per day."[87] And when Mazzantini was gored in
Seville, "the municipal authorities . . . put sand in the streets around his hotel
to prevent the noises and vibrations of the carriages from bothering him.
One had to see the unending flotillas of coaches of the most select Sevillian
fans and elegant and aristocratic ladies . . . expressing interest in his condition and signing the white sheets posted on the door of the hotel."[88]

Less tragedy attended the amputation of Frascuelo's pigtail (*coleta*). Cutting the coleta marked a bullfighter's retirement, and when Frascuelo retired
he divided his in three parts, which he gave to the editor of *La Lidia*, to his
son, and to the archbishop of Madrid, "the Family, the Church, and the
Bulls," as Andrés Amorós remarks. In 1882 *El Tendido* had reported rumors
that Lagartijo was planning to "leave his pigtail to the Virgin of the Pillar in
Zaragoza next October"; these rumors resurfaced two years later, and *La
Lidia* noted that "the sword, cape, suit of lights, and even the pigtail are
solemnly promised to very well-known people."[89] The amputation of Guerrita's coleta in October 1899 lacked these religious overtones but reflected his
celebrity with equal effect: His wife cut the pigtail before an audience that
included some friends who had traveled from Madrid to Córdoba just for

this ceremony, and the news was "transmitted by telegraph all across Spain." José de la Loma, bullfight critic for Madrid daily *El Liberal,* was one of those present, and he wired the following report:

> As soon as he arrived in Madrid, Guerrita hid himself in the house of his friend Noval to avoid unwelcome visits and treacherous reporters. He left in the ordinary train from Valencia, catching the express at Alcázar and arriving here at seven in the morning. Today, at midday, in the hall of his house where many friends of the celebrated bullfighter had gathered, his wife, Madame Dolores Sánchez, cut Rafael's pigtail. The members of his cuadrilla, in tears, hugged him. He was much moved. His friends then shouted a "viva" to Guerrita.[90]

When word of Frascuelo's impending retirement came out, it moved the famous composer of *zarzuelas* (operettas) Francisco Asenjo Barbieri to write a poem entitled "Frascuelo's Pigtail":

> Don't cut it off Frascuelo,
> Frascuelo, don't cut it off
> Look, without a *coleta*
> One cannot make *coleo*
> And the man who cuts it off
> Cannot please the fair sex.[91]

Barbieri had already written a zarzuela entitled *Pan y toros* (Bread and Bulls), which included three bullfighters of the late eighteenth century as characters, and this was but one of a plethora of literary works about the bullfight. Nicolás Fernández de Moratín, one of eighteenth-century Spain's leading authors, wrote an "Ode to Pedro Romero" in which he painted the bullfighter as a Classical hero. In the nineteenth century, foreign writers such as Lord Byron, Théophile Gautier, and, above all, Prosper Mérimée (*Carmen*) as well as Spanish authors (Mariano José de Larra, Fernán Caballero, and Luis Coloma) wrote about the corrida. But it was only in the last third of the century, and especially after 1890, that the number of works about the bullfight, and especially novels, became significant: More than one hundred bullfight novels appeared between 1890 and 1910.[92]

These novels had bullfighters as protagonists, but the way they represented them changed over time, moving from "a romantic hero, full of positive values to the critical and negative treatment of the last novels." The "typology of the hero" was the creation of foreign Romantics who "uncovered the possibilities" of the bullfighter for Spanish writers. By the end of the century, however, literary naturalists such as Vicente Blasco Ibáñez produced books such as *Blood and Sand* with "a hero who was more fragile and exposed to disrepute," and they were followed by much more critical authors who focused on "the conflicts, problems and failures of the hero" to produce "a drastic demythification" of the bullfighter.[93] On the other hand, in 1922 *Blood and Sand* was made into movie starring Rudolph Valentino, which served to create a new myth of the bullfighter and convey it to vastly more people than would ever read the novel.

Bullfighters were a mainstay of the *cuplé*, the cabaret song that was a hugely popular form of entertainment in the early twentieth century. Commercially produced escapism, these songs "limited themselves to exploiting profitable veins . . . which is why this 'mass production' returned untiringly to the well-trod paths of the dead bullfighter, the woman deceived, the femme fatale . . . and the tragic love affair." Characteristically, the cuplé was set in either Madrid or Andalusia, and in the latter "the bullfighter is the supreme hero, the spiritual reserve of the virtues of the race in the face of danger and death."[94] In his memoirs, novelist Pío Baroja described the popularity of such songs, and of the bullfight as one of their themes. Such songs were popularized in the cabarets of the major cities, but "students and traveling salesmen" carried them to smaller centers.[95] Bullfighters were less prominent in the zarzuela, although in 1870 Guillermo Cercereda wrote one about Pepe Illo, who was killed in the ring in 1801. The 1896 Madrid revival included a bullfight scene that featured a live calf.[96] Luis Carmena y Millán compiled a list of 118 dramatic works and 75 pieces of music with bullfight themes. Many of them were dedicated to individual bullfighters, *pasodobles* such as Juan Crespo's *Bombita chica* and Federico Chueca's *Guerrita*; Bernardo Gómez's mazurka for piano *Frascuelo*, or T. J. Bartoli's polka *Mazzantini*.[97]

The bullfight penetrated this "high" literary tradition much more slowly than it did the world of less formal, popular culture. Beginning in 1771 with José Cándido, the first important bullfighter to be killed in the ring, and continuing into the twentieth century, the figure of the matador, and especially of those who died in the ring, inspired a continuous stream of ballads (*romances*), popular epics (*cantares populares*), and narrative songs, both in written and oral form.[98] The vagaries of the oral tradition often produced various versions of a single ballad, but written or oral, these songs and poems shared similar features: "Besides the personal qualities of the bullfighter, the most common themes refer to his valor and fearlessness, the episodes of his struggle with the beast, the goring, the death and burial of the matador. Others include homages before the tomb."[99]

Even in Catalonia there was enough interest in the bullfight for it to be incorporated into the shadow puppet theater, a local form of popular culture. And this happened in the 1860s, well before massive immigration from southern Spain. The Cuyàs family had such a theater and published its own Catalan-language magazine, *L'entretenement*, that included a poem describing the performance entitled "The Great Bullfight."[100]

Celebrity could accompany a bullfighter into death, and the funerals of some leading matadors became public events. When José Redondo, "El Chiclanero," died of tuberculosis in March 1853 at the age of thirty-three, his burial was a mass event. Hours before the service "an immense crowd surrounded the church of San Sebastián," and the procession to the cemetery included "the state carriage of the governor of Madrid, Sr. Ordóñez, . . . some carriages of titled nobles . . . followed by up to one hundred carriages occupied by friends and fans of the famous bullfighter. . . . The number of individuals of all classes who went on foot before and behind the cortege was extraordinarily large. We cannot think of any analogous ceremony or event that can compare to it; the streets through which the procession passed were packed with people and so were all the balconies."[101]

El Chiclanero's funeral paled beside that of Frascuelo in March 1898. The news of his death "spread rapidly through Madrid" and drew so many people to the funeral home that "it was necessary to call in the police to prevent an invasion by the crowd . . . eager to see the body of the man who had been a true popular idol. A half hour later various special editions were on the streets." When the body had been prepared, "hundreds of people, in their majority from the lower class, filed before the corpse in an hour and a half." Fifty police officers were present to keep order, but there was a small riot, which led to a number of arrests and a visit from the governor, who, "in light of what had happened and finding someone dying in the street, prohibited anyone else from entering."[102]

On the day of the funeral, and despite the rain, "very early in the morning the area around the mortuary was populated by people who had risen before dawn to get a good spot"; guests who came by carriage had to leave them

behind, as the streets were impassable. Young boys wandered the streets selling "the last portrait of Frascuelo." By one in the afternoon there were an estimated ten thousand people in the streets, and when the procession finally got
under way, the civil guards at its head could barely open a passage through the
multitude. The carriage was "imperial, magnificent, of ebony" pulled by eight
horses with black velvet trappings. At the Puerta del Sol, in the heart of
Madrid, it took "the Civil Guard on horseback and the governor himself" to
open a wedge through the crowd. The presence of U.S. ambassador Wood-
ford drew special notice. With tensions rising between his country and Spain
over Cuba, "the authorities had adopted special measures to prevent the
occurrence of any disagreeable incident." When the funeral was over, the
ambassador "got down from his carriage and began to distribute alms."[103]

Status

Bullfighters were celebrities, and this status brought widely held expectations. Successful bullfighters, and perhaps less successful ones, too, acquired
a set of hangers-on, forerunners of the rock band's roadies and groupies. In
his autobiography, Juan Belmonte, the great star of the 1910s and 1920s,
described his "complex clientele":

> The *mozo de espadas* is the commander in chief of the campaign, and he con-
> trols an army of veteran subordinates. Immediately after him comes another
> very important personage called the "assistant to the mozo de espadas," who in
> his turn is surrounded by his friends and a horde of auxiliaries who don't travel
> with the cuadrilla but are acquired temporarily at every bullring. The last
> members of this chain of servants are almost unknown to the bullfighter him-
> self. . . . If, for instance, the matador wants to send a telegram to somebody, the
> mozo de espadas gives it with the money to his assistant, the assistant passes it
> on to "the man who looks after the capes" [who] gives it to an assistant of his
> own, and sooner or later there is somebody in this complicated series who tears
> up the message and keeps the money.

The bullfighter's obligations were "almost infinite, ranging from the purely
material and economic to the moral and the spiritual. A combination of the
two is one of the heaviest burdens: that of patronizing weddings and baptisms.
I don't know why a torero should have to be a kind of universal godfather, but

everyone thinks he is entitled to bring his children to the torero to be baptized or married."[104] Belmonte added that he refused to do this, "with a firmness that was almost rude," but when the petitioner was particularly obdurate, he sent his brother "or one of the members of my cuadrilla" as a stand-in.[105]

But bullfighters, the stars at least, were not beholden to their clients alone. As the custom of holding bullfights to raise money for charity or for disaster relief became increasingly common after about 1870, they were also expected to display a much more public patronage through their generous response to these worthy causes.[106] Thus, in July 1882 *El Tío Jindama* reported that Frascuelo "has given 2,000 reales to the municipal government of Barcelona for the families of those who died in the explosion of the textile factory on Amalia Street" and that he would "take part, without receiving any payment" in a bullfight to raise money for them.[107] The chronicler of the career of Rafael Guerra, "Guerrita," pointed out that he performed in twelve fund-raisers between 1888 and 1898 and that when he was not able to take part in one in 1895 he made a donation of 5,000 pesetas.[108] When asked to make a donation to the hospital in Valencia, in whose bullfights he had agreed to participate, he replied that he would take less than his normal fee of 6,000 pesetas: "I leave it to your conscience to pay me the amount you think right, with the difference to benefit the poor."[109] The matadors who worked in the patriotic bullfights that were held in 1898 and 1921 did so without pay.[110]

The bullfighter's generosity could also be highlighted by contrast to the miserliness of others. Bartolomé Muñoz, the promoter of the Madrid bullring, was much criticized for charging the organizers of charitable corridas for using the facility. This led Guerrita to announce that he would refuse to sign any contracts with Muñoz, and this promise "to punish such an abominable and antipatriotic act" was applauded by *La Lidia*: "While he and his colleagues, driven by charitable sentiments, risk their lives to raise money for our sick soldiers, you laugh at them pocketing many thousands of pesetas."[111]

Not all such acts of generosity were connected to special bullfights. While living in the town of Chinchón, near Madrid, Frascuelo helped the victims of an especially brutal winter, when there was much unemployment, in the manner of a bishop of the Church one hundred years earlier: "He went to the main square, bought 'all the bread that was brought from Villaconejos' or ordered bread to be baked, and announced that people could get it at his house." In a different vein, when the old Madrid bullring was torn down in 1875, Frascuelo bought the boards that enclosed the fighting area and gave them to the town to use in the corridas that were held in its main square.[112]

And in 1906 Rafael González, "Machaquito," celebrated his wedding by "founding two poorhouses, one in Cartagena and the other in Córdoba, which will serve as a haven for poor and incapacitated elderly who . . . have need of a place where they can receive the necessary help during the last years of their lives." Machaquito was "a truly supernatural being . . . a truly charitable man," but what made him stand out so for the author of this report was the contrast between his generosity and its absence among his colleagues, who "think of nothing but having a good time or hoarding the money for a secure and comfortable retirement."[113]

This generosity was for public consumption, but bullfighters were very careful to protect their "interests." In 1890, Lagartijo sued the Madrid promoter because he was late in paying him his fee; he won and got 40,000 reales in damages on top of the 47,000 he was owed. Mazzantini, for one, was not above a little blackmail, as he explained to the director of the Valencia hospital why he could not work an upcoming charity fund-raiser: "I would not be stopped from giving your Committee a demonstration of my interest if it were not for the circumstance of not yet being contracted by the promoter for the July bullfights; it would be reckless for me to expose the possibility of this contract to the inevitably unfavorable contingencies of killing one bull in a charity bullfight." If, however, a contract for July arrived in time, he would take part.[114]

During the first two decades of the twentieth century it became increasingly common for matadors to give away tickets to friends and admirers. César Jalón, who himself benefited from this practice, wrote that "this chapter of their public relations budget grew to an inconceivable degree. . . . Their managers would sign a chit for tickets and the amount would be deducted by the promoter from their earnings. . . . Many . . . do their duty of cheering on their matador and even that of booing his rivals," but on occasion the recipients of these favors would scalp them instead. According to Jalón, bullfight critics "were at the head of the line" for free tickets, and he claimed to have known only one critic who never took a ticket from a bullfighter.[115]

This highly public generosity was part of the larger question of bullfighters' public image and its fluctuation between the poles of roughness and respectability. Into the 1840s, the popular perception was that bullfighters were rowdy and disreputable. Cossío described the matadors of the first few decades of the century as having:

> an irregular and boastful style of life of confused and brazen manliness, of rowdy carousing that did not recognize even the minimum required for dignified socia-

bility. Good times with wine and women, socializing with the worst elements of society, rejoicing in shameless audacity, preferring bluster to valor, risking the pistol or the knife, governed by wine and the most violent passions . . . were considered obligatory qualities of the taurine profession. . . . The bullfighter's bravado in the ring became confused with his behavior in the street.[116]

José Blanco White, a liberal writer from Seville who fled to England in 1808 and became a Protestant minister, presented bullfighters as lower-class toughs whose behavior "joined the licentiousness and superstition" common to their class. The "Bullfighter" was the first entry in the classic compendium of Spanish types, *Los españoles pintados por sí mismos*, which reads in part: "Amusing free-spenders, happy and gay by the nature of their art, they spend and triumph and go overboard to such an extent that when [a bull gores them] they can whisper in its ear 'do me in, it's all right . . . I've had enough.'"[117]

Writing at the end of the 1870s, Sánchez de Neira noted that until the 1840s, "bullfighters were considered vile," implying that they had since risen in public esteem. He himself made the case for their respectability: They dressed well, they treated at bars, and few got into trouble with the law. Indeed, only 5 of the 15,973 prisoners in Spanish jails in 1878 were bullfighters.[118] A few years later, *El Tendido* cited bullfighters' respectability in defending them from charges of being "social scum" that appeared in a Socialist paper in Seville. Admittedly their "valiant character" made them "somewhat quarrelsome," but this was their "sole defect." Hardly any bullfighters committed crimes, especially "robbery, housebreaking, or fraud"; in contrast, "they are good fathers and family men, and even though they are often wined and dined by society ladies, there has yet to be a single case of one abandoning his family, which shows . . . that they fulfill their social duties with faithful rigor."[119] And in 1873 the *Ilustración Española y Americana*, a highly popular illustrated weekly, reproduced José Villegas's painting *The Bullfighters' Chapel* accompanied by the following comment: "This pious custom . . . stands in marked contrast to the skepticism and irreligiosity that today are spreading with lamentable rapidity."[120]

This greater respectability began with Francisco Montes, the "superstar" (*astro-rey*) of the 1840s. Montes had such prestige that when, on April 9, 1850, he gave a dinner for a number of leading fans, the guest list included "titled aristocrats, members of the Lyceum, writers, bankers, and other well known people." This dinner took place only a few days after Montes had had an audience with Queen Isabella II, and for a while there was even talk that he would be given a title.[121] In the 1870s "famous bullfighters" joined leading politicians and famous writers at key social events, such as the inauguration of the palace of the marquis of Alcañices.[122]

By this time, bullfighters themselves actively sought respectability. Before leaving for a tour in Cuba in 1886, Mazzantini gave a speech in which he boasted of having started a "revolution" that showed that "bullfighters do not have to be vulgar and gaudy nor live amidst orgies or scandalous uproar . . . that they were worthy citizens; that bullfighting was not the enemy of culture and education; that they could wear tuxedos and suit jackets, too." José Bilbao's portrayal of Guerrita, published in 1902, is a virtual negative of the former image: "He has never been a gambler, a womanizer, a drunk, a libertine, but rather a serious and upright man; above all, he has saved the money he earned through his honest labor."[123] Angel Carmona, "Camisero," abandoned the traditional bullfighter's garb for the "clothes of the ordinary citizen" after an unpleasant experience on a train: Returning to Madrid after a fight in Valladolid, he and his friend Lagartijillo Chico shared a first-class compartment with a bishop who ignored Camisero and spoke only to his companion. The reason: "Lagartijillo Chico dressed elegantly, like a marquis, and I wore my short jacket, like a bullfighter." From then on he wore his former clothes only in the countryside.[124]

The lesser members of the profession claimed a similar respectability. According to the president of the banderilleros' union, his members were "different from the bullfighters of yesterday. The days in which the bullfighter was a *bullfighter* in the street as well as in the ring are over. Today we dress the same as everyone else . . . and our life is methodical and orderly, without raucousness. There are no bashes! . . . We have abandoned the tavern and we read books."[125]

This new, "improved" bullfighter was not to everyone's liking; some people wanted their heroes to continue to be "bullfighters in the street." *El Toreo* was in this camp. In December 1901 it printed an article entitled "How Bullfighters Should Dress," which argued that bullfighters "should appear as such in all aspects of his life," which meant continuing to wear a short jacket, tight pants, and flat hat. The villain was Mazzantini: He was "the first to introduce the change in the clothes bullfighters wear in the street . . . which exercised a pernicious influence on his colleagues." And the influence was not just a matter of appearances: "The genuine character of the bullfighter, squandering his money . . . happy and extravagant, gave way to the modern character: meticulous and calculating, sober, modest, looking down on wine and gambling, favoring cocktails, and as knowledgeable as anyone about the state of govermment bonds."[126]

La Coleta printed an almost identical complaint from a correspondent in Chiclana (Cádiz), although his villain was Montes. The "modern matador" had abandoned the traditional dress for fashionable shirts, ties, and jackets, and as a result he was "unrecognizable in the street." Moreover, he now traveled by train, "in first class, surrounded by all the comforts that good taste demands." At his destination, he "forgets about any discussion of his art; rather, he chats about the opera that debuted last week, about so-and-so's dowry and so-and so-so's speech." Moreover, the modern bullfighter was boring: "No more bashes in taverns; no more downing one glass of sherry after another. None of that exists any more! That style has been lost forever." By contrast, the bullfighter of the past "was a bullfighter in everything . . . 'he smelled like a bullfighter', as the saying went."[127]

Blaming Montes for this change in appearance was quite ironic, since it was Montes who was largely responsible for defining what the bullfighter's working dress should be. The suit of lights originated in the everyday clothes of the popular classes of eighteenth-century Madrid, but while fashions changed, bullfighters' outfits did not, and they thus became increasingly archaic and distinctive. At the same time, bullfighters "felt freer to indulge their imaginations in adding rich adornments"; Montes was central to this process, "introducing tassels and sequins" as well as mandating the short jacket with embroidered shoulder pads. According to Cossío, Montes "lived up to his reputation as the great legislator of the corrida, promulgating the bullfighter's clothing so effectively that today it remains without any major modification."[128]

El Liberal's version of the critique went like this: "Then bullfighters drank manzanilla, smoked expensive cigars, drank coffee, and spent one thousand pesetas on a Manila shawl that they gave to the first girl they came across. Today they drink tea, take their wine cut with water so it doesn't irritate their stomach, take tranquilizers to calm their nerves, and smoke Turkish cigarettes, which are milder than those sold by the Tobacco Monopoly."[129]

The dichotomy between those who were "bullfighters in the street" and those who were not was embodied in the two rival stars of the 1880s and 1890s, Frascuelo and Lagartijo. While both were undeniable masters of their profession, Frascuelo enjoyed a genuine popularity that his rival did not. For one critic, the reason was precisely their very differing lifestyles; while Lagartijo "lived quietly, was a man of few words, hated showing off, and dressed modestly," Frascuelo came much closer to fulfilling expectations of what a bullfighter was "supposed" to be, although in a more upmarket way: he was "always a fashion plate, he paraded along the Castellana [one of Madrid's main streets] on a prancing Andalusian horse, flirted with the most stylish women on the sidewalk of San Jerónimo Street, and ate every day in a fashionable restaurant." Even when his daughter got married, Frascuelo wore a short jacket instead of the conventional frock coat.[130]

And as for Guerrita, what one admirer saw as virtues many fans found offputting; "his sullen and withdrawn character . . . his lack of inclination to throw his money around, which earned him the reputation of being 'greedy,'" were adduced as reasons for his not engaging the empathy of fans that his undeniable talent would otherwise have earned him.[131]

For all their differences in style, Lagartijo and Frascuelo apparently did have something in common: amorous adventures that gave the public plenty to gossip about. "The successes, and scandalous, foolhardy escapades of Rafael Molina [Lagartijo] (who, according to one joke, placed more picks than his picadors), spread through the salons, cafés and theaters. . . . On occasion the woman involved took pleasure in showing off the liaison, like the statuesque beauty from the aristocracy who showed up in her box wearing the same colors that Frascuelo wore in *corrida*."[132]

But these laments for a lost style inevitably led somewhere else: complaints that the quality of their performances had declined because bullfighters were no longer concerned about "art" and were in it only for the money. For *El Toreo*, "It seems that before anything else, the bullfighter of today does his accounts and says 'so much money for so many fights. I need so much and when I get it, I'm out of here.'" *La Coleta*'s bullfighter of the past "didn't get through his work with three half veronicas for which he received 6,000 pesetas(!). Not at all. He went out to face bulls of the greatest ferocity and power. He lavished valor, art, and grace onto every move. He *received* bulls, not pesetas."[133] *La Lidia* denounced Antonio Carmona, Gordito's comeback as "driven solely by the desire for greater profit and the pleasure of adding a few thousand pesetas to his fortune."[134]

Bullfighters' greed formed part of more general critiques of the state of the corrida around the turn of the century. After taking promoters, breeders, and the authorities to task, *El Toreo Chico* lashed out at the matadors: "The bullfighter is the first to congratulate himself for helping out the destitute, but when it comes to . . . helping out a ruined promoter his nobility disappears. . . . The day will come when either bullfighters and breeders will have to reduce their monetary and *professional* demands by at least half or they themselves will have to get together to entertain the public."[135] Pascual Millán summarized this sentiment in his remark that in the matadors of the day "the public sees a man who earned a living fighting bulls rather than a bullfighter." He went on to compare the 1890s with the 1870s: "Then one saw a bullfighter in the ring; today one sees the bullfighter who turns his art into riches. . . . Today the bullfight is nothing more than getting away without injury and continuing to exploit the trade. Greed has invaded from the breeder to the last peon."[136] Even so, there did remain the occasional exception, such as Gallo, "a bullfighter in his tastes, in his essence, in his gestures, in the atmosphere with which he surrounded himself."[137]

This disappointment was not limited to professional bullfight critics, for whom stars of the present were outshone by larger-than-life heroes of the past. The sense that by the end of the nineteenth century matadors had become mercenaries was also present in popular culture. The following song, which was recited in 1945 by Francisco Gallego, a seventy-one-year-old shoemaker from Badajoz, treats these erstwhile popular idols harshly, lumping them in with some much less admired figures:

> The famous Mazzantini
> Has returned to Spain
> Covered in gold and silver
> From his contract abroad.
> The money that is minted
> Is for the bullfighters;
> For this reason bullfighting
> Is the best career.
>
> These little things
> Have their charm,
> Which is why
> Bullfighters live in Spain.
> That is how I know
> That in Spain
> There is no money left

> Because it has all been taken by
> The sacristans,
> The politicians
> And the bullfighters.[138]

Despite their celebrity and their newfound respectability, it was very much the exception for bullfighters to become active in other areas of public life. One of the very few to do so was precisely Luis Mazzantini, who went into politics after retiring from the ring in 1905. (Mazzantini was undoubtedly aided by his middle-class background—his father was an engineer—and his education.) He was elected to the Madrid City Council in 1905 and became deputy mayor four years later. After World War I he served as civil governor in Guadalajara and Avila. He also found that the world of politics had a rough and tumble all its own from which his prestige as a bullfighter was no protection. As governor of Guadalajara in 1919 he undertook a program of administrative reform that immediately brought him into conflict with local politicians. He fined mayors who failed to send their budgets for his approval, and in an attempt to deal with grain shortages, he refused to grant permits to export cereals from the province. Guadalajara was the political fief of the Liberal leader the count of Romanones, and Mazzantini was a Conservative: Romanones's clients demanded that he rid them "as quickly as possible of such a disastrous governor." In December, after only four months in office, he was transferred to Avila, but there he lasted only four months as well.[139]

Bullfighters were celebrities and popular idols, but neither as individuals nor as a group were they viewed uncritically. Assessments of matadors, and of the corrida, too, had an importance that went well beyond the spectacle itself. For many Spaniards, both bullfighters and bullfighting were bellwethers of gender relations within Spain as well as of the virility of the nation as it faced an increasingly competitive international climate.

three
3

In the first volume of the seven that make up his classic encyclopedia *Los toros*, José María Cossío devoted a brief chapter to what he called *señoritas toreras*, little lady bullfighters. The phrase is clearly pejorative, and was meant to be; Cossío found this topic distasteful, but he included it because the obligations of the encyclopedist required that he do so: "If the most masculine qualities and serious moral values are what characterize the bullfight and give it nobility, . . . the activity of the little lady bullfighters is a parody of the bullfight. . . . I will attend summarily to this history, and with the repugnance of anyone who has to deal with a subject that is in conflict with Nature itself."[1]

For Cossío, bullfighting was clearly a gendered activity: Not only was it something that men did, it embodied male qualities and virtues. The participation of women violated—*profaned* might be a more appropriate word—the masculine nature of the bullfight. But the existence of the "little lady bullfighters" was not merely an attack on the essence of the corrida. More seriously and dangerously, it was also an assault on the nature of Woman and thus a threat to one of the foundation stones on which Spanish society was based. Spanish women were not legally equal to men, and the disadvantages were magnified for married women. Beyond the law, there was a set of expectations that defined, and constrained, the activities that were deemed acceptable for women. The role that was prescribed for Spanish women was identical to that prescribed for women in other European countries as well as in North America: to get married and be a good wife and mother. In the secular world only one type of public activity, charity work, was considered acceptable, and then only because it was seen as a logical extension of women's role in the family.[2]

Killing bulls was clearly inappropriate behavior for women as, for that matter, was watching bulls being killed. This was pointed out repeatedly, but despite the denunciations, women were always present as bullfighters and prominent as spectators. Bullfight critics and social commentators railed against the participation of women in the spectacle, but they did not go away. Indeed, after about 1890 they became both more common and more popular. More significantly, Spaniards were prepared to ignore these proscriptions, to the extent of paying money to watch women cross the established borders of gender. The appearance of the team of Catalan women in Madrid in 1898 drew such a crowd that "Dulzuras," the reviewer for *El Enano,* wondered whether "women will be responsible for regenerating [the bullfight]. . . . Today the women have drawn more people to the bullring than have come to any other fight this season." His colleague in *El Toreo* reluctantly "yielded to the evidence. The public has tired of novilleros, and the girls amuse them more."[3] Was it the thrill of being party to the violation of a taboo? Or were the gender Jeremiahs out of touch with an increasingly consumerist society in which such prescribed norms were being undermined by the growing commerce of leisure?

A Virile Nation?

For many people who wrote about bullfighting, and particularly for those who defended it, the corrida was an eminently masculine spectacle that contributed to the virility of the nation. There was some commentary of this sort in the last decades of the nineteenth century. In his novel *Ricardo,* Emilio Castelar, who had been president of the First Republic, has his young protagonist go to a bullfight, where he strikes up a conversation with an old man. When Ricardo says that he dislikes the spectacle, the old man replies: "I cannot abide it, especially from the lips of a young man. That's how the generations become effeminate to the point that men become women and women become nothing at all." And in a defense of the corrida published in 1878, Manuel López Martínez affirmed that "the problem with society today is not the energy and virility of the men but the feminization of customs."[4]

The humiliating military defeat at the hands of the upstart United States in the Spanish-American War of 1898 led many Spaniards to question the virility of their nation, and this loss of national virility was one of the tropes of the literature of the Disaster that followed the war. Thus, Joaquín Costa, the leading voice in the Regenerationist movement, spoke of Spain as a "nation of women" and a "country of eunuchs" with a "castrated public opinion."[5]

In this context, the bullfight could be presented as more beneficial and more needed than ever. For one reviewer of the count of Navas's *El espectáculo más nacional*, published in 1899, the bullfight was a national tradition that belonged to a "people that was virile, happy, boisterous, healthy and full of life."[6] Bullfight newspapers were especially prone to see the *corrida* in this way. An article in *El Toreo Chico* entitled "The Crisis of Bullfighting" lamented that "for years bullfighting has been experiencing a true crisis that will at least partially do away with the virility, the greatness, and the majesty of the spectacle." The next year, the same magazine published an editorial, "The National Festival," that argued in defense of the bullfight that "we believe that it is even humanitarian to support all those spectacles that tend to maintain the innate energies of a virile nation, such as Spain has always been."[7] In 1904 another magazine criticized suggestions to impose a tax on bullfight tickets: "So that is how to achieve the moral and material betterment of our country: increasing the tax on a healthy, virile, genuinely Spanish spectacle, the only noble and dignified thing left to our race, to discourage people from going to the bulls."[8] For one of *La Coleta*'s correspondents, the bullfight was the sign that "the virile energy of the race" survived, however "decadent" the country might appear.[9]

Critics of the bullfight were charged with attempting to feminize Spain. One author contrasted the bullfight, "a sanguinary spectacle, if you like, but virile and robust," with such "corrupt, effeminate, and degrading entertainments" as horse races and circuses.[10] A tract published in 1877 claimed that eliminating the bullfight would reduce the country to "a state of weakness and feminity," and twenty-six years later *El Toreo Chico* denounced opponents as "more or less effeminate people."[11]

Such arguments were not always made so defensively. In 1907 *La Coleta*, another bullfight magazine, published an article on the origin of the bullfighter that argued, on social Darwinist grounds, that sports such as bullfighting helped preserve "the virility that is so necessary for the peaceful but energetic struggle among modern nations . . . and without which, by the law of nature, they perish, absorbed by others. . . . Civilization and the humanist may temper the cruelest features, but they cannot remove one atom of the valor and . . . virility of our country for all types of struggle in modern civilization or current progress."[12]

Even the crowd who went to watch could be seen as virile. In reporting on a bullfight in the Madrid suburb of Tetuán de la Victoria, the correspondent for *El Toreo* wrote that "the Madrid fans went to the bullring with great enthusiasm and a half hour before the bullfight began the animation and boisterousness of a virile people reigned everywhere." The point was made more forcefully in a report in *Respetable Público*. When Bombita appeared afraid of the bull he was fighting, the crowd reacted: "The knowledgeable public made a virile protest," But not everyone was so angry, and "the *chorus of virgins* applauded like crazy."[13] In his memoirs, the bullfighter Camisero spoke approvingly of the rowdiness of the bullfight crowds of the past: "That's how bullfights were . . . and should be, stormy and passionate. . . . If it is not going to be that way, then abolish [the bullfight] once and for all and forget all this cant that . . . has left it mannered and girlish, not how bullfights are supposed to—and always were—for men with 'hair on their chest,' for vigorous, valiant, and manly *machos*."[14]

Manliness was also a characteristic attributed to those who defended the bullfight against its enemies. At the crucial moment of the dispute over the Sunday Rest Law in 1904 and 1905, Pascual Millán described the conflict as one between true men and immoral women: "When the government saw that all those hurt by the [law] adopted virile measures" it yielded, but "if after the upcoming cabinet meeting they ignore us, we will fight as MEN fight. . . . We will proceed with true virile spirit; if we do not, we will appear in the eyes of cultured Europe as the worst class of broad . . . just like those sluts who sold their shriveled bodies in public and could not enter into the temple of Citeria."[15]

If the bullfight helped keep the nation virile, it did so by contributing to the manliness of individual Spanish males. Bullfighting helped turn boys into men. The corrida was certainly popular among young boys. Foreign visitors described how Spanish children played at bullfighting "as ours do at leapfrog," as one put it in 1832, and an American who spent *Four Months Afoot in Spain* in the 1920s wrote that "every red-blooded Spanish boy dreams of becoming a bullfighter and would not think of being unfamiliar with the features, history, peculiarities, and batting av——, I mean number of *cogidas* or wounds of the principal fighters. Rare the boy who does not carry about his person a pack of portraits of matadors such as are given away with cigarettes. On the playground, no other game at all rivals 'torero' in popularity."[16] Juan Belmonte, the great star of the 1920s, confirmed the popularity of bullfighting as a game for children in his hometown of Seville: He played at it "because it was the natural thing for me to do: in those days the boys of my age did it, just as today [1937] they are always playing at soccer."[17] By the 1890s, if not before, Madrid toy stores were selling bullfighter action figures, made by a French company. [18]

But the bullfight was especially important to boys, although it meant different things at different ages. Before adolescence it could be a fantasy about the future, as it was for the great poet Rafael Alberti, who was born in Cádiz in 1902:

> When at the age of eleven, when a boy nourishes his dreams of becoming a torero, there is no such thing as fear. During math or Latin a few of us would go into the fields behind the school building . . . all set to separate one of the young bulls from the herd or take on the first animal that decided to charge. . . . Whenever we did have a bullfight it consisted of some awkward passes with a velvet jacket, various spins and tumbles and a few well-placed kicks that were later transformed into painful aches and black bruises. . . . And then there followed the illusory conversations and enthusiastic commentary. Such conversations were filled with words and expressions like 'the bullring's dim, dark emergency room, iodine, the intestinal mass, gangrene, a fractured femur or instant death from shock(!),' a vocabulary we picked up from reading bullfight magazines. . . . What a marvelous period in our lives, when we innocently and seriously dreamed of a future filled with glorious afternoons, our pictures appearing in magazines and our handsome faces displayed on matchboxes.[19]

The bullring remained important as boys moved into adolescence and approached manhood. For young males from the middle and upper classes of late-nineteenth-century Almería, "it was their point of attraction, where they gathered at any time of the day to hold those exercises so appropriate for the development of their activity and strength . . . as well as for their intellectual and moral education. . . . It was their gymnasium, the riding school, their school of arms, and all other sports necessary for a truly male (macho) puberty." And this type of adolescence molded morally sound and virile men:

> In the spirit of those youths the ideal of the struggle for victory in all their sporting endeavors was strong . . . everything that, with the passage of time and the forging of serious men, we have recognized. That strenuous stage of

life had an educative role in the moral order and the vigorous and healthy constitution of that group of young men who, fond of virile exercises, stayed away from gambling and other vices that lead to the degeneration of men.[20]

These Spaniards were giving vigorous sports the same role in "recreating manhood . . . instilling moral as well as physical virtue" as were late-nineteenth-century Americans.[21]

Bullfighters were the embodiment of masculinity, although it seemed that they had always been more masculine in the past. As an old man, Carlos Roure remembered the bullfighters of his youth as "more manly . . . and more valiant than those of today or of thirty years ago. . . . To be blunt, they were not the least bit effeminate." [22] In comparing Frascuelo and Lagartijo, the stars of the 1880s, with their inferior successors of the early twentieth century, one critic found that their physiques differed: "The herculean and muscular figure of the bullfighters responded logically to their ability; they were athletes forged in iron and not emaciated sissies."

> The bullfighter of yesterday was synonymous with the strong, athletic, muscular and healthy man; the very model of the thin-legged and narrow-waisted peasant, the wriggling body full of sculpted beauty. . . . Today [a bullfighter] who does not look like a traveling salesman seems a hick wearing his Sunday best or a scrofulous boy who carries the sign of degeneration in his face. . . . So this is how the virile legend of the hero of the Spanish festival has wound up.[23]

Even bullfighters' nicknames no longer carried the masculine message of earlier, and better, times; back in the 1880s "they used truly male nicknames and not childish ones that used the diminutive ending."[24]

Opponents of the bullfight could completely invert these gender identifications. One member of parliament did just that as part of a verbal assault on what he called the "national shame." While he was particularly concerned with the effect of the corrida on those who watched it, he also noted that the matadors' gestures in the ring struck him as "hermaphroditic."[25]

Women Bullfighters

For all the talk of bullfighting and masculinity, there were always some *toreras*, women bullfighters. Indeed, the figure of the torera is virtually as old and continuous as the professional bullfight itself. None ever became a star, and very few earned much respect, but they were always there, a small and marginal but permanent part of the history of the corrida.

Initially woman fought on horseback, not on foot. The first woman to fight bulls professionally appears to have been Francisca García, who was married to a professional banderillero. In 1774 she petitioned the city of Pamplona for permission to fight there: "Due to a special spirit I have fought on horseback and have garnered much applause over the ten years in which I have performed in the cities of Cádiz, Valencia, Granada, and Murcia as well as in other capitals." Her request was denied, as it was the following year as well, as the city fathers felt that such activity was improper.[26] The next woman bullfighter was Nicolasa Escamilla. She was much better known because she fought in Madrid, and her performances were noted by a number of writers, including José Daza, author of one of the first treatises on bullfighting, who praised her work.[27] Goya also put her in one of his *Tauromaquia* lithographs, with the caption, "Manly valor of the celebrated [Nicolasa Escamilla] in the bullring of Zaragoza." An Asturian woman named Teresa Alonso participated in a bullfight organized by Joseph Bonaparte in 1811; Andrea Cazalla fought dressed as a Turkish princess in 1818, as did Antonia Fernández in 1820 and María and Benita Fernández in 1822.

Many women got their start in the *mojigangas*. (So did some men, Frascuelo among them.) These plays with bullfight interludes that were performed in a bullring during the winter when regular bullfights were not held enjoyed a vogue in the 1830s and 1840s. In *Camacho's Wedding*, "a group of peasants from La Mancha, preceded by a small drum and clarinet, accompany Camacho, his bride, and the bridesmaid. Then come Don Quijote and Sancho Panza, who join the party. . . . After the dance, they go to a food-laden table that stands in front of the bull pen, and when they have sat down to eat, a three-year-old bull is let loose."[28] The use of regional costume as well as exotic, foreign dress, such as Turkish and Chinese, was habitual among the women who took part in these performances, but men dressed this way, too.

The number of women bullfighters increased notably in the 1830s. In 1832 Teresa García and Manuela Capilla appeared in Madrid. Four years later it was the turn of Mariana Duro and Magdalena García. The posters described them as "valiant and manly amateurs . . . who will attempt to prove that their sex, although weak and delicate, can be determined, intrepid and daring . . . and that neither controlling a horse nor wielding a lance is an obstacle to their presenting themselves calmly before the beast and defeating it." And so that the crowd could determine "which was the more intrepid," they dressed in different regional costumes, Duro as a Valencian and García as a village girl.[29] Manuela García fought in 1837, and Carmen Ortiz fought in 1839.

That year also saw a major breakthrough: the first full team of female bullfighters, composed of Francisca Coloma, Josefa García, and Ramona Castillar. They were not very successful, but they were followed a few years later by another team headed by the first woman who was able to make a career in bullfighting, Martina García. Born in 1814, she was orphaned at four. When she was fourteen she went to Madrid, working first as a servant, then as a cook in a bar. It is not clear when she took up bullfighting, but in 1845 she appeared in Madrid at the head of her own team. She also appeared with a number of the leading male bullfighters, including the great Francisco Montes. Her career was a lengthy one, longer than those of most men. She appeared in the last bullfight to be held in the old Madrid ring in August 1874 and, incredibly, continued fighting until 1880, when she was sixty-six.

The 1830s were something of a golden age for women bullfighters. According to Pascual Millán, from 1836 to 1840 women were the "spirit of the fights using younger bulls . . . the attractive part of the spectacle and only they were able to fill the bullring." He explained this anomalous situation as a creation of the civil war between liberals and absolutists that had begun in 1833 and ended in 1840. The brutality of this Carlist War created a "new type of woman thirsting to fight." But unlike earlier women bullfighters, these did not behave like women; they had "lost all female dignity . . . they took so little care of their appearance that it got to the point of their being obliged to wear *appropriate clothing* . . . to avoid their showing things that were better left hidden when they were hit by a bull."[30]

During the 1840s, '50s, and '60s, there were fewer women fighting bulls, but they never disappeared entirely. Martina García continued to make a living, as did Rosa Inard, another veteran, and a handful of others worked occasionally. There was something of a revival in the years after the revolution of 1868 and during the Second Carlist War, but for Millán this was but a pale and farcical repetition of the 1830s: "The politically absurd . . . should reflect itself in spectacle, and it did." Moreover, the women involved were ridiculous: "treading underfoot all the respect that as women they deserved . . . pretending to be men and turning themselves into the laughingstock of the public in the bullring." Even Martina García, whom he earlier described as an "institution," had become "a senior citizen disguised as a bullfighter."[31]

Things changed in the 1880s as a small number of women managed to achieve a reputation as decent bullfighters. These women often took the nicknames of the leading male stars: La Guerrita, La Mazzantini, and La Reverte, among others. Ignacia Fernández, "La Guerrita," was a domestic servant before she took up bullfighting; she became the first Spanish woman to fight bulls in Latin America when she signed for a season in 1898, and remained until 1910 because of the large amounts she earned there. The last two decades of the century saw two further breakthroughs, both attributed to Dolores Sánchez, "La Fragosa," the most famous female bullfighter of the period: She fought wearing the men's suit of lights, and she had a team composed entirely of men, including one who later became a well-known matador in his own right. La Fragosa began her working life as a seamstress, but she was able to earn enough money as a bullfighter to afford a comfortable retirement.[32]

The popularity of these women and their acceptance among the people who bought tickets, if not among the critics, led to the most interesting and successful phenomenon of the all-woman team, the Catalan Lady Bullfighters. Las Noyas, as they were known, were the creation of Barcelona bullfight promoter Mariano Armengol. He had already put together a team of "Boys from Barcelona" when, in 1894 he was approached by a "dozen girls led by Julia Carrasco, who asked that I organize and teach them the difficult art of bullfighting as I had done with the boys." Amused by the idea and sensing a business opportunity—"it was a great novelty that would easily be successful"—he agreed, and there followed weeks of training. After a slow start the girls "made such rapid progress that even I was amazed," which he attributed to "a degree of interest (*afición*) that is almost incomprehensible in a woman." After only five months they made their debut in March 1895 in the bullring of Barcelona and were so well received that they made nine more appearances there, "all of which were sellouts." Their success was not limited to Barcelona: "Contracts began to fall on them like rain: Valencia, Cádiz, Jerez de la Frontera, Alicante, Cartagena, Valladolid, Bilbao, Játiva, Castellón, Zaragoza, San Sebastián, Logroño, Albacete, Murcia, etc., and, finally, Madrid on September 12, 15, and 19 [1895] with all the tickets sold for all three."[33] In all, forty-five fights in their first year and sixty-eight in 1897. They continued fighting for twelve seasons before they retired. In 1898 they signed for twenty-two fights in America, and they returned each year afterward.

Critiques

Women bullfighters sold tickets, but they were never easily accepted, especially by bullfight critics and other insiders. The unprecedented success of Las Noyas and of other women, such as La Guerrita, led one of the great stars of the time, Guerrita, the man, to warn promoters that he would refuse to fight in any ring in which his female namesake or the Catalan women had fought within the previous year.[34] Even Mariano Armengol himself admitted that "these women have had their detractors, and why not? I am the first to recognize and affirm that women should not dedicate themselves to such a risky and male profession."[35]

One charge was that women degraded the bullfight. Cossío called their participation a parody, and in 1897 one Arturo Llorens wrote that "I have had a profound aversion to all the women who have dedicated themselves to bullfighting, especially the Catalan team. . . . I consider it a sacrilege that a woman's feet tread the same sands that have been immortalized by the great bullfighters of the past and those of today."[36]

The damage that women bullfighters might have inflicted on the corrida paled beside the possible consequences for Spanish society as a whole. Women bullfighters not only degraded the corrida, they also degraded their gender by engaging in activities that fell outside the female sphere, and this posed a threat to the gender structure, one of the basic pillars of Spanish society—as of all European societies. Father Sarmiento responded to the presence of Nicolasa Escamilla in the late eighteenth century by noting indignantly that "this phenomenon has brought ignominy on the devout female sex . . . and an outrage to the indiscreet bearded sex, which permitted such a monstrosity to happen in public. Compare her with those little girls from Galicia who are put in charge of a cow and manage to spin all day while making sure that the animal keeps out of the grain."[37] But Escamilla also had a defender. For José Daza such female manliness could only be a good thing, since it added to the strength of the nation: "We find such manly and valiant acts in Spanish women, from the most sublime peaks [of society] to the deepest valleys of the humble. They are capable of emulating the greatest foreign armed host. A single Spanish woman in this school of Mars is more important than all the rest."[38]

Such openly favorable statements would not be repeated in the nineteenth century. In February 1849, following the performance of some women bullfighters in Madrid, *El Clamor Público* denounced such "repugnant" spectacles as "disparaging the dignity of women in a shameful way."[39] This point was made at some length in an editorial in *La Lidia*. A number of women had become bullfighters, believing that "fighting bulls is no different from darning socks" when, in fact, this was a "profession inappropriate for the sex that nature gave them."

> To permit the presence of women in the ring is an absolute insult to their sex. Women have another mission in the world . . . the moral order of their households, the tasks proper to their sex, the education of their children in the ways of God. Considering that their mission on earth is none other than to uphold the family, they should not be in the bullring exposed to the demands of the crowd. . . . Never again must women take up the profession of bullfighter, which humiliates them and denigrates those who watch.[40]

The home, not the bullring, was their proper place. In November 1886 the bullfight paper *La Nueva Lidia* published a portrait of Dolores Sánchez, "La Fragosa," but this did not mean that the paper approved of women bullfighters: "Let the fair sex concern itself with sewing, washing dishes, and the other domestic tasks; and let the ugly sex fight bulls and take the blows that this entails."[41] This sentiment was also captured in a popular verse dedicated to La Fragosa:

> Her name is La Fragosa
> Dolores Sánchez
> Lady bullfighter
> Who is pretty tough.
> But thinking it over
> Would not La Fragosa
> Be better off washing dishes?[42]

The consequence of women not remaining in their proper domain was a total disruption of established gender roles. According to *El Toreo Cómico*, having a woman kill bulls was the same as "a bishop giving birth or request-ing a lieutenant of the Civil Guard to work as a domestic servant." It imag-ined a world in which husbands did the shopping and washed clothes in the river while their wives were off practicing their passes and promoters would have to publish notices such as the following: "The corrida announced for today cannot be held because the leading female matador is indisposed, hav-ing given birth to a child."[43] The violently anticlerical *El Motín* had its own version of this nightmare. A cartoon showed a woman dressed in a suit of lights watching her husband on his knees before a statue of the Virgin, their daughter at his side; the caption read: "The woman to fight bulls and the man to pray."[44]

But there could be some leeway for a woman who was alone in the world. When María García fought in Madrid dressed as a man, the promoter had included in the contract her statement that "she has no father or mother, is free from all obligations, and can do with her person whatever she believes convenient."[45]

Women bullfighters also threatened sexual confusion. To many they were mannish, and they were often described in the press as manlike (*varonil*). This could be a term of praise, but another frequently used word, *marimacho*, was unambiguously disapproving. One of the numerous satires of the bull-fight academy created by Ferdinand VII in 1830 included an article that read: "Women will not be admitted as students unless they drink wine, smoke, and can prove that their inclinations and energies are male, taking this in its most honest meaning."[46] One French author who saw women bullfighters in action described them as "grotesque transvestites," while a Spaniard who attended a fight in Almería in which La Reverte performed alongside men called the spectacle a "bordello."[47]

Girls, whose sexuality was not yet fully developed, were less dangerous. The critic "Dulzuras" was a staunch opponent of women bullfighters, and in a review of Las Noyas he urged their manager to end their careers soon: "Once they lose their enchantment as *girls*, they will become the butt of jokes; this has happened to one of the sisters . . . who is already a real woman."[48]

Women in the bullring could also lead to affronts to public decency. In 1811 the minister of the interior tried to prohibit Teresa Alonso from fighting in Madrid on the grounds that "public decency and decorum must be pro-tected, and they are violated by this spectacle."[49] An 1839 advertisement for a bullfight that included a team of women was careful to mention that "the women fighters will wear clothes adequate to let them perform their roles with the comfort and the decency that are necessary." But such care was not always taken. In 1853 *El Enano* commented on a performance by Magdalena García that "public decency suffers, especially when they roll on the ground or have to jump over the boards, since those who are on the other side take advantage of the situation to examine the parts of their bodies where they think they might have been wounded." It also included a bit of doggerel that made the same point:

> When they raise the darts
> And roll on the ground
> They show certain things
> That should remain hidden.[50]

José Solana described an incident in which a wandering team of female bull-fighters caused a scandal in one village. "They revealed things that should not be seen, and the mayor called the leader into his office, fined her, and then let her know that they would not be allowed to fight again unless they wore pants that were closed or they dressed as men."[51]

Women bullfighters could cause scandals of another sort. In October 1884, a female appeared in Tarragona, but the first bull of the afternoon knocked the torera down a number of times, and she refused to continue. The crowd began to demand its money back and "threw seats, bottles, and even stones from the stands into the ring." The president finally decided to refund the money but only to find that part of the receipts had disappeared, which led to further trouble and the use of the Civil Guard and four companies of soldiers to empty the ring. The promoter and the women bullfighters were arrested, but the lesson that *La Nueva Lidia* drew from the afternoon was "Female bullfighters and man-sized scandal."[52]

Some women bullfighters did earn respect. In 1851 the *Heraldo de Madrid* announced Martina García's upcoming fight describing her as "famous" and "intrepid." [53] After her death the author of a history of the Madrid bullring wrote that she "had no art. She barely used her left hand, but she was valiant and she did what she could to kill."[54] Ignacia Fernández earned a biographical sketch in *El Toreo* that attributed to her "the most essential quality required, that of valor." It also suggested that with proper coaching

she could be much more successful and "realize all that woman who dedi-
cates herself to the bulls can: save enough to start a business and not have to
depend on anybody." (On the other hand, "Dulzuras" claimed that valor was
"a quality limited to men.")[55] One of *El Toreo*'s critics also had kind words
for Las Noyas: "They fight with more art than some bullfighters from the
ugly sex."[56]

Women on Display, 1890–1910

The increased presence and commercial viability of women after 1880 was
not limited to the corrida; rather, it was part of broader changes in behavior
and attitudes in Spanish society, or at least in the major cities. These changes
centered on the greater public visibility of women. During the 1880s they
moved into office jobs with the government and large businesses such as the
railroads, but their presence was particularly marked in the realm of commercialized entertainment. In the theater, the last decade of the nineteenth
century and the first decade of the twentieth saw the systematized use of the
female body to lure customers into theaters and music halls. At the same
time, the content of the cuplés, the songs that constituted the most popular
form of entertainment, and the gestures accompanying their performance
became "almost exclusively erotic."[57]

   These developments prompted a moral backlash. In Madrid, "the vigilance
of the authorities [over music halls and theaters] produced fines, closures of
locales, and all sorts of prohibitions." The capital was not unique. In
Barcelona, cabarets and music halls were denounced as centers of moral
degeneracy and prostitution. Thus, the author of a book entitled *Barcelona
sucia* (Dirty Barcelona) blamed music halls for "the decline in marriage and
consequently the fall in population and the rise in the incidence of tuberculosis, syphilis, and alcoholism." And in Asturias, Catholic women's organizations constantly lobbied the authorities to clean up such entertainment.[58]
This atmosphere would also explain the decision of the Real Maestranza of
Sevilla in 1913 to install "foot covers" in the boxes of the bullring. These
"twenty-centimeter-high boards" were intended "to prevent degenerates in
the stands from looking at the ankles of the women who were sitting there."[59]

   The concern for moral standards penetrated the national government as
well, especially when Antonio Maura's conservatives were in power, from

1904 to 1905 and from 1907 to 1909. Maura and his interior minister, Juan de la Cierva, undertook a wide-ranging program of "conservative socialization" intended to turn Spaniards into worthy citizens of a democratic society, although critics saw it as an attempt to kill "Spanish happiness." The measures taken included a 12:30 A.M. curfew on theaters and a ban on informal village bullfights (*capeas*), although the second provoked violent opposition and was quickly abandoned.[60]

This context explains the government's decision to prohibit women from fighting bulls. During the nineteenth century there had been intermittent— and ineffective—attempts to prohibit women from fighting bulls, at least in Madrid. The first came in 1811, while Joseph Bonaparte was on the Spanish throne. The minister of the interior sought to keep Teresa Alonso from the ring, arguing that "the same reasons that prohibit children and the aged from appearing in the ring must also be applied to women; but, above all, we must attend to the decency and public decorum that are violated by such a spectacle, whose influence on morality is well known."[61] The king overruled the minister, and Teresa Alonso was allowed to fight. The next attempt came in February 1849. Following a polemic in the press over women bullfighters, the civil governor of Madrid issued an order banning *novilladas* (bullfights with young bulls) in which women took part. The ban was largely ignored, and three years later, when another civil governor issued the first formal regulations, women were not mentioned.[62] In 1880 yet another civil governor of Madrid considered prohibiting women from appearing in novilladas, but he did not ever issue the ban.[63]

On June 25, 1908, Juan de la Cierva invoked legislation protecting women to suspend a bullfight in the Madrid suburb of Tetuán in which María Salome Rodríguez, "La Reverte," was to take part. Two weeks later, on July 4, de la Cierva issued the following circular to all civil governors:

> Public opinion has protested on various occasions against the practice of women taking part in bullfights, and if one can be pleased that the law does not expressly prohibit this, it constitutes a spectacle that is not proper and so opposed to culture and any delicate sentiment that in no case should the government authorities permit this offense to morality and good customs to take place. Thus, His Majesty has ordered that Your Excellency make use of Articles 22 and 25 of the provincial law and refuse to authorize any bullfight in which women are to take part.[64]

The political context also explains the response to the prohibition. The conservative paper *ABC* applauded the decision "because we cannot imagine women other than dedicated to the tasks proper to their sex,"[65] but there was, surprisingly, considerable support for the toreras, or at least for La Reverte.

The suspension of the bullfight on June 25 prompted a series of positive evaluations of La Reverte. The *Heraldo de Madrid* called her "valiant" and "a professional, known in all the bullrings of Spain, for whom bullfighting is the only way of making a living and who has more than demonstrated her abilities."[66] And *El País* pointed out that La Reverte "has been fighting bulls for twelve years and has killed in the rings of Madrid, Tetuán, and Carabanchel [another suburb of the capital] and in all the others in Spain" and that she "is a bullfighter who is in better physical condition than most of the men who are in the ring today." [67] The praise continued after the ban was announced. Writing in *El País*, "Mangue" said that La Reverte "has a history of success that cannot be matched by any two [male] bullfighters of her time."[68]

The wittiest response to the prohibition came from the liberal paper *El Imparcial*, in an article entitled "La Reverte in London" written by the well-known bullfight expert and author Mariano de Cavia. After observing that de la Cierva had robbed La Reverte and "other brave women" of their livings, he made the connection between their situation and the feminist movement. Female bullfighters constituted "one of the most arrogant and bizarre manifestations" of the "varied and interesting aspects that feminism offers." He then proffered some advice to La Reverte: She should overcome her "patriotic scruples" and "hurry to take out British citizenship" because "the active and intrepid feminism of Free Albion offers her a magnificent position."

Thousands of suffragettes, of those terrible suffragettes, who have London and all the United Kingdom in such a commotion, would acclaim La Reverte as their director and captain. What Spanish bullfighter has ever had such a formidable cuadrilla or such a colossal legion of supporters?

Because it is true . . . that at the same time as Spanish women are being banned from the bullring, English women have thrown themselves into the fight [*toreo*] with a determination and a vigor that is without precedent in the history of the popular arena [redondel]. This uprising of the skirts promises to make the English Revolution of the seventeenth century and the French Revolution of the eighteenth look very small indeed. . . . Those valiant suffragettes show unequaled daring and skill in playing the cape, picking and placing darts [*toman de capa, pican y banderillean*] in the Parliament and government of Great Britain.

Like the Black Prince in the fourteenth century and Lord Wellington in the nineteenth, who came from England to fight [*torear*] for the good in Spain, now a Spanish woman can go and help out her suffragette comrades, leading and completing the bullfight [*lidia*] they are putting up against the egotistical John Bull, a name which . . . promises much to our *torera* because we all know that *bull* is English for *toro*. . . .

To London then, sister, to redeem the poor downtrodden English women. Spanish women will enjoy those distant triumphs without even thinking about the conquest of political rights.[69]

All this was less a matter of support for La Reverte than politically motivated criticism of de la Cierva and Antonio Maura's Conservative government as a whole. In the same article in which it announced the ban, *El País* took dead aim at Maura's reputation for clericalism: "Alleging morality and good customs, these Conservatives will end up making it impossible for Spaniards to live in Spain. Only Belgians—and Jesuits—will be left!"[70]

After threatening to sue the minister, La Reverte announced that she was really a man and began an unsuccessful career as a male bullfighter. Presumably her/his skills had not changed, but La Reverte was much less a draw as a man than as a woman. She then spent many years working as a field guard named Agustín Rodríguez before returning briefly and ingloriously to the ring in 1934, at sixty years of age, as La Reverte.[71] The differing success of La Reverte as female and male bullfighter suggests that, for all the stated opposition to women matadors, for some Spaniards at least, the idea of a woman bullfighter had its own appeal, as Mariano Armengol had guessed.

Women in the Crowd

Bullfights were popular among women, and they were always a significant share of the spectators. In 1760 Edward Clarke noted that in Madrid women of both "the first quality" and "the common people" attended, and a few years later Jacobo Casanova de Seingalt commented on the popularity of the bullfight among the women of Zaragoza.[72] These observations were repeated in 1800 by Pepe Illo, the great bullfighter of the late eighteenth century, who wrote in his *Tauromaquia* that "women of the upper and lower classes talk about these events and are present in the bullrings."[73] And in the nineteenth century a succession of foreign visitors repeated this observation. For example, in 1850 William George Clark saw "a fair sprinkling of the softer sex in the balconies" at the Madrid bullring; a few years later Théophile Gautier noticed "a great number of women present" at a bullfight he attended in Málaga. In 1875, an English clergyman wrote that the women "are generally numerous."[74]

Such observations are confirmed by numerous artistic representations. Paintings, and especially lithographs, of crowds on their way to the bullring or watching the fight frequently give women a prominent place.

Many foreign visitors were accustomed to women leading a more cloistered existence, and they were surprised—and often troubled—by the habitual presence of women at the bullfight. Their comments reveal much about how men from other countries expected their women to behave. In the 1770s Richard Twiss commented on the inconsistency contained in women's enjoyment of the bullfight:

> If women acted consistently, it would be wondered at how those who would either faint, or feign to faint at the sight of a frog, a spider, etc., can delight in spectacles so barbarous as these are, where they are certain of seeing a number of bulls expire in agonies, horses with their bellies ripped open, men tossed on the beasts' horns or trampled to death, and every species of cruelty exhibited; but as they do not act consistently, the wonder ceases: the greater the barbarity and the more the bloodshed, the greater enjoyment they testify, clapping their hands, waving their handkerchiefs and hallooing. . . . I have seen some women throw handfuls of nuts into the area of combat in hopes of causing the men who fight the bull on foot to fall over them. But as no general rule is without its exceptions, I own with pleasure that I am acquainted with many Spanish ladies who were never present at a bullfight, neither did they ever intend to see one.[75]

The abbot Léon Nicolas, who visited Spain in 1865, could not understand how women could attend: "A people can only lose softness of manners at seeing so much blood run, and I cannot conceive that a woman, the mother of a Christian family, could take her daughter to see such butchery. That a young woman should applaud such cruel suffering and contemplate such horrors with a dry and indifferent eye . . . It's incredible."[76] Godard's countryman Théophile Gautier did not share his disapproval, but he knew that many would:

> According to our notions it appears strange that women can like to witness a performance in which the lives of human beings are every moment in danger, where blood flows in large pools, and where wretched horses are gored until their feet get tangled in their own entrails; a person unacquainted with the true state of the case would be very likely to imagine that women who could do this were brazen-faced, shameless creatures, but he would be greatly mistaken.[77]

John William Clayton, who toured the "sunny south" at about the same time as Godard, saw a different kind of danger: "The maiden's cheek might well redden as the graceful forms of the strong young men, with their sinew swelling round and fair beneath the tight jackets of satin, the coloured pantaloons and the silken hose, passed erect below. . . . Some young ladies of haughty grandees were actually listening in such a place to whispers of love from gallant young nobles while they reclined luxuriously among cushions and flowers."[78] Rubén Darío, the great Nicaraguan poet who visited Spain while serving as the Paris correspondent for *La Nación* of Buenos Aires in the 1890s, also felt that the bullfight aroused a threatening sensuality in women: "The *corrida* is yet another example of voluptuousness . . . [there is] a truly sadistic enjoyment among certain women who attend the bloody spectacle."[79]

Some foreigners claimed that women were losing interest in the bullfight, but this was only wishful thinking by people who saw the corrida as totally worthless. Lady Mary Elizabeth Herbert, the baroness of Lea, who visited Spain the year after Godard, saw few women at the bullfight she attended in Seville and expressed the hope that this was "a sign that the corrida no longer has such attractions for them. . . . It is simply horrible and inexcusably cruel and revolting. It is difficult to understand how any woman can go to it a second time."[80] For John Lomas, "it is a pleasure to mark that . . . the diversion is steadily losing the favour of the fair sex. The average Spanish woman now lifts up her voice against it and in many plazas she is only conspicuous by her absence."[81]

While some foreigners talked of women in general, others drew distinctions between women of different classes. Edward Clarke said that the women of the upper classes were "feasting, with these bloody scenes, those eyes which were intended only to be exercised in softer cruelties" but only noted the presence of lower-class women, even when they had "children at their breasts."[82] Richard Ford did not think that women were harmed by going to bullfights, but he did feel that the experience differed according to the women's social position: "The better classes generally interpose their fans at the most painful incidents and certainly show no want of sensibility. The lower order of females, as a body, behave quite as respectably as those of other countries do at executions."[83] And Hugh James Rose noted that "ladies who still attend these performances are always to be seen in the boxes, it not being considered *comme il faut* for women of the higher classes to appear elsewhere." He also saw—and criticized—a change in the dress of these respectable women: "Many of them [have] put away the graceful mantilla and wear the hideous bonnet and hat. When women arrive at this bonnet-and-hat stage of civilization, they ought to give up bullfights along with the mantilla."[84]

T. M. Hughes also distinguished among women of different classes when he made an unusual proposal to tax bullfight tickets as a means of discouraging attendance. The tax was to be progressive, according to the cost of the seats, with the women who sat in the boxes to pay the most: "a peseta for the lowest class, two pesetas for the next and three for the highest class; the boxes where fine ladies go to gaze at the butchery to be taxed at a dollar per head."[85]

The anonymous author of *Madrid in 1835* saw women as having a special moral influence that they could use as a weapon against the *corrida*:

> Why should they not exert themselves and try to reclaim their [men] from this savage passion by absenting themselves from all such diversions, and thus stigmatizing them as unworthy of their presence? Why should such velvet cheeks be suffused with pleasure at the writhing of tortured animals and the perils of brutal gladiators? That some diminution has taken place in the partiality of the ladies for bullfights cannot be denied but it is by no means such as to promise an entire cessation of their presence and countenance.[86]

Some Spaniards shared these concerns. In the eighteenth century a number of writers expressed their disapproval of sexual mixing at the bullfight. The Benedictine monk Martin Sarmiento went so far as to propose separate bullfights be held for men and women: "I wager that if the bullfights in Madrid were divided into two equal parts, one to entertain the men . . . the other to entertain the women . . . there would not be as many bullfights or as many lazy people in attendance."[87]

Some nineteenth-century opponents of the bullfight shared the hope that women's moral influence could be harnessed against the corrida, as it could against numerous other social ills. The Madrid Animal Protection Society, which was founded in 1874, created a special women's section because women, "through their legitimate influence, the delicacy of their sentiments, and because of their place of honor as the teacher of their children, will contribute greatly to the desired end and will be the most powerful element in the victory over evil instincts." Antonio Guerola, who wrote an antibullfighting tract for a contest sponsored by the Barcelona Animal Protection Society in 1882, saw public opinion, and above all the opinion of women, as the key weapon against the corrida: "Using the laws of fashion and good taste, it is women who can best establish that it is not good to go to the bullfight. By staying away from the bullring and by speaking against it, they will do so much good and also benefit their own sensibility, which cannot bear mortal agonies and the shedding of blood."[88] Three years later, José Navarrete sought to recruit "educated ladies" for his Society for the Abolition of Bullfights. Among his other concerns was the immorality of the bullfighters' tight-fitting suits of lights, which "show their form and incite the women."[89] At the same time, he claimed that few women, at least few "who have any opinion of themselves," were attending. And if those who did happened to be attractive, this "only proves that a woman can be beautiful and have perverse taste."[90]

José Solana also disapproved of women going to the bullfight, especially when their interest was hypocritically joined to an exaggerated religious piety. Even so, he saw it as a phase that passed when they took on the responsibilities of mature women:

> More than a few Spanish women are in the stands, enthusing over the bullfighters, standing and applauding and shouting like men; sometimes they take

off a shoe and throw it, along with a fan, into the ring to show their interest in the bullfighter. What most excites and inflames them is when the bull is picked, and when they see a horse looking like a bloody rag, they laugh, unable to contain their cruelty. . . . All year these same broads go to hear Father Calpena preach; they confess and take communion frequently; they wear a veil and scapular in processions and end up by getting married and losing their interest in the bulls when their houses fill with children.[91]

Three of Spain's leading women writers also criticized the presence of women at the *corrida*. In her poem "Los Toros en España," Carolina Coronado chided them:

> The women, the *sweet ones*, the *pampered ones*,
> *Delicate hearts of milk*,
> Gloat as they contemplate the bloody
> Flesh of the good bull riddled with wounds,
> The chest of the horse torn to shreds[92]

Fernán Caballero, the pen name of Cecilia Böhl de Faber, twice raised the issue of women in an impassioned letter against the bullfight she sent to *El Heraldo de Madrid* in August 1852. She criticized those ladies, "the sensitive ones who scream, who shudder, who cover their face, but who *go to see the bulls*" and, even worse, take young children with them. Then she called on women, "who have the holy mission of sweetening, refining and ennobling the sentiments of men," to present themselves as "the ardent adversary" of the cruelty of the corrida.[93] Finally, Concepción Arenal, the country's most active advocate of philanthropy and social and penal reform, denounced the taste of some women for the bullfight: "It is certain—and let it be said with shame—that many women go to the bulls, but they belong to the plebs and to the aristocracy, to the badly dressed mob, or to the elegant crowd. There are exceptions but this is the rule. The women of the royal family also go."[94] (Arenal also felt that bullfights were dangerous for the working class, an irrational entertainment that caused them to fritter away money necessary for their family's well-being. Bullfights were acceptable for the affluent, but a vice for the less well off.)

While not everyone criticized the presence of women at the bullfights, few were prepared to actively defend it. Among the foreigners, Charles R.

Scott was the most forthright. While he admitted that it might be better if they did not attend, he saw little difference between Spanish women going to the corrida and English women attending the analogous spectacles in their country.

> Surely some allowance is due, considering their want of such breakneck sights as horse-races and steeple-chases? And—apart from the cruelty to animals—I see no greater harm in the Spanish Lady's attendance at a Bull-fight than our fair countrywomen's witnessing such national sports. The *Toreadores* are certainly not exposed to greater risks than the jockeys and gentlemen whom taste or avocation leads daily to encounter the dangers of the field for the entertainment of the public![95]

A Badajoz correspondent for the *Boletín de Loterías y de Toros* was unique in finding a positive cultural referent for them. "On entering the ring we want to see all the people there, and above all our beautiful Extremaduran women, whose delicate sentiments can only be reconciled with the corrida on the assumption that they have the valor of the women of Sparta."[96] Spartan women, of course, raised warriors for that most virile of states, but in all the rhetoric over whether or not women had a place in the bullfight, the possibility that contemporary Spanish women could make a similar contribution was rarely suggested.

Whether they were watching or performing, Spanish women had a more important place in the bullfight than other women had in the athletic spectacles of their countries. The one comparable case, at least so far as performance goes, were the women who took part in professional rodeos in the United States and Canada beginning in the 1890s. In her book *Cowgirls of the Rodeo,* Mary Lou LeCompte explains the surprising presence of those performers as the product of the West, a region with distinctive economic realities and different ideologies of gender from those of the urban East.[97] Spanish toreras came from the lower classes, where bourgeois strictures about respectability did not hold sway, but if this helps explain why there were women prepared to fight bulls, it does not account for why either the men who controlled the business of the bullfight or the political authorities allowed them to do so.

For the politicians this was a relatively insignificant issue, and when a politician did ban women bullfighters, it did not earn him much applause.

The bullfight world itself was divided. Mariano Armengol, the creator and manager of Las Noyas, was the perfect embodiment of this ambivalence. In the same article in which he said that women should not fight bulls, he explained that he had agreed to take on the aspiring young women because he sensed a business success. For bullfight entrepreneurs such as Armengol and the men who ran the bullrings, the key lay precisely in the fact that they were running a business. If women bullfighters sold tickets, then the promoters' personal scruples, where they existed, were set aside. In the moment of truth in which profit confronted considerations of morality and gender, it was profit that cut the ear.

four The corrida created crowds. Week after week, or even day after day, thousands of people headed to a single place with a single purpose: to see the bullfight. An unexceptional fact, but not in the eighteenth century, or especially the nineteenth, and certainly not in the eyes of the authorities, for whom crowds were a danger, the bearers of disorder and the leading edge of revolution.

Throughout the century and across Europe, the "crowd" was the object of concern and, increasingly, serious study. According to Mark Harrison, early-nineteenth-century English people looked on the crowd with a mixture of "awe and anxiety," but the latter clearly predominated: "Notions of contagion, regression, criminalization and susceptibility to suggestion are all episodically present in early nineteenth century accounts."[1] And in France there was a tradition dating from the eighteenth century that equated "the crowd with the poor and the poor with the insane, the imbecile, the ferocious beast, the barbarian."[2] The demonization of the crowd reached its peak in the last decades of the century, when the subject drew the attention of a series of intellectuals, of whom Gustave LeBon was the most famous. As they saw it, "the crowd was awesome, almost invariably terrifying. As they described the crowd's savage behavior, these crowd psychologists encapsulated many of the fears of their well-to-do contemporaries. Their crowds loomed as violent, bestial, insane, capricious beings."[3]

Bullfight crowds could live up to such fears. The worst instance took place in Barcelona on July 25, 1835. The crowd was angered by the fecklessness of the bulls, which one commentator said were "more like lambs," but in the context of civil war and fears of attacks on the city by the forces of the ultraclerical Carlist pretender to the throne, the anger turned into anticlerical rioting in which churches and convents were destroyed and priests killed. These events entered popular culture in a Catalan-language song:

> On Saint James's Day
> In the year of '35
> There was a riot
> In the bullring.
> There were six bulls
> That were weak
> And this was the cause
> Of the burning of the convents.[4]

The connection between the bullfight and the anticlerical violence was not as straightforward as the song would have it. People in the crowd may have had other complaints against one of the promoters, Mariano Borrell, who was a leading wholesaler of salt cod; they began to voice their displeasure by chanting "cod, cod." There is also a strong likelihood that the killings and church burnings were not entirely spontaneous, but provoked by Liberal agitators.[5] Nevertheless, the government saw fit to close the bullring, and it remained closed for fifteen years.

The events in Barcelona were unique, and even less destructive disturbances were unusual. The bullfight crowd was not generally riotous, but it was far from decorous. It was boisterous and rowdy, but usually good humored. On the day of the corrida the crowd could dominate the city, even in Madrid. If this caused anxiety, it was less because it was dangerous than because it was novel. In the mid-nineteenth century, masses of people "thrown into the maelstrom" of the city streets was "the primal modern scene."[6] Going to a bullfight was an eminently modern experience. What was it like?

Advertising

Bullfights were widely advertised. The most important medium has always been, and remains, the poster. These first appeared in the 1750s, and for almost a century they consisted of unadorned text that listed the date and time, ranches providing the bulls, ticket prices, and the names of the bullfighters. In these early posters, the bulls and the ranchers received top billing, and the bullfighters came afterward. But as the matadors increasingly became the central figure in the bullfight, they also came to dominate the posters.

Until the middle of the eighteenth century bullfighters were announced by a town crier. The first posters appeared around 1760, but for some eighty years these generally consisted of text alone. It was only in the 1840s that illustrations became a standard component. Initially these were crude and unattractive, but they quickly became more sophisticated. By the middle of the century the posters in some provincial towns were being colored by hand and printed on colored paper. In the 1870s bullfighters' portraits began to appear, and shortly afterward posters were characterized by the massive use of bright colors, as in commercial art. The designers began to sign their posters, as if they were works of art. By 1890 posters were using photoengraving, and there were printing houses that specialized in bullfight posters.[7]

The posters were displayed widely; foreign visitors were certainly struck by their prominence. Alexander S. Mackenzie commented that "the immense handbill which announces it, and which, by covering more space than those of all the theaters and masquerades put together, shows its superior importance, stares you in the face at every corner," while Clark wrote that "in Spain these things are not done in a corner. In my first stroll through the city I observed placards stuck up in prominent places in the streets."[8]

The construction of the country's railroad network offered new opportunities. Posters were put up in train stations outside the city in which the bullfight was to be held. The organizers of Madrid's annual Welfare Bullfight sent posters to the Ferrocarril del Norte, the Ferrocarril MZA, the Ferrocarril del Mediodía, and the Ciudad Real-Badajoz line asking that they be put up in the main stations.[9] But the availability of the railroads was itself an attraction, especially for bullfights held in smaller centers. Thus, in 1861, the city of Valladolid sought to entice potential promoters for its annual bullfights by playing up the city's rail connections: "In addition to the benefits accruing to this type of spectacle from the Palencia, Alar del Rey, Reinosa, and Santander railroads, this year there is the added advantage of having the forty kilometers of the Sanchidrian-Burgos line open."[10]

The impact of the railroad was noticeable almost immediately. In 1852, only four years after the construction of the first line in the country, one Madrid newspaper reported on the recent bullfight in Valencia that "the movement by train has been extraordinary during the three days of the fights. On the twenty-fifth all the trains carried fourteen cars and by nine at night some ten thousand travelers had been on board."[11] By 1860 the railway companies were putting on special trains on bullfight days. The promoter of the Pamplona ring marked the opening of the Pamplona-Tudela line by holding two celebratory corridas; the company reciprocated with "a special train and a considerable reduction in prices as well as making it possible for travelers to return home after the bullfight." For Antequera, trains meant that "when the day came the city was inundated by more than five thousand elegant outsiders."[12] Andalusian Railways put on special low-priced trains for bullfights in Málaga in 1880, and posters for bullfights in Cádiz in 1887 included an announcement that "desiring to bring more animation to the bullfight, the railroad Company has put on recreational trains from Sanlúcar." When Guijuelo inaugurated its bullring in August 1909, a special train carried more than four hundred people from Salamanca and other towns on the line.[13]

The railroad also helped internationalize the corrida. People from France attended the bullfights during San Sebastián's summer season as early as 1852, but trains made this much easier. Jacinto Benavente recalled that during the summers he spent as a child in the northern resort city of San Sebastián in the 1870s, "on bullfight days the trains from France arrived bursting at the seams."[14]

The railroad also permitted matadors to increase the number of appearances they could make. Without the train, it would have been impossible for Guerrita to fight in San Fernando, Cádiz, and Sevilla in a single day.

Ticket Sales

Tickets for individual corridas were sold at centrally located box offices. In Madrid, the bullring's ticket office moved from time to time, but it was always in the heart of the city. In 1857 it was in Preciados Street, just off the Puerta del Sol, the very center of Madrid. At the end of that year the building that housed the box office was to be torn down, and the empresario, Justo Hernández, requested permission to move to the Puerta del Sol itself. When the city architect authorized a temporary structure that measured eight feet by ten, Hernández complained that he needed at least twenty-four by twelve: "It is not a question of building something ugly, rather it is a matter of building something more attractive than what we have now, and avoiding as much as possible the repugnant scene offered by one of the busiest spots in the capital."[15] By the time the British traveler Henry Blackburn visited the

José Jiménez Aranda, "An Incident at a Bullfight." Courtesy of the Baroness Thyssen-Bornemisza.

Eugenio Lucas Villamil, "The Old Madrid Bullring—Sunny Day." Courtesy of the Baroness Thyssen-Bornemisza.

Alfred Guesdon, View of the Madrid Bullring, 1860s. Librería Amieva—México Collection, Madrid.

Wine label featuring Lagartijillo, early 20th century. Author's collection.

Wine label featuring Antonio Carmona, el Gordito, 1879. The caption on the sides reads "Con este vino mato yo," or "This wine's a killer." Author's collection.

Advertisement for "Famous Bullfighters" brand cigarette paper with portraits of leading matadors, 1920s. Author's collection.

Banquet for Bombita at Llhardy's, one of Madrid's most fashionable restaurants, before his departure for America. *Los Toros*, November 25, 1909. Courtesy Hemeroteca Municipal, Madrid.

Satire of bullfighters' greed. The matador, who carries a ledger on his back, has skewered the promoters, the breeders, and the fans. *El Toreo Cómico*, December 29, 1890. Courtesy Hemeroteca Municipal, Madrid

Portrait of Dolores Sánchez, La Fragosa, *La Nueva Lidia*, November 2, 1886. Courtesy Hemeroteca Municipal, Madrid.

Postcard of an all-women's section in the stands of the bullring, early 20th century. Author's collection.

"The woman fights bulls and the man prays for her." Cartoon from an anticlerical newspaper criticizing the disturbing effect of male religiosity on gender roles. *El Motín*, October 5, 1895. Courtesy, Biblioteca Nacional, Madrid.

"To the corral!" The crowd expresses its disapproval by throwing objects into the ring. *La Lidia* October 6, 1884. Courtesy Hemeroteca Municipal, Madrid.

Photograph of aftermath of riot caused by suspension of a bullfight, *Los Toros*, May 18, 1910. Courtesy Hemeroteca Municipal, Madrid.

The bullfight as political metaphor: anti-French cartoon from the Napoleonic War. Courtesy Museo Municipal de Madrid.

Royal bullfight held to celebrate the marriage of King Alfonso XII in 1878. This was the first such event held in the bullring instead of the Plaza Mayor. *La Ilustración Española y Americana*, January 30, 1878. Courtesy Biblioteca Nacional, Madrid.

Poster for the royal bullfight held to celebrate the coming of age of King Alfonso XIII in 1902. Courtesy, Biblioteca Nacional, Madrid

Scene from the 1902 royal bullfight. *Illustrated London News*, May 31, 1902. Courtesy York University Libraries.

city in 1864, the ticket office was in Alcalá Street, "a little wooden structure, resembling those in the Palais Royal in Paris, for the sale of newspapers."[16] There it remained for the rest of the century.

Despite the convenient location, making a purchase was often neither easy nor pleasant. Edmondo de Amicis, an Italian visitor, commented that "on Saturday morning, before dawn, they commence to sell tickets. . . . A crowd collects before the doors are opened, yelling, pushing, and knocking each other about; twenty policemen with revolvers in their belts are scarcely able to keep decent order; there is a continuous stream of people until night."[17] De Amicis had not seen the worst; six years later, in his bullfight encyclopedia, José Sánchez de Neira noted dryly that the situation at the ticket windows "has been much regularized, as the authorities intervened with armed force, including cavalry."[18]

But the police were always needed, particularly on special occasions. Every year, shortly before the annual Welfare Bullfight, the president of the provincial deputation, which sponsored the event, wrote to the civil governor to ask him to assign police to the box office. In 1879 he wrote: "In order to avoid the abuses that can derive from the agglomeration of people due to the sale of tickets for the bullfight, I ask Your Excellency to assign three pair of agents of public order at the ticket office set up in the Palace of this corporation."[19]

These problems were not limited to the capital. In 1853, Francisco Flores Arenas described his experience of going from Cádiz to the town of Puerto de Santa María to see a bullfight. When he got to the box office it was "besieged by more than one hundred people elbowing each other, grabbing each other, and even slugging each other at times to get rid of those who by stealth or by force had gotten ahead of them. From that congested throng there issued smothered shouts, laments, curses; some got on the shoulders of others and these turned on their aggressors, who fell into the midst of the tumult, further increasing the disorder and the uproar."[20]

For those who could not go to the ticket office, or who did not want to endure the commotion, there were other ways of acquiring tickets. Scalping made an early appearance. The mayor of Valencia denounced scalping as early as 1815, but the practice had certainly been around for a long time by then.[21] In 1833 authorities in Madrid noted that scalping brought "notorious prejudice to the public and discredit on the authorities" and proposed to "take measures" against it. Whatever measures they took were ineffective: In 1868 the civil governor prohibited "the scandalous abuse of scalping tickets for public spectacles." His plan was to use scalping as a kind of unemployment insurance, licensing people to resell tickets, "taking account of their previous histories and their difficulties in finding work in their respective trades." Limits were placed on the amount they could charge beyond the actual price of the tickets, with the difference considered as "a reward for the service received by those people who prefer to buy tickets from scalpers than go to the places where they are sold." Anyone caught scalping without authorization was to have their tickets seized and divided between welfare institutions and the police officer who had arrested them. When counterfeit tickets turned up in 1880, the authorities and the promoter urged fans to buy tickets only at the box office "or from authorized scalpers wearing a hat with their number."[22] The civil governor of Sevilla tried to "avoid the unjust speculation that harms the public" by banning scalping in 1876.[23]

A variant on reselling tickets at inflated prices was to rent a box and then sell individual seats to the public. This was banned in 1813 and again in 1849.[24]

Despite such measures, scalping continued to be an integral part of the business of bullfighting. Some people blamed scalpers, "buying up tickets to sell again at exorbitant prices," for much of the trouble at the ticket office.[25] Bullfights that held special interest were a gold mine. The reappearance of Frascuelo in Madrid in June 1882, after an absence of two seasons, was one such occasion: "Early in the morning of the Friday before the fight, there was a real riot in Seville Street, caused by the crowd that sought a spot in the line outside the ticket office. The Civil Guard, on horseback, charged with sabres drawn." Little surprise, then, that scalpers "became celebrities, demanding exhorbitant prices," as much as 25 pesetas for a seat in the sun.[26] Tickets to the annual Welfare Bullfight were always at a premium. In 1873 one José Noriega wrote to the organizing committee offering to buy five hundred tickets and pay 2 reales above the face value. He was, he added not entirely convincingly, "guided solely by the philanthropic desire to contribute . . . to the better relief of those in need . . . the Committee can rest assured that they would never be used for speculation." There is no record of the committee's answer.[27] And in 1884 there was even a judicial investigation of the sale of counterfeit tickets.[28]

But scalpers had to judge correctly what the traffic would bear. The June 1, 1858, edition of Madrid's *Diario de Avisos* commented on one corrida that began with "slight attendance, because the scalpers were asking too much for the tickets." Once forced to lower their prices, the scalpers sold tickets more briskly.[29]

It was not always clear just who the scalpers were. In 1884 *El Globo* claimed that unemployment had turned workers into scalpers and made possible new levels of service: "The true aficionado receives the tickets he needs in his own house . . . without the risk of the police confiscating them." It also reported a visit from licensed scalpers complaining that the people who made a killing on tickets to the recent Welfare Bullfight "have never belonged to the guild" but had worked "in the shadow of some unknown municipal or government insignia."[30] Two years earlier the *Diario de Valencia* noted that scalping was thriving, in spite of having been prohibited by the civil governor, and claimed that some of it was being done by "industrialists [and] more or less respectable people" who had received tickets from the organizers "on the condition that they were not to be exploited."[31]

The line between scalping and legitimate business was narrow. Ticket agencies existed by the 1880s, if not earlier, but their methods were not always above suspicion. In 1889 the Madrid police closed down the "General Agency for Spectacles" because of numerous complaints of abuses. According to the chief of police, these abuses were "worst with bullfight tickets. The employees are all former scalpers, known to the police. They fill Seville and Alcalá streets and set up an office in a refreshment stand there. . . . When my men recognize them, they answer back rudely, saying that they have authorization." He went on to note that the box office lacked "the conditions of decency required of a place to which a distinguished public flocks to pay a greater price for tickets so as to avoid inconvenience."[32]

To the Bullring

On the day of a bullfight, a city was more animated than usual. This was particularly so for smaller centers where corridas were not regular events. To the excitement of the locals was added the presence of numerous outsiders. The railroad made this easier, but it had been going on for a long time. When three bullfights were held in Jerez de la Frontera in June 1794, the crowd included many people from Cádiz and Puerto de Santa María, "in spite of the excessive prices one had to pay for carriages and horses and of not finding at any price places for even a fraction of them to sleep."[33] The anonymous author of *Toros: Descripción poética* prefaced his account in verse of a bullfight in Murcia in 1839: "As these spectacles were infrequent there, places in an extensive radius are in motion and the aspect of the capital . . . is most admirable for its animation and the extraordinary crowds. The immense flow of spectators is strange for some, but new and surprising for almost everyone."[34] Later, in the poem, he described the scene:

> From nearby towns come,
> Inundating the wide roads
> Hoping to conclude their journey
> Before the sun rises in the east,
>
> Between the crash of the speedy carts
> Racket, clamour, jokes, and banter,
> They arrive happily at the city
> As the red disk of the sun appears.
> And adding to the life and din
> The sharp grating of the iron wheels
> And the clattering of the horses
> Mix with the festive hubbub,
>
> . . . .
>
> Today the capital is a great theater
> Of amusing and confusing scenes:
> The new arrivals go hurriedly
> To give their fatigue some respite,
>
> They hurry to the inns and cafés, where a thousand glasses
> Whose mere fragrance dazzles the brain,
> Each toasting as she pleases
> Amid the bacchic din.
>
> The most sober and moderate people
> Go through the city; and meet
> On the corners to study the prices
> And the novelties the posters proclaim.[35]

Bullfight day was noticeable even in Madrid. For Spaniards, the biggest problem was the traffic. *Madrid en la mano*, a guidebook for foreign visitors, mentioned "the continuous movement of the omnibus, carriages, and coaches that make it very dangerous to move along Alcalá Street for an hour before the bullfight begins." And almost forty years later, *La Ilustración Española y Americana* commented on the beginning of the 1888 bullfight season by criticizing the "coming and going of the carriages that, without any concern, run over the peaceful pedestrians."[36]

Foreigners found the experience much more overwhelming. Their descriptions emphasize the movement and the confusion and read as though they were struggling to find an adequate vocabulary to describe a kind of scene with which they were totally unfamiliar. It was alien, and not just because it was taking place in a foreign country; they had no experience from home with which to comprehend it. Richard Ford tried it this way: "The wavering line of the Calle de Alcalá becomes the aorta of Madrid through which a dense mass winds like a colossal snake to its prey. The hurry and scurry, the dust and merry mob are neither to be painted with colours nor with words; such are the reds and yellows, the fringes and flowers, the picturesque swarms, the sights and sounds, the driving and running, the screaming and crowding."[37]

A swollen river that pulled people along was a favorite metaphor. In 1836 Alexander S. Mackenzie described Alcalá Street as a "swollen current which extends, one vast river of human heads, to where the view at length terminates, at the outlet of the Gate of Alcalá. There is nothing left for a quiet person, disposed to go with the crowd, and do like his neighbours once caught in the vortex, but to abandon himself to the onward movement and float forward." For Lucien Boileau it was like "two moving banks of a flooding river, the sidewalks of the immense inclined highway of Alcalá are covered with a swarming throng of strange heads and dress. In the middle flowed a wave of horsemen, carriages, omnibuses and vehicles of all sorts, followed crazily by pedestrians four and five abreast."[38]

By the twentieth century this seems to have changed. The crowds along Alcalá remained pretty much as they had been, but now foreign observers had a ready vocabulary with which to describe them. The metaphors gave way to similes based on experiences from home. J. Enoch Thompson, the honorary Spanish consul in Toronto, described his trip to the bullring in Seville as "something like watching the English public going to the Derby."[39] An American visiting in 1931 found a different but analogous comparison:

> By 4 o'clock a very perceptible movement of traffic sets towards the eastern quarter of the city, where the Plaza de Toros is situated. Motor cars, taxis and horse-drawn vehicles hurry along . . . the street cars bound in that direction are crowded with passengers . . . It is an ordinary throng, however, and its general aspect might be that entering a baseball game at home. . . . It is just a multitude of everyday folk attending a professional sport and desiring to be amused on a holiday afternoon.[40]

The scene outside the bullring itself appeared chaotic: "It is early but lines of ticket buyers curve like the tail of a kite from the wickets. Policemen keep a moderate degree of order, and I believe are on the look-out for pickpockets. Water sellers, orange sellers, sellers of sweatmeats. Lottery ticket sellers, and sellers of pillows pester you mercilessly."[41] Yet, for all the crowd, it was easy enough to find one's seat. Foreigners were impressed by the organization. Philip Marsden commented that "the system of tickets and entrances was admirably worked out and there was no confusion. Even unskilled as we were, we found the right entrance for our red tickets." And De Amicis noted that "every seat in the tiers is numbered, every person has a ticket, so the entrance is made without the least disorder."[42]

Such an effective system was relatively new. The first bullfight of the 1849 season was marked by "people from the bleachers invading the covered stands and taking over the seats for which others had paid, knocking over every living thing and respecting no one, not even the ladies."[43] In March 1889 the promoter who ran the Madrid bullring informed the provincial deputation of his intention to paint numbers of the seats in red paint, "so as to avoid the problems we have had until now, when the spectators occupy seats other than those they should; prevent people from sneaking in without tickets and convince both the Authorities and public opinion that we do not sell more tickets than there are seats."[44] That same year, the civil governor of Sevilla urged the Maestranza to more effectively separate the "sun" section from the "shade" to prevent further "disturbances that originate from there not being a truly effective separation between seats in the sun and in the shade."[45]

At the Bullring

The assault on the senses did not relent once the spectator had entered the bullring. The movement of the crowd abated, but it was replaced by a stunning panorama and a deafening level of noise.

The immediate impact was visual; thousands of people gathered together beneath a brilliant sun in the compact space of the arena. This was a scene that lent itself well to the rich, descriptive language of novelists and poets. Alexander Dumas wrote that "on entering the arena . . . we stopped, dazzled, blinded, reeling. Whoever has not seen this blazing Spain does not know what the sun is; whoever has not heard sounds of the arena does not know what noise is. . . . On entering that circle in flames, our first impulse was to turn back. We had never seen . . . so many parasols, sunshades, fans, handkerchiefs."[46] For Rubén Darío: "The spectacle is sumptuous, there is no denying it; so much color, golds and purples, beneath the golds and purples of the sky, is singularly attractive, and the vast circus in which work those jugglers of death, resplendent in silks and metals, gives off a Roman courage and a Byzantine grace." Darío also cited Théophile Gautier: "I assure you that it is a spectacle to be admired, twelve thousand spectators in a theater so vast that God alone could paint its backdrop with the splendid blue that he takes from the urn of eternity."[47]

People with less gifted pens were no less moved. To Edward Hutton, an American in Seville in 1924, "The Corrida itself is certainly one of the sights of the world."

> The great amphitheater, half in shadow, is full of people in every sort of splendid costume. Above is the soft sky, below, as in Rome of old, the golden sand of the arena, and everywhere around you the people of Seville. Before you, on the sunny side of the circus, thousands upon thousands of poor folk, splendid in many colours, with yellow, red, green and crimson handkerchiefs, parasols, mantillas, embroidered with flowers. On the shady side, thousands and again thousands in every sort of costume, the white mantilla predominating among the women, though it is overwhelmed by the innumerable sombreros of the men.[48]

But this same sight could be seen in a different light. For an opponent of the bullfight such as José María Salaverría, the scene was not impressive but tacky, less European than Oriental: "Not a single cloud disturbed the clean blue sheet of the sky. In that clean, radiant atmosphere the vigorous colors of the crowd and the floating decorations were jauntily and barbarously the same as in those crude Oriental scenes. The colors were all sharp and strident: the flags yellow and bloodred; the parasols blue, red, green; the fans polychromatic."[49]

Observers were, if anything, even more struck by the noise. To the thousands of spectators were added the music of the brass band and the voices of the vendors: "The cry of the man selling 'el helado' (ices), 'panales y agua' (a sort of sweet meat that is dissolved in the water), nuts of different sorts, etc., rises every now and again over the hum of thousands of voices. . . . 'Quien quiere agua....a? Agua fresca y panale....s. El hela....o'. These cries and many others mingle with the ring of merry laughter."[50] Katherine Bates, who toured Spain in 1900, described a "tumult of voices . . . so loud and insistent as often to drown the clashing music of the band. The cries of various vendors swelled the mighty volume of noise. Water-sellers went pushing through the throng. Criers of oranges, newspapers, crabs and cockles, almond cakes, fans and photographs of the *toreros* . . . strove with all the might of their lungs against the universal uproar."[51] The range of refreshments and other items available was wide: "oranges, crabs and cockles," "photographs of toreros," "newspapers, fans and strange kinds of shellfish," cushions for rent, and, of course, programs and scoresheets, "a printed leaflet divided into columns for noting the strokes of the spear, the thrusts, the falls and the wounds."[52]

Before the fight began, the vendors were in the arena itself: "Down in the glaring sand, the orange sellers are plying their trade. Should you want fruit, you raise your hand and immediately, with unerring aim, the fellow down below throws an orange into your lap. Then you fling your coppers. Very seldom does any dispute occur over payment."[53] During the fight, the vendors wandered through the stands, but not everyone considered this a welcome service. In his *Tauromaquia*, Francisco Montes had proposed that vendors be put on a much tighter leash:

These men swarm around, thinking they are authorized to bother people who are seated peacefully, entertained and even absorbed in the fight; they block the view, step on them, get them dirty and wet, stun them with their loud shouts . . . the numbers of such people should be limited and they should have a fixed place from which they are not permitted to move, nor should they be allowed to announce their wares.[54]

A similar complaint was voiced in the *Boletín de Loterías y Toros* in 1881: The crossfire of oranges and coins disturbed the fans and should be prevented; orange sellers should be restricted to the gates of each section, as were the people who sold buns.[55]

The overall effect, especially for someone experiencing it for the first time, could be overwhelming. Thus said the sophisticated Italian writer Edmondo De Amicis:

> The circus is crowded full, and presents a spectacle of which it is impossible to form an idea unless one has seen it: it is a sea of heads, hats, fans and hands waving in the air; on the side where the better classes sit in the shade all is dark; on the other side, in the sun, where the common people sit, a thousand brilliant colors of vesture, parasols and paper fans—an immense masquerade . . .
>
> It is not a buzzing like the noise of other theaters; it is different: it is an agitation, a life altogther peculiar to the circus; everybody is shouting, gesticulating and saluting each other with frantic joy; the women and children scream . . . the discordant cries of the crowd are augmented by the howls of a hundred hawkers, who are throwing oranges in every direction; the band plays, the bulls below, the crowd outside roars; it is a spectacle which makes one dizzy, and before the struggle commences one is exhausted, intoxicated and stupefied.[56]

Crowd Behavior

The Spaniards still had plenty of energy, and having paid their money, the crowd exercised the right to express their opinion. What the anthropologists call aesthetic distance, "the sense that while in their seats the drama on the stage is not happening to them; they are observers, never participants," was a concept that seemed foreign to many bullfight fans.[57]

The variety and rowdiness of their chosen modes of expression can be glimpsed from the authorities' repeated prohibition of certain kinds of behavior. The poster announcing bullfights in Madrid in 1818 forbade the throwing of "orange peels, stones, sticks, or anything else that might harm the bullfighters . . . nobody, without distinction of class or status, neither before nor during the corrida, in any part of the bullring, may throw dogs, cats, or other dead animals, nor anything else that might offend . . . the pub-lic."[58] Similar orders, although without the mention of dead animals, were repeated in decrees by the mayor. These also tried to limit the range of the crowd's verbal expression. Thus, on June 6, 1841, the mayor of Madrid issued a "Warning to the Public." Prompted by "the excesses committed by some of the people who attended the last bullfight, held on May 31, in detriment to the decorum owed to the public and the respect owed to the authorities," the mayor ordered "due moderation among the spectators, avoiding any words that might offend the public or the bullfighters."[59] Sometimes such prohibi-tions could be more specific, as when the poster announcing the bullfight on October 10, 1852, stated that "it is absolutely prohibited for the spectators to direct insults or unbecoming language to each other or, equally, to criticize or make fun of the suits or decorations that anyone is wearing, or to beseech anyone to take off or put on any piece of clothing."[60]

It proved impossible to quiet the crowd. On occasion the crowd's com-ments could take a political turn, as when former prime minister Luis González Bravo was given a rude reception at the Madrid bullring shortly after falling from power. According to novelist Benito Pérez Galdós, "undoubtedly the discordant symphony with which he was greeted last Sun-day helped him decide quickly to take the road to Paris, frightened by the speed with which the people of Madrid reduced a fallen tree to bits of wood."[61]

Usually the crowd concerned itself with what was taking place on the sand and at times even became a participant in the bullfight it had paid to watch. The bailiff, who received the key to the bull pen from the president of the corrida, was a frequent target of abuse. Commenting on a bullfight in Valencia in 1860, Charles Davilliers wrote that "these men did not seem to enjoy great popularity, as their approach was greeted by outburts of shrill whistling and torrents of abuse."[62] Davilliers's description was positively understated compared to that of Alexander S. Mackenzie:

And now the *verdugo*, or common hangman, was introduced amid the groans, shrill whistling and execrations of the populace. . . . Having received [the key] he departed to give egress to the bulls, saluted by a renewed exhibition of the ill-will and detestation of the canalla, who thus sought to take satisfaction in advance for the insult he was likely to offer one day to many of them, when he should adjust the iron collar of the garrote to their necks. . . . As the bull furiously entered, the alguazils hastened to escape, putting their horses to full speed. In going out, they also received a share of the same epithets which had been so freely bestowed upon their brother worthy, the hangman, whose office begins with the culprit at the point where theirs terminates. The alguazils are, moreover, employed to levy fines, and distrain upon the poor and, as they are great miscreants, who use the arm of justice about as conscientiously as the myrmidons of a Turkish pacha, they are looked on in any thing but an amiable light by the mob, who avail themselves of their moment of liberty, as they sit in judgement on the benches of the amphitheater, to vent their hatred, against the baser instrument of a despotism which sits in unheeded supremacy above them.[63]

But it was the performance of the bullfighters that most exercised the crowd. A particularly fine piece of work could provoke great enthusiasm, as Hugh James Rose saw: "The audience have gone mad; they are standing up, screeching, stamping and yelling. Hats, cigars and money are thrown into the ring in a perfect shower; handkerchiefs and umbrellas are waved, and the great crowd heave with excitement."[64] But to judge by the reaction of foreign visitors, it was the crowd's response to bad work that was most striking.

The audience . . . became most clamorous. One tells him to make haste, that it is growing late, that the diversion is delayed; another, emboldened by the importance of having paid ten cents at the door, that he is robbing him of his money; while an old woman, sitting near me, assured him in a loud shrill tone, that he was as fit to fight bulls as she was, and that he had better . . . go to the tavern of Tio Pelao and call for a bottle, which he might possibly have the courage to empty. Meantime, the words *ladrón* [thief], *grandísimo tunate* [great villain], *bribón* [vagabond] and *cobarde* [coward] resounded in a discordant chorus on all sides. . . . At length their impatience became ungovernable; and although the poor fellow presently succeeded in killing the bull, they ordered him out of the arena, with cries of *"afuera! afuera! hombre de poca verguenza! a la cárcel!* [out! out! man of little shame! to jail with you!][65]

The range of epithets was almost endless. Gautier heard "butcher, assassin, brigand, thief, galley-slave, headsman"; De Amicis reported "poltroon" and "impostor."[66] And the editor of a collection of popular songs listed *asaúra* [offal], *mamarracho* [scarecrow], *zapatero* [shoemaker], and *burro* [donkey] as some of the more frequently used insults.[67]

Occasionally a bullfighter would answer back. In February 1863, Tomás Caro was fined by the president for "directing indecorous gestures to the public after killing a bull."[68]

Betting could also lead to trouble. In June 1815 the count of Montezuma, the *corregidor* of Madrid, issued an edict prohibiting betting because at a recent corrida this had led to "heated disputes among various individuals over the merits of the various herds whose bulls were fighting that day, producing a general unpleasantness for the pacific spectators." Betting on a bullfight was never institutionalized, and although it is rarely mentioned, informal wagering may have been common. An account of an 1882 fight began with mention that the hours before the corrida began were filled with "the typical incidents, with arguments and wagers over whether Guapito would perform better than Pando. . . . "[69]

But what was there to bet on? Certainly not on whether the "winner" would be the bullfighter or the bull, since this outcome was all but guaranteed in advance. The quotations cited above refer to wagers on the relative performance of the bulls from one ranch against those of another. This was also the case with the first attempt to create an institutionalized system of wagering, in 1901. Under this system, 1,542 tickets were put up for sale at 5 pesetas each; the purchasers bet on one of the bulls scheduled to preform in that week's corrida. Seventy-seven people backed the winning bull and took home 80 pesetas each. This system was used one more time, in July 1912.[70] The bullfighter Enrique Vargas proposed a different approach in a pamphlet published in Mexico in 1908: This involved a points system that would allow fans to bet on the performance of matadors and banderilleros. His system was never put into practice.[71]

The crowd did not always stop at verbal abuse; it also threw things at the targets of its displeasure. The range of projectiles was as varied as the range of insults. In 1841 and 1846 the mayor of Madrid issued an edict prohibiting the throwing of "orange peels, sticks, hats or any object that could harm the bullfighters," but foreign visitors noted a larger inventory: "fans, hats, sticks, jars full of water and pieces of the benches torn up for the purpose," "orange peels and cigar stumps," and "cushions."[72]

Occasionally events could get out of hand. In Jerez in 1872, Gordito had to confront a hail of "stones, bricks, and canes" as well as "all classes of insults" from a crowd that blamed him for a picador's having been knocked from his horse and gored. During the opening corrida of the 1879 season in Madrid, the second bull of the afternoon was a disaster, and the president ordered fire darts to perk him up. This only made things worse: "A large part of the crowd shouted terribly and threw hundreds of oranges into the ring." Frascuelo ordered all the bullfighters out of the ring, for which the president sent him to jail. In Vinaroz (Castellón), a crowd angered by a shortage of horses for the picadors went so far as to rip out bricks from the bullring itself and hurl them at the bullfighters.[73]

Members of the crowd might even invade the ring, usually when the poor quality of the bulls became too much to bear. Salamanca saw such a disturbance in September 1870:

> The sixth bull was meek in every sense of the word, and the crowd came down from the stands in disorder and invaded the ring. The authorities responded weakly at first, and it became impossible to contain the uproar. The Volunteers were unable to clear the crowd; so were the Civil Guard, and the poor bull was stabbed to death.[74]

There was a similar incident in Madrid: "Fed up with all the cows the promoter had provided," the crowd "tumultuously invaded the ring after having thrown all the projectiles that came to hand." In June 1908 the crowd at Seville's Maestranza ring became "indignant" when the president refused to return a meek bull to the pens: "Some jumped into the ring to insult the bullfighters." When it began to rain, "the public broke the benches, the railings, and anything it could get its hands on and stoned the bullfighters."[75] In Barcelona in August 1902, the invasion of the ring included an attack on one of the bullfighters, who escaped by jumping over the boards and taking refuge in the rooms of the ring's concierge.[76] Six years later, the city saw another "scandal." Provoked by bad bulls, the crowd "began to protest loudly. Things turned ugly and bottles began to rain down." The fight was suspended, but that just made matters worse. Frustrated by their inability to locate the promoter, some fans turned on others. "In box 6 there was a phenomenal dispute and the police had to intervene and separate them with saber blows. Some people from the sun side tried to assault the bull pen."[77]

Such incidents, and especially those triggered by inadequate bulls, seem to have become more frequent at the end of the nineteenth century. This would coincide with the great increase in the number of ranches and the decline in quality that followed the expansion of the corrida after 1875.[78]

At times, invasions were prompted more by enthusiasm than by anger: In Seville in 1881 a group of fans jumped into the ring and tried to fight the last bull themselves. "At the same time, they fought the municipal police who, sabers in hand, undertook to . . . disperse them, but not without feeling the downpour of cucumbers, tomatoes, and other vegetables of the season."[79] And there was a similar episode toward the end of a novillada in July 1908. While the final bull was dying,

> various spectators jumped into the ring and tried to "fight" it using jackets, pants and hats. . . . A number of policemen entered the ring to evict them and arrested one who disobeyed them. The arrest of this future matador produced an enormous effect on the public, which began to protest and even throw bottles. The police officers . . . jumped into the stands on the sun side from which some bottles had been thrown and began to lash out with their sabers. . . . The Inspector of Police occupied the ring at the head of a platoon of officers and arrested some of the rioters, which calmed things down. One police sargeant was hit on the hand by a bottle and one fan was injured in the foot.[80]

Other sorts of problems could also lead to trouble. In August 1852 a fight with novillos in the town of Leganés, just outside the capital, produced a brawl between spectators from the town and others from Madrid. But that was not all: *El Clamor Público* reported that "as a result of this set-to it seems that some people from Leganés who sell vegetables in Cebada Square [in Madrid] left because some of the people who were beaten up wanted to avenge themselves." Nor was this an isolated incident, for the paper called on the authorities to take some action "and take precautions whenever there is a festival in a surrounding town because rare is the occasion in which there are no fights or broken bones."[81]

Disorderly or riotous crowds were the authorities' nightmare, but like nightmares, they rarely returned during the light of day. In Madrid, the president of each corrida logged a report with the mayor's office. Two hundred sixty-four such reports are available for the years between 1823 and 1869. On only seven of these occasions did the president note any misbehavior at all, and these were all minor: two fans arrested for "insults and aggression" toward police officers; a "state of effervescence" among the crowd due to a meek bull, and on the busiest day, "ten incidents, none serious, arising out of people having their umbrellas open while it rained. Two or three were arrested."[82]

Partisans, "Real Fans," and Others

To talk about the "crowd" as if it were a single entity is misleading. Top bull-fighters all had their fans, and this partisanship could be extremely intense. Toward the end of the eighteenth century the French traveler Jean François Bourgoing reported that "during my first residence in Madrid, the amateurs were divided between . . . Costillares and Romero, as elsewhere between two celebrated actors. Each party was loud in its praises, as positive in its deci-sions as ever were with us the Gluckists and the Puccinists."[83] In the 1860s the great rivalry was between El Tato and El Gordito. Both were from Seville, but El Tato was the idol of the Madrid fans, and by 1867 "El Gordito and his team could not move without whistles, shouts, and other expressions unknown since the times of the royalists." There was even a special newspa-per set up and "other means" brought to bear to force El Gordito to break his contract and leave the capital. But El Gordito was the favorite in the provinces, and "in some places the authorities had to put the troops on alert" when Tato was in town. Two decades later the rivalry was between Guerrita and El Espartero. "In the Casinos and Clubs there were long, grave, and above all noisy debates over whether Guerrita was better than El Espartero. . . . The competition caused incredible excitement. In Sevilla the two groups got into such a state that more than once they came to blows, and it was nec-essary to protect one idol from the ire of his rival's fans. Guerrita was escorted from the bullring by armed guards: He had performed admirably and the victory made the *esparteristas* furious."[84]

Francisco Montes felt that such partisanship often went too far, disrupt-ing the proper order of the spectacle and even leading to unneccessary injuries.

> We know that, unfortunately, the rivalries that partisan and imprudent specta-tors foment among the bullfighters with their resolute shouts and applause are frequent; for this reason, on many occasions when one bullfighter's party is dominant in the bullring . . . they protest against the bull being killed by the person who should do it and oblige him to hand the sword over to the mob's

favorite—and it is always the mob that acts this way—so that he can shine with a bull that belonged to another.[85]

Montes spoke with authority. In April 1834 the mayor of Madrid sent a note to the police to inform them that "at tomorrow's bullfight there might be some problem because of the presence of Francisco Montes . . . please take the necessary measures to prevent the partisans of one bullfighter or the other from upsetting the peace or from reaching the point of some thoughtless people mistreating he who they identify as the object of public animadversion."[86]

At least one bullfight magazine saw such excessive partisanship as harmful to the development of the bullfighting art. For *La Nueva Lidia,* this meant that bullfighters could "rest on their laurels and look with indifference on what they owe the art" because they knew they could "count on the applause of their passionate admirers." More dangerous was the impact this could have on the future.

> No one is concerned to support, protect, and encourage the youngsters who sooner or later . . . will replace today's eminences. If instead of disdaining them and pointing out only their defects, the public animated them with its applause, there could be no doubt that the art would gain each day. But these youngsters are bereft of any such stimulus; they see that their errors are not forgiven nor their improvements celebrated, that the public and the intelligent fans ignore their existence. . . . Let us call a truce to this passion . . . and concern ourselves less with the present than with the future, which is approaching rapidly.[87]

Partisanship was not the only line of division. From early on, the bullfighting public divided itself into two blocs: the real fans, known as *aficionados* or *entendidos,* and the rest. The former were those for whom bullfighting was an art with rules and standards against which the matadors could be judged; the others were, in their eyes at least, the uninitiated who wanted nothing but crude spectacle and vulgar emotional stimulus. The publication of guidebooks, such as the *Tauromaquias* written by the great bullfighters Pepe Illo in 1796 and Francisco Montes in 1836, formalized a learned standard that was beyond both the economic means and literacy levels of most of the lower classes.

The emergence of "true fans" and their aesthetic appreciation was not unique to the corrida; it had a counterpart in such a distant sphere as classical music concerts in Paris. The audiences for those spectacles learned to listen in a new way early in the nineteenth century. The 1820s saw the emergence of a "code of respectability" that valued "self-control" and frowned on rowdiness. Respect for this code of silence was one way of distinguishing oneself from the vulgar mass and constituted one of the "boundaries . . . that clearly marked the social terrain."[88]

The differentiation of the bullfight crowd was well in place by the 1820s. The author of the pamphlet describing the royal visit to San Sebastián in 1828 was well aware of it. The bullfight held in King Ferdinand's honor gave everyone plenty to talk about: "the aficionados . . . polemical discussions of the charges, of the observance and infraction of the rules of tauromachy. While the knowledgeable ones examined the comparative merits of the athletes, the rest of the public enjoyed the bull, which hurled itself against the barrier five times in an attempt to jump over it."[89] The anonymous compiler of the very detailed diary of the bullfights held in Madrid between 1827 and 1830 frequently invoked the division between the aficionados and the "people." Thus, after one "very poor" bullfight, "the people left disgusted and the aficionados more so." Another day, "the people left happy, but not the intelligent fans."[90] Francisco Montes himself made this distinction when he criticized the "novelty-loving mob" for its inappropriate demands, such as "demanding that a bullfighter who is watching the fight come out to kill or place darts."[91]

In the 1880s, Sobaquillo invoked this distinction when he defended the bullfight from its critics with the argument that the crowds were made up of learned people seeking to apply their critical judgment:

> This select crowd does not go to the bullring moved by idle curiosity or unhealthy appetites . . . [it is moved] by judgments and ideas that cannot be confused with the caprice of the moment because they depend on a technical education and a group of special laws, as occurs in the hunt . . . in which intellectual vitality is combined with serenity of spirit, and personal grace with muscular vigor.[92]

In an editorial on the role of the president, *La Nueva Lidia* remarked that "there is nothing more difficult for the president than reconciling the taste of the lay public with that of the truly intelligent. . . . Today the profane outnumber the intelligent in the Madrid bullring, and their extravagances and lack of knowledge of the art often drown out the voice of intelligence." A few months later the paper went even further and divided the crowd into three groups. "Good-time fans" went to the bullring "only to drink, eat, and raise a ruckus . . . they don't understand anything the see." The polar opposite were the "intelligent fans," who brought reason and judgment to bear on everything, from the lineup for the next fight, "reading it more than once, studying the matadors and the bulls" to the post-corrida assessment: "On leaving they make their summary . . . and spend two or three days studying the condition of the bulls and the work of the bullfighters." In the middle were the "passionate fans," who may or may not have understood the fine points but had eyes only for their idol, "whom they consider to be superior to all bullfighters of the past or future."[93] José de la Loma, a longtime bullfight critic, was unable "to explain to myself the attitude of the public in Madrid and in the provinces against the best bullfighter of the day [Bombita]. . . . I have thought about the Sunday Rest Law, which provides the corrida with an enormous contingent of ignorant people who always go against what sensitivity and justice have commonly agreed."[94]

The distinction between true fans and the rest could even affect the actual content of the corrida. This was the case in the ongoing conflict over whether or not dogs should be set on cowardly bulls. In the eighteenth century this was a common practice: "If nothing can excite his courage . . . and the cries of *perros, perros* redouble . . . [E]normous large dogs are let loose on him, who get hold of his neck and ears. . . . The dogs are thrown into the air, fall down again stupefied, and sometimes mangled, into the arena; they get up again, recommence the combat, and finish in common by dragging their antagonist to the ground, where he perishes by an ignoble blow."[95]

By the 1830s, the general public and the "true fans" had very different views on the use of dogs. At the first fight of the 1835 season, the "public showed its desires, and asked for dogs." These were provided at the second corrida, but the Hospital Commission, which owned the bullring, was having second thoughts and asked the mayor to decide the issue:

> To provide this favor at every corrida would only produce the ruin of the bull-fight, which would be converted into a continual fight between dogs and bulls in which . . . the art of the pick, the darts, and the kill, which are in the hands of the bullfighters and which most of the spectators come to see, would cease

to exist. For these reasons dogs were replaced by fire darts many years ago . . . because this way the darts and the kill still remained. It has continued this way for a long time without the public having remembered the dogs with the determination they showed the other day. . . . Order the measures you think useful to conciliate the taste of the public without compromising your Authority and without prejudice to the brilliance of the events in which the majority of the true fans of the bullfight are interested.[96]

The president of the commission, the marquis of San Martín, also noted that the use of dogs "disgusted the true fans who, in order not to be deprived of seeing the bullfighter kill the bull . . . prefer the use of fire darts. . . . It is very easy to yield to the demands of a certain number of spectators who, against the taste of the true fans . . . always clamor for dogs." The mayor's decision was to use dogs judiciously: "to prevent authority from being compromised . . . employing [them] with much economy, only on a bull that will not charge the pick and when the crowd shows a determination difficult to silence."[97]

The question of the dogs did not go away easily. On March 15, 1853, *El Enano* denounced the "brutal custom" of using dogs: "The abolition would be well received by all the fans who otherwise are deprived of seeing the matador kill the bulls, which is what they most want to see."[98] In 1862 the promoter of the Madrid ring informed the government that he had decided to "accede to the wishes and requests of the true fans and eliminate the use of dogs," but two years later, Francisco de los Ríos reported on a corrida at which he had presided that "dogs are absolutely necessary" for some bulls.[99] The dispute between true fans and the others emerged again in 1868: On March 28, one Joaquín Verdier wrote to the mayor of Madrid to complain about the use of dogs and to request that in the future unsatisfactory bulls be removed from the ring. Dogs had been banned in 1855, in response to the "desires and at the demand of the 'true fans' so that the arts of putting darts and killing would not be lost," but the ban lasted only until July 1864 when, for some unknown reason, dogs were kept in readiness. It was downhill from there, as "with reason or without, the public was always ready to demand what it knew was available, and dogs have been set on many bulls that did not deserve it."[100] The use of dogs was prohibited in the early 1880s, but posters for corridas in Seville continued to remind the public of this at least as late as 1883.

The Desirability of Crowds

The bullfight crowd, its behavior, and its effects were the subject of much discussion, especially in the latter part of the nineteenth century. Critics were concerned about the general potential for disorder, but they also found crowds dangerous on two other grounds: the challenge they posed to morality and the principle of authority, and the dangers of class mixing. On each point, however, the critics encountered opponents who were prepared to argue not only that the crowds were not dangerous but that they could even be beneficial.

Such debates were not unique to Spain. In the last decades of the nineteenth century, social critics in Europe and North America confronted a new kind of crowd, one produced by commercialized leisure spectacles, and the particular set of "problems" it brought. In Britain, "the development of professional soccer and its concomitant spread to a largely working class audience . . . aroused fear and anxiety in the minds of respectable and upper class commentators." And in the United States, sports spectatorship was denounced by some as damaging the virility of the nation. For Ernest Thompson Seton, founder of the Boy Scouts of America, "spectatoritis [turned] robust, manly, self-reliant boyhood into a lot of flat-chested cigarette smokers with shaky nerves and doubtful vitality," while for others the baseball stadium joined the tavern and the brothel as "haunts of dissipation" that undermined moral and physical virtue.[101] Sporting events also revived the public mixing of classes that "had previously been the hallmark of the street"; for some this provided yet another cause for concern.[102]

The behavior of the bullfight crowd, and especially the lack of respect it often showed for the decisions of the person presiding over the bullfight, was a concern for both supporters and critics of the corrida. In 1864, the civil governor of Barcelona sent a long letter to the minister of the interior on the subject. He himself "detested" the corrida and had developed the practice of "presiding only once in each of the provinces I have governed." His immediate concern was that public officials were given tasks for which they were unqualified and which could bring them discredit.

> The President attends not only to maintain order, as in any public gathering, he also plays a role in the event, and a very awkward one at that. . . . The decision to move from one act of the fight to another is left to his discretion . . .

and all this turns him into a kind of Director of Bullfighters, not merely lowering his authority but also running the risk of having his decisions rejected. . . . A Governor or Mayor has to make immediate decisions . . . on matters in which he is not expert . . . before people who are and exposing himself to a criticism that is often tumultuous and scandalous . . .

If the critiques of the President were within reasonable limits I would not complain; I know full well that the actions of public authorities are subject to criticism, and I am the first to listen to and learn their lessons when I see truths and not insults. But in the bullring it is not like that. The nature of the spectacle, the midsummer sun, our southern blood, and, above all, a custom as ingrained as it is censurable, turns murmurings into taunts and shameless insults. Men, and not always from the lowest classes of society, who would tremble before an authority in his office, in the bullring heap the most scandalous insults upon him.

His solution was to create a "bullfight jury" composed of "three intelligent people" to sit apart from the president and direct the corrida.[103]

Identical arguments were voiced by other opponents of the bullfight. In a prize-winning essay for the Animal Protection Society of Cádiz, Fernando de Antón emphasized the damage to the principle of authority: The crowd "fills [the president's] ears with terrible insults, attacking his authority so that at that moment the multitude loses the respect and consideration it owes to constituted authority."[104] Antonio Guerola, who wrote an antibullfight essay for the Barcelona Animal Protection Society, had himself been civil governor of Málaga, and was concerned about the fact that it was someone with political authority, a mayor or civil governor, who was required to preside over the bullfight: Such a person "is under no obligation to know anything about bullfighting. . . . As happens many times, his lack of knowledge may expose him to strident whistles and insults that affect the decorum of his position." Guerola proposed creating panels of experts to direct the fight and leave the governor with only the responsibility of maintaining order.[105] Three years later, José Navarrete expressed similar concerns, asking, "Can bullfights not be held without the authorities directing them . . . without the representatives of the law being whistled at, insulted, and even stoned when they do not know that the bull has been wounded enough?"[106]

Concern for order, and especially for the prestige of public officials, was shared by the corrida's advocates. Francisco Montes had contemplated this problem earlier in the century. He did not see the crowd as a problem, but he did admit that the lower classes got carried away at times. "We know that the lack of control and obscenity of the mob is scandalous when they are together in the bleachers and, almost drunk, they give themselves to their great shrieking." Montes felt that the crowd's pretence to "sovereignty" could be eliminated by "the presence of sufficient armed force and a few exemplary punishments." It was appropriate for the civil authority to preside at the bullring, but he proposed that that person be advised by someone "with a complete knowledge of bullfighting."[107]

The question of the presidency was raised repeatedly in the bullfight press in the last two decades of the nineteenth century, and their comments were surprisingly similar to those of the critics. Thus, *El Tendido* expressed its concern over episodes in which the crowd insulted a public official who was presiding over a bullfight, but also found it necessary to "say a few words in defence of the public." Their upset was perfectly undertandable, since "on very few occasions do the worthy people who fill the role have the necessary knowledge of what a bullfight is." The solution: "Assure that presidents are always intelligent about the bullfight."[108] *El Toreo Chico* took a different tack. The bullring was "the only place in which Spaniards can direct at the authorities whatever insults come to our lips; it is not prestigious for any town councillor, who represents the governor, to be the object of the public's ridicule." The paper rejected the frequently bruited idea of a committee composed of a breeder, a bullfighter, and a critic because in many places this would not be practicable, and if it were, there was little likelihood that "three Spaniards would agree on anything to do with the bullfight." Instead, it proposed the "Portuguese" solution: A public official attends, but solely to maintain order, while the direction of the bullfight is left to a "highly competent expert" who is paid by the promoter.[109]

For critics, the challenge to the authority of the president was only part of a more general danger to morality. J. M. Salaverría connected the demands of the crowd to excessive eating and drinking, and he left no doubt of the imminent danger he saw in this: "The crowd wanted more fight. . . . They protested, whistled, shouted; they would have hit and kicked the president; they injured him with rude remarks and demanded justice at the tops of their voices. And while the popular torment unfurled . . . up in the stands the men drank avidly the wine they had brought in wineskins and bottles, and some ate as well, cutting their food with large, shining, and very sharp knives."[110]

José de Navarrete was even more explicit. The bullfight was the locus for general dissolution, with the liquor store, "a seat in the stands, and the restaurant or the whorehouse, inseparable." Who, he asked, did not spend "three of four hours" before the fight wolfing down "crayfish, slices of salami, olives" along with "three dozen shots of sherry"? Who did not take more wine along to the bullring, go for a large meal afterward, and then finish up with "little women of the finest quality?"[111]

Such fantasies were rebutted with claims that the bullfight crowd was respectable, not dissolute. According to Sobaquillo, "the vast majority of the people who fill the bullring can read and write and many have academic degrees or eminent titles in all the noble careers." Nor did it behave any worse than the crowds at other events, especially the theater. "We have seen worse rows at the Teatro Real than any at the bullring, with seats flying onto the orchestra and the stage; we have seen debuts such as *La Africanita* in which the public brawled with the police, knife in hand . . . and every day the foreign press reports tumults and disorders . . . and when the Comic Opera of Paris cannot present *Lohengrin* for fear of the ferocious intolerance of the anti-Wagnerites."[112]

Others saw the assertiveness of the crowd as something positive, and judged the bullring an oasis of democracy, an opportunity for the crowd to "rule." This was the opinion of Prosper Mérimée, the author of *Carmen* and a frequent visitor to Spain: "In the bullring, and only there, the public commands as if it were sovereign and can do and say whatever it likes."[113] Such views were shared by a number of English tourists. Lady Louisa Tenison, who toured Castile and Andalusia in the early 1850s, wrote:

> Within these precincts everything bows to the will of the sovereign people; within its sanguinary area they reign undisturbed. Governments rule with a rod of iron, but on the threshold of the bullring their authority ceases, and here indeed may be found that freedom of which they are always boasting. . . . The freedom which exists within the bullring is exactly in an inverse proportion to that which reigns without.[114]

Richard Ford, author of the most authoritative nineteenth-century guidebook to Spain, claimed that at the bullring even the king could be seen to bow to the voice of the people: "Often when royalty is present an [extra] bull is clamoured for, which is always granted by the nominal monarch's welcome sign, the pulling of his royal ear; in truth, the mob here is autocrat, and his majesty the many will take no denial."[115]

There were Spaniards who expressed this position too, usually to rebut the critics of the corrida. The anonymous author of *El Respingo* denied Antonio Guerola's charges that the authorities did not receive the proper degree of respect from the crowd:

> The president will lose none of his prestige in acceding to the demands of the crowd as soon as they manifest themselves because then the vociferous demonstration turns into universal applause. I understand that once a decision has been sustained for some minutes it is impossible to retract it, but acceding at once to a demand which has become general does not harm authority in any way. Most spectators are not riotous; they would appreciate this favor and acquiescence and would take the President's side and support his future decisions. . . . The disrespectful letting go of the crowd, which would be punishable outside the bullring, does not really mean anything. It comes in the heat of the uproar, without any forethought or premeditation, and most of the time a smile from the President disarms what, to judge from the confusing clamor, might be taken for a riot.[116]

In a similar vein, Sobaquillo answered Navarrete: "Neither the king who is whistled at nor the mayor who is insulted take offense, and they allow themselves to return a thousand and one times to face up to the same opprobrium."[117]

Defenders of the bullfight also presented it as a badly needed locus of contact between the classes. Looking from the outside, Richard Ford saw the bullring as the one place in Spain where the principles of a liberal society were fully realized: "All ranks are now fused into one homogeneous mass of humanity; their good humour is contagious . . . the liberty of speech is perfect and . . . all is done in quite a parliamentary way."[118] In arguing to have the Barcelona bullring reopened fifteen years after the riots of 1835, the civil governor presented class mixing as a benefit: "Far from causing immorality, it adds more than a little to the culture and morality of the less educated part of the public."[119] Miguel López Martínez, a member of the Supreme Agricultural Council, rejected the arguments of those who saw the "union of the various hierarchies" as wrong and argued that, unlike the opera and the races, with their separate audiences, the bullfight brought various sorts of people together: "Nowhere else can one see such a spontaneous demonstration of the community of joy among all people." The Madrid daily *La Epoca* agreed: "The bullring is the only place . . . where people act with independence and without hypocrisy. . . . There is no clique, nor party spirit, nor governmental convenience; even acquired merit is not considered."[120] The most elaborate argument of this sort came from Sobaquillo:

> The bullfight makes Spanish society the most democratic in the world. At the bullring the grandee of Spain mixes with the least laborer, the rich with the poor, and the person of the most cultivated intelligence with the stupidest: all united with the ties of the same enthusiasm. The bullring is the only place where all our political, religious, and regional divisions are blurred and eliminated, where on Sunday the absolutist meets the demagogue, the priest—with habit or without it—is friendly with the violent anticlerical, where common affection for Lagartijo can bring together Romero Robledo and his most furious opponent, where the Catalan feels Castilian and the Basque becomes Andalusian, the American and the Portuguese feel once again their tie to the Spanish fatherland.[121]

Such arguments for the democratic function of class mixing echoed in that contemporary epitome of democracy, the United States. Defenders of baseball spectatorship claimed that "the spectator at a ballgame is no longer a statesman, a lawyer, broker, merchant or artisan but just plain, everyday man with a heart full of fraternity and good will to all his fellow men," or that "persons of every economic, social, religious or intellectual class touch shoulders . . . They are just human beings with the differentials of rank or vocation laid aside." Or, in the words of Zane Grey, prolific author of westerns and once a minor-league baseball player, "Here is one place where caste is lost."[122]

Not everyone considered this sort of popular sovereignty or class contact to be a good thing. Adolfo de Castro cited a book, *The True History of Asar Nonato*, allegedly written by one Vargas Machuca and published in Tangiers, which described bullring democracy most negatively: "There . . . it is permitted to shout, to speak insolently and obscenely, to insult anyone, throw oranges and chunks of cabbage. . . . It is, it has been said, the only place in which there is absolute sovereignty and no superior authority is recognized."[123] Nicolás Mariscal condemned the corrida for turning

repectable people into ruffians, "adopting language, habits, and customs suitable for ruffians or *even gypsies*." For children and youths above all, the bullring was a school of bad conduct: "From the moment they enter to the
moment they leave, they hear nothing more than gross words and dirty and
obscene interjections."[124] For José María Salaverría, the bullring blurred
social distinctions, creating a being that was at once monstrous and childlike.
"Select society" sat in the shade, and the "people massed together in sun," but
"from afar and above, in the last rows, the human whole appeared to be
formed from the same material, in agreement in its demonstrations of
unhappiness and joy; a pile of homogeneous beings . . . the enormous monster of the multitude. When the time had come, the crowd began to express
its impatience by means of shouts, clapping, and angry gestures; but then the
band struck up a pasodoble and the crowd calmed down like a child who is
easily humored."[125]

The noxious effects of the crowd were brought out in a parliamentary
debate in May 1922. For deputy Bastos, the bullfight was a "national disgrace" that had serious consequences for those who attended. "When the
public gets together in that place it loses all the conditions of civilization and
becomes a totally savage horde. It respects no authority . . . and insults [the
president] with the grossest phrases . . . it insults all the members of his family and his caste. . . . I know many people of good sentiments who, five minutes after they enter a bullring, get excited, exalted, insult everybody. . . . The
evil is not that all who attend are barbarians; the evil is that they are not but
that the bullfight stimulates them to these extremes of barbarity."[126]

The question of class contact was nicely set out in a long poem published
in 1846 describing a bullfight in the city of Murcia. The anonymous author
presents a critic and a fan debating the merits of the corrida. They eventually
get around to the presence of both ordinary people and the better sort at the
same event. The critic begins with a vitriolic attack on the lower classes:

> Who but a bullfight fan
> Would tolerate such riffraff,
> The shoving, the foul-smelling farts,
> The bitter, nauseous belches
>
> From stale suppers of undigested
> Chickpeas and nuts, wine and fruit,

The disgusting tobacco smoke
And other such nasty delicacies

So that even if their nostrils were bronze
They are oppressed by fetid torture?
An elegant spectacle! Who suffers,
Who tolerates such rabble

This infernal bedlam, pushed together
The magistrate and the public prostitute,
The lady of quality and the lowlife
And the people who, above all, bray?

Obscene multitude that freeing its
Licentious, immoral, rude tongue
Delivers itself to disorder, loses control,
And the barbarous shouting of immense crowds

Stuns the eardrum and
Stupefies the wise philosopher
Who looks on his fatherland with disdain
And deplores and is shamed by its lack of culture.[127]

The fan responds that each occasion offers its own experience, and that while the theater, the salons of the elite, and even the Sunday sermon each has its virtues, the bullfight offers something special:

But if one wants
The most immense multitude of all,
We go to the Bulls, to the Bulls,
The *non plus ultra* of brazenness and license.[128]

But it has it over other events, which,
Although many people attend them,
At times their pleasure lacks focus,
Loses intensity and is weakened.
Our diversion is not like that.

> The more people who attend
> The easier to assimilate it, turning
> An infinite number of people into one.
>
> When this prelude is over,
> And the hour to agitate the furies arrived
> There is a center and focus of expectation;
> The most critical moments of the fight
>
> Will affect with a strange impression
> The burning brain of the crowd
> And at the great and wavy blows
> It will shiver with immense enthusiasm.[129]

The author, who dedicated the poem to Francisco Montes, was clearly a fan, but he left the last word to the critic, who repeats his lament for the philosopher shamed by Spain's lack of culture.

Throughout the nineteenth century and into the twentieth, Spaniards debated the desirability of the crowds that the corrida created. But these debates were only part of a larger and longer-running controversy over the bullfight itself: How should the government deal with the corrida? Should it be allowed to exist at all?

The history of the opposition to the corrida *five* is almost as long as that of the bullfight itself. The arguments against it have been primarily religious, economic, and moral, although their relative importance has changed over time. Until the eighteenth century the religious argument, that bullfighting was un-Christian, was the most prominent. This was the basis of the prohibition contained in Pius V's bull of 1567, *De salutis gregis domini* (On the Health of the Lord's Flock).

> Although the Council of Trent prohibited the detestable practice of duels, we know, however, that they are still legion those who in . . . public and private spectacles, fight incessantly with bulls where there are deaths, mutilations, and great danger for their souls.
>
> As we consider how very opposed these exhibitions are to piety and Christian charity . . . we prohibit, under pain of excommunication, that all princes, ecclesiastical as well as lay, royal, or imperial, permit these bullfights.
>
> If anyone dies in the ring, let him remain without ecclesiastical burial. We also prohibit the clergy, secular as well as regular, from attending such spectacles, under pain of excommunication. We annul all oaths and promises to run bulls which have been made in honor of the Saints.[1]

Philip II did not permit this bull to be published in Spain, and two of Pius's successors softened the prohibition: In 1585 Gregory XIII prohibited bullfights in religious festivals while lifting the sanctions on everyone except the clergy, and eleven years later Clement VII limited the penalties to the regular clergy alone. In 1680, Innocent XI ordered Carlos II to ban the bullfight; the Council of Castile refused, but did suggest that the clergy be prohibited from attending.

On this matter, anyway, Spaniards were not inclined to pay the popes much heed. No sooner was *De salutis*

gregis domini known in Spain than a Franciscan published a book in which he defended the bullfight. And some professors at the University of Salamanca, all ecclesiastics, argued that "it was not a mortal sin to watch bullfights."[2] Nor did Spaniards listen to the criticisms of churchmen closer to home. As archbishop of Valencia in the 1540s, Tomás de Villanueva repeatedly attacked the bullfight, which he called "bestial and diabolic," but when he was canonized in 1685 many towns included bullfights among the celebratory activities.[3]

The Eighteenth Century

During the eighteenth century, just as the professional bullfight was developing, the attacks on the corrida became much more intense than they had been in the past or would be in the future. At the same time, the nature of the critique changed to become primarily economic. These arguments were shared by influential political figures who convinced Charles III to impose severe restrictions on the bullfight and then his successor, Charles IV, to ban it entirely.

The bulk of the criticism came from intellectuals who formed part of the Spanish Enlightenment. Father Martín Sarmiento criticized the "libertinism and indecency" of having men and women mixing in the crowd, something that not even the Moors, "who were so careful to keep their women locked up," did, but he was more concerned with the effect of the bullfight on work discipline: "Each bullfight is the excuse for three days of wasteful leisure: the night before, because of the anticipation; the day itself and the day after, when they rest from the exertions of having yelled and screamed. . . . On those days no one works or earns any money, but they eat more than is necessary and drink *ultra condignum*, and far from anyone earning a cent, they spend many dollars in order to be lazy."[4]

A similar argument was repeated by Pedro de Campomanes, an influential minister, in his *Discurso sobre la educación popular*, published in 1775. Campomanes recognized that the "innocent recreations" of the artisans were "an essential part of police and good government," but he was concerned about their effect on the economy and on the working classes and proposed that they be limited to Sundays.

> Bullfights are not a diversion that should be permitted to the laborers, workers, and artisans when they take place on working days because they lose the wage

for the day and spend that for three or four and ruin their families. If bullfights take place over many weeks, then jobs that have been undertaken are delayed and those who have commissioned them are left empty-handed, even when they need the product right away.[5]

The religious and economic arguments against the corrida could collide head on, as they did in the city of Cádiz in 1781. Bishop Juan Bautista Severa, founder of the Congregation of the Christian Doctrine against Luxury, Entertainments, and Pastimes, sent a petition to the king requesting that the government prohibit bullfights on religious holidays because "many people break the Third Commandment; . . . they miss Mass and profane the entire holy day with this diversion." The Crown acceded to the bishop's request and on July 3, 1781, issued a decree banning bullfights, fairs, and markets on religious holidays. This prompted the city government to protest that the measure would be economically harmful because holding bullfights on workdays "would leave the artisans and laborers inactive, damaging their subsistence and that of the State."[6]

Other Enlightenment figures also attacked the bullfight. Father Benito Feijoo mentioned it only in passing, to say that the breeding of fighting bulls had led to a shortage of mules. This introduced what would become one of the foremost arguments against the corrida: that it was harmful to agriculture. José Clavijo y Fajardo devoted two essays to the bullfight in his periodical *El Pensador*, denouncing it as an affront to religion and human decency as well as a danger to the interests of the state. Like Sarmiento, he criticized sexual mixing in the crowd and pointed to the harm done to agriculture and the amount of work lost in other sectors. Clavijo also shamelessly exaggerated the brutality of the bullfight crowd, claiming that they stoned cowardly bullfighters.[7] José Cadalso dedicated one of his *Moroccan Letters*, in which an imaginary Moroccan visitor wrote letters to a friend describing his impressions of Spain, to the bullfight. After seeing a corrida he understood the Spaniards' ferocity in war. "From childhood they amuse themselves with something that would cause men of much valor to faint the first time they saw it."[8] Gaspar Melchor de Jovellanos, perhaps the most outstanding Enlightenment intellectual, said that the bullfight "did not have the least relation or the remotest beneficial influence on public education." The idea that prohibiting it would cause "any real loss in the moral or civil realm is an illusion."[9]

The most famous attack on the bullfight was contained in the pamphlet entitled "An apologetic defense of the flourishing state of Spain," popularly known as *Bread and Bulls*. This first circulated clandestinely in the 1790s, while Spain was at war with revolutionary France and was published only in 1812, when constitutional government had been established. Written by a marginal figure of the Spanish Enlightenment, León de Arroyal, the pamphlet attacked every aspect of Spanish life. Spain was "old and shrewish . . . the most despotic and confused monarchy known to history . . . decrepit and superstitious."[10] There was nothing good to say about Spain, and the bullfight was to blame for it all:

> In that august amphitheater, the only place the Spanish people celebrate their assemblies, I see such good taste and delicacy. The bullfights are the sinews of our society, the fuel of our patriotism, and the workshops of our political customs. . . . These spectacles that . . . make us unique among all the nations of the world embrace all the agreeable and instructive elements you could desire. . . . Scorn as heretofore the skills of the jealous foreigners, abominate their turbulent maxims, condemn their free opinions, prohibit the books that have not got by the Holy Index, and sleep restfully in the pleasant warblings of the pipings with which they mock you. Let there be bread and let there be bulls and let there be nothing else. Enlightened government, bread, and bulls are what the people call for, bread and bulls are the diet of Spain, bread and bulls thou should give them that thou may do with them what thou would, *in saecula saeculorum*, Amen.[11]

The various strains of Enlightened critique came together in José Vargas Ponce's *Dissertation on the Bullfight*, which was written in 1807 and presented to the Royal Academy of History, although it remained unpublished until 1961. Vargas Ponce's tract repeated all the familiar charges against the bullfight while adding little that was new or original. The corrida was supported by "blind custom" and opposed by "all the wise men of the century." It had an incalculable influence on the national character, producing "hard-heartedness, exiled sweet sensibilities, and forms men as cruel and vicious as the spectacle they watch."[12] The bullfight was not a national spectacle, but only a regional one, and the differences between those regions where it was popular and those where it was not were abundantly clear:

> In the provinces where this barbarous and cruel distraction is not known we find that the people work harder and are better farmers as well as being softer

and more docile than in those where they give themselves over to the furious frenzy of the bulls. . . . In [the former] there are hardly any murders, while in the latter there is scarcely a night without brawls nor a loose woman who in the history of her love life cannot recall any number of knife fights nor a tavern in which punches are not as common as glasses of wine.[13]

The bullfight hurt agriculture and took workers away from their work; it hurt religion when corridas were held on holy days. Finally, it tarnished Spain's image in the rest of Europe.[14]

Few were prepared to defend the bullfight publicly. Playwright Nicolás Fernández de Moratín argued that all nations had some form of fighting wild beasts; in Spain the beasts were bulls, and fighting them had made the people valiant.[15] Curiously, a foreigner, and probably the most influential intellectual figure in Europe during the eighteenth century, also saw value in the bull-fight. In his *The Government of Poland*, Jean-Jacques Rousseau recommended "frequent open-air spectacles in which, as in ancient times, the different ranks would be carefully distinguished but in which all the people would take equal parts. Look at Spain, where the bullfights have done much to keep a certain vigour alive in the people."[16] Antonio Capmany echoed Rousseau's arguments in his 1815 "Apology." Every country had "entertainments adapted to the climate, to the customs of the people," and in Spain this was the bullfight. Such national customs had to be defended at a moment when "fashion . . . has taken away so much of what we called our own: our music, our dance and our theater . . . our language will soon disappear."[17]

By midcentury the government was prepared to listen to the critics. A decree of 1754 stated that no bullfight could be held without authorization from the president of the Council of Castile (equivalent of the prime minister). This led to requests such as that from the hospital of Zaragoza, which in 1751 had been granted the right to hold two bullfights a year for six years to raise money "for the maintenance of the poor," for permission to continue.[18] Or that from the city of Salamanca, which had been given the privilege of holding three corridas per year and needed the money to pay off the debt on the construction of the Plaza Mayor. When bullfights were not held, the city was 232 reales short in payments to its creditors, money that came from renting the balconies in the plaza. "It is not fair that people who loaned money in good faith, believing that with the rentals and product of the bullfights they were assured of repayment, find themselves deprived of their legitimate assets." The city was also concerned for the breeders, since when bulls passed three years of age, "it is impossible to accustom them to labor, so that if the bullfights are not permitted, their owners will not be able to derive any benefits from them."[19]

In 1768 the count of Aranda, president of the Council of Castile, proposed that all bullfights be suspended on the grounds that they hurt the economy. The matter was passed to a special committee of the council, most of whose members were adamantly against the bullfight. José Moreno recommended that the corrida "be banned and as far as possible be extinguished from memory." The bullfight was inappropriate for a "Catholic, pious, and obedient nation," and bullfighters risked their lives "not in defense of religion, their King, or their Fatherland but to divert a yelling crowd that is out of control."[20] José Herreros used economics to argue for a "total and complete prohibition." A ban would not hurt breeders, who could use their animals "for other and equally useful purposes, pulling carts and plows," as well as for hides and meat. In any case, there were very few breeders, perhaps eighty in the entire country, and they were usually wealthy so that any harm would be less noticeable.[21] Luis Orries could find only one possible reason for permitting bullfights: the value of the animals that were sold as bulls, but even this was deceiving, since "in the many years that [a bull] grazes, two or three generations of cows could be raised." On the other hand, he could find a number of reasons for banning the bullfight. First of all, fighting bulls were useless for any other purpose. Second, the corrida was a "barbarous spectacle" that depends on "an infinity of bloodthristy people prepared for any evil, such as bullfighters." Finally, bullfights had economic and social consequences: "On these days, and the evenings before, people are totally distracted from their work, by which they provide for their families; the disorder leads the plebs to sell their most necessary goods for a pittance in order to enjoy themselves."[22]

One member of the committee, Francisco de la Mata Linares, offered a vigorous defense of the corrida. He challenged Aranda's claim that the bullfight was responsible for a shortage of cows for useful purposes and that this constituted "a threat to the state." There was no evidence of such a shortage nor any reason to believe that banning the bullfight would lead to there being more. He pointed to Salamanca and Ciudad Rodrigo, which produced more fighting bulls than any other region but still had sufficient draft animals. Raising fighting bulls was economically beneficial, not harmful: The high price paid for fighting bulls "sustains the ranchers and permits them to pay the rent on their pasturelands." Draft animals were sold in smaller numbers and fetched only half the price. If bullfights were prohibited, stockraising would suffer, and "there will not be enough animals for farm work, haulage, and other needs . . . nor will there be enough meat, the demand for which has increased greatly."[23]

De la Mata did not limit himself to the economic arguments. The bullfight was tremendously popular, and if it led to some people missing work, this was common to all entertainments. Finally, the bullfight revealed the "spirit and ability of the Nation" as well as displaying that God put all creatures at the disposition of humans.[24]

Despite the committee's support for a ban, bullfights continued to take place. There were further discussions within the government, including a special high-level committee composed of various ministers, which led, in 1773, to a proposal to ban bullfights within two years. This was never enforced, but it was the background to Charles III's decree of November 1785 prohibiting corridas in which the animals were killed, except when permission had been specifically granted in the past in order to raise money for religious or useful purposes. The decree was repeated the following year, but now it prohibited all bullfights except in Madrid, "even in towns that have a perpetual or temporary concession for useful or pious purposes."[25]

Such measures were not accepted quietly. The 1786 decree was ignored in a number of villages in Seville. Campomanes, president of the council, had it publicized again, "but in spite of this, bullfights in which the bulls were killed were held in Jerez de la Frontera and Puerto de Santa María." The ban continued to be ignored the next year, when Ronda held a bullfight, so "the Council of Castile . . . decided that the Decree be communicated and circulated once again, and the Courts and Justices of the Kingdom be charged with its strict enforcement."[26]

The Royal Chancellery of Granada, the principal court in the south, heard many cases of illegal bullfights, and these illustrate the problems the situation of limited legality could cause. They also reveal the tensions between a centralizing, reformist government and local custom, which was often defended by members of the local elite.

In 1784 the parish priest of Rota charged local officials with permitting bullfights on the feast days of San Juan and San Pedro for which the corregidor had refused permission. The priest's concern was that when bullfights were held on religious holidays "fewer people go to church." In this instance, corridas "provoked scandal among the residents and the neighboring villages, reduced the Devotion of the people, impeded their fervor for the holy rosary, and offended the authority of the Church." The mayor and his deputy claimed that there had been no bullfight; they had only allowed some calves and young bulls to run through the streets, which was not prohibited, and that they had done so in order to raise money to pave the main entrance to the town, which was impassable because of the rain. They were fined.[27]

The town of Valle de Abdalajes came to the court's attention in 1788. Some "resentful" residents of the city of Antequera, including "people of the first quality and of the nobility," had requested permission to hold bullfights there, and when this was refused, they organized them in this nearby village. On the third day, one of the bleachers collapsed during the fight, and in the confusion a couple of people were seriously gored by the bull.[28]

In 1790 the court investigated the town of Caravaca (Murcia) for "abuses committed by the Marquis of San Mamés and other residents." The previous year, after a request to hold bullfights had been turned down, they held them anyway, "on their own authority and totally ignoring that which had been ordered." The case was a complex one and the investigation lengthy. The occasion for the bullfights was the coronation of Charles IV. The town hall did not have the money to put on the celebrations it had wanted, which included a general illumination, a masked ball, and a Te Deum mass, so when the marquis, who was the president of the Brotherhood of the Holy Cross, offered to pay for the bullfights out of his own pocket with any profits to be used for the brotherhood's church, the town government accepted.

The marquis and the local officials claimed that they had not intended to hold full bullfights in which the animals were killed, since these were prohibited, but that after the corrida had begun the crowd demanded that the bulls be killed and the man who was presiding yielded to prevent a possible riot. According to his testimony, "There arose an excessive and universal clamor from the men, women, and children who shouted 'Long live our King and let the bulls be killed' . . . they were threatening the bullfighters . . . which put me in a tough spot, and as I saw an imminent risk of a greater disturbance and wanted to prevent a riot . . . I decided to tolerate it." Another witness asked, "Who would have been able to contain such a throng, carried away by the joy of celebrating the coronation of His Majesty . . . especially when they had his portrait before them and this filled them with even more love? And who, seeing their hearts set on the bulls being killed . . . would not have yielded to prevent greater fatalities?" The mayor summed up the defense when he stated that "the force of a determined crowd is irresistible."[29]

The question returned to the Council of Castile in 1791. When the Maestranza received the privilege of holding twenty-four corridas, the chief royal official in Sevilla protested to Madrid and called for a new prohibition. Juan Pablo Forner, a judge in the royal courts in Seville, was ordered to investigate. Forner's report was a powerful defense of the bullfight: The public needed entertainment; if these entertainments were policed to prevent "scandal and disorder," and corridas were, they would also provide other benefits: "Spectacles and festivals are not incompatible with affluence. On the contrary, they facilitate trade, encourage consumption, and the people, anxious for diversions, double their efforts to acquire the necessary money."[30]

Such disputes and the large number of requests for exemptions from the 1785 decree prompted Charles IV to raise the issue again in 1804. The governor of the Council of Castile argued that bullfights "always cause much harm to the State": They hurt agriculture by causing a shortage of draft animals and of pasture, and they led people to take days off work. Beyond this, bullfighters had become so "inept that they are constantly in immediate danger of losing their lives," and between bad bulls and bad bullfighters the corrida had ceased to entertain and only annoyed the public. He recommended that bullfights be banned everywhere but Madrid and other *reales sitios,* "in order to conserve the memory of an old and singular spectacle for the Ambassadors of other powers, and other foreigners, some of whom admire while others criticize it." Where they were still permitted they should be fewer and shorter, so as to save on bulls and horses, "animals too useful to be wasted."[31]

The governor's submission provoked a lengthy response from a member of the council, Simón de Viejas. He began by questioning the governor's grasp of economics: "It is an axiom of economics that whatever is most used is most produced, since the security of consumption stimulates the industry." When bullfights were freely allowed there was no shortage of animals, especially in Castile, which produced fighting bulls. Putting restrictions on consumption would only throttle production and lead to higher prices. Viejas also challenged the critique of bullfighters' skills: If bullfights were allowed, "the art of fighting them . . . would be considered a trade and men would take it up the same way they take up tailoring . . . and all occupations that offer security." As to the charge that bullfights kept people away from work,

Viejas argued that this was a matter of "domestic economics and prudence, areas where governments should never intrude." If people abused such "innocent recreations," it was not the fault of the bullfight.

> Otherwise, neither should beautiful women go out on the street nor men carry money in their pockets, since one provides opportunities for the lustful and the other opportunities for thieves. And this ignores the fact that the government would not be consistent, since there are only eighteen bullfights per year, while there are two theaters open all year, one of which is open even during Lent.[32]

Viejas offered one positive "political" reason for retaining bullfights, which can be summarized as "if not bread, then circuses." In hard times, such as those in 1804, the people blamed the government for high food prices; banning the bullfight would only produce more dissatisfaction. "When we face the situation of being unable to give the People the satisfaction they desire, it is necessary to provide entertainments that make them think of other things and as little as possible of the government."[33]

These arguments carried little weight with the rest of the council, which decided that "the end of bullfighting . . . is urgent and necessary."[34] On February 10, 1805, Charles IV issued a royal decree that announced an "absolute prohibition" of any bullfight in which the bull was killed. The partial bans decreed by his father had been ineffective, and as the "political and moral evils" inherent in the corrida continued to flourish, he had decided to "abolish a spectacle that does not conform to the humanity of the Spanish people; which causes damage to agriculture because of the obstacles it poses to the raising of livestock and the backwardness of industry because of the sad waste of time among artisans on days in which they should be working." The ban applied to the whole country, "not excepting the Court," and those places that had the privilege to hold bullfights to raise money for "pious or useful" ends could suggest forms of reimbursement to the Council of Castile.[35]

The Nineteenth Century

This ban did not last long, but the bullfight's restoration to legality came from a most unexpected source. In 1808 Napoleon invaded Spain and, after forcing Charles IV and his son Ferdinand to abdicate, placed his brother, Joseph Bonaparte, on the throne. It was this French king, José I, who, in 1811, authorized bullfights once again. The 1805 decree was not formally repealed, but it was ignored from that point on. Not everyone was happy with this situation. In 1814 the mayor of Vitoria opposed holding bullfights to celebrate the return to the throne of Ferdinand VII because of the danger they posed to public morality. He

> observes sadly the perversion they have wrought on the customs of a country considered to be the cradle of innocence and warns that in spite of vigilance a multitude of prostitutes have come here with the cover offered by the troops and the liberal system, and that his zeal is not sufficient to correct these disorders; that the bullfights in question will stimulate vice to such a frightening degree that it will not dissipate in years.[36]

There were no further serious attempts to prohibit the bullfight. Even when key government officials personally opposed the corrida, their policy was one of reluctant toleration. Javier de Burgos set the tone in his *Instructions* of November 30, 1833, which created the country's modern administrative system. Bullfights were discussed as one of a number of "public diversions," but they also received a special mention that revealed de Burgos's ambivalence toward them.

> Among these spectacles there is one in which men risk their lives, in which useful animals are destroyed, in which hearts are hardened, and which the progress of public reason will sooner or later eliminate. The administration ought to accelerate this beneficent process indirectly, witholding from this class of spectacle any protection other than simple tolerance while giving full protection to those [spectacles] that serve the interest of civilization and prosperity.[37]

The corrida had unique implications for public order, which brought it to the attention of government officials and led them to impose a degree of state intervention unusual for liberal regimes. The initial regulations came from local and provincial officials whose objective was to prevent disorder by preventing the conditions that antagonized the crowd. This meant paying close attention to the practices of the promoters. The following incident, which took place in Madrid in August 1848, displayed the dynamic that could lead from promoters' cutting costs to a riot. After a series of inadequate bulls had been returned to the pens, there was none left to continue the *corrida*.

The public demanded another bull, which the president granted. But the promoter did not have any more animals and once again sent out the one-eyed one that had earlier been withdrawn amidst the shouts and whistles of the crowd. The public went crazy, demanding "Another bull," "Out with the one-eye" ever more loudly. . . . The governor ordered that the promoters be arrested. . . . This was done immediately, and they were taken across the ring by the municpal police amidst the biggest racket that has ever been heard. . . . This is how the bullfight ended.[38]

The 1840s and 1850s were a critical moment in this respect. The recovery of the bullfight from decades of decline in the context of a definitively established liberal system seeking to create a sweeping new economic freedom tested the limits of laissez-faire.[39] The *Tauromaquia,* written by the great matador Francisco Montes in 1836, included a set of proposals to regularize and regulate the spectacle, among them the creation of an official called the *fiel* whose job was to make sure that bulls were as advertised: "to see that they have the brands of the ranches that the promoter has announced and avoid deceiving the public, as happens every day." Montes also recommended applying a special brand to animals that had fought in novilladas: This would prevent ranchers from selling them to be used in other fights, where they posed great dangers to the bullfighters.[40]

Eleven years later, Melchor Ordóñez, the civil governor of Málaga, became the first official to actually regulate bullfights. His decree consisted of fifteen articles, of which four were directed at the bullfighters and the rest at the promoter. None referred to the crowd itself. Ordóñez was in no doubt about the source of any potential problems: The way to keep the crowd well behaved was to guarantee that promoters acted honestly and that the fans got what they paid for.[41] The promoter was threatened with fines for selling more tickets than the ring held, knowingly buying less than top-quality bulls, having bulls that were younger than five or older than eight years of age, and not having the ring's service personnel decently dressed.[42]

Ordóñez was moved to issue his decree by ongoing problems at the Málaga bullring. The ring had been built in 1839 by Antonio María Olivares, who was also granted the right to hold ten bullfights per year. In January 1850 he was involved in a major dispute with the civil governor and the city council, complaining to the Ministry of the Interior in Madrid that over the years the "authorities," which undoubtedly included Ordóñez, had "so altered the conditions that the promoters flee from taking on the ring." Such "arbitrary behavior" had to be ended, and he urged the creation of a committee of a breeder, a bullring owner, and a top bullfighter to design a set of regulations "to set the rights and duties of all who are involved in the bullfight."[43]

If Olivares had had trouble with Ordóñez, he was having even more with city hall, which had the backing of Ordóñez's successor. The conditions that the local authorities were trying to impose make it clear that the practices addressed by Ordóñez's regulations had not been eliminated. The city was demanding that the promoter have on hand one bull more than the number scheduled to fight, that the bulls all be from the ranch and of the category advertised, and that he not sell tickets beyond the ring's capacity. But it was also entering into new territory, requiring that he reduce ticket prices by 20 percent. The city justified its initiative by asserting its role as the public's "teacher." The promoter was charging "the largest amount that is charged in the best rings of the peninsula. In this case, who represents the public? Who is its teacher? There can be no doubt that it is Public Authority, and it is up to that Authority to prevent any taking advantage of the public's eagerness." Moreover, public order was at risk: "Men of all classes meet with a degree of liberty found only at this class of spectacles." In these circumstances it was up to government to ensure that the promoter was not giving *gato por liebre*: "guarantees that what is offered is delivered and that the prices bear some relation to it."[44]

The civil governor agreed that such measures were entirely justified. "The promoters have always defrauded the expectations of the public, giving them bad bulls that were only adequately fought and demanding payment totally out of relation to the merit of the performance." Specifying the source of the bulls would protect both breeders and public: "It is well known that not all breeders' bulls are equal and that some ranches have better reputations than others. . . . Therefore, if the public is offered first-quality bulls from, say, Veraguas but in order to save money the promoter brings bulls from an unknown ranch, he cheats the public, and if he advertises them as Veraguas he is also bringing that ranch into disrepute." Overselling the arena was "a notable abuse" and one that made possible "upsets, discomfort, and even tragedies."[45]

The ministry disagreed. Madrid put the defense of economic freedom ahead of consumer protection and local concerns about possible disorder. The city's proposals had "deprived [the promoter] of indisputable rights and have put unmanageable constraints on this class of industry." Setting ticket prices was nothing less that "an attack on property"; this had been raised in other jurisdictions, and the Royal Council had always ruled that "the ability to set ticket prices belongs exclusively to the owner or promoter of the ring."[46]

Concerns about promoters' shady practices also led authorities in Seville to intervene. In April 1864 the civil governor reacted to reports of "deplorable events" outside the bullring, "all the result of some of the public having been denied entry into the ring, even though they all had tickets, because there were already more people inside than the building can accommodate," and he ordered the city to take measures to "ensure tranquillity and punish the promoter for having committed a great abuse." He later ordered the municipal architect to ennumerate the seats so that the mayor's office could stamp the appropriate number of tickets for each fight. Three years later, the city council created a Bull Pen Commission to ensure that the bulls were of the age advertised.[47] Bulls continued to present a problem the following decade. In April 1876, the governor had been unsure whether to authorize a corrida "because of doubts that the bulls had sufficient age and qualities." This required "precautionary measures to prevent the repetition of such situations, which can affect public order," but these were elusive. On July 3, 1877, the governor wrote to the mayor that the previous day "real bulls had been advertised but poor novillos appeared, and two of them were one-eyed. This produced notable disgust in the public, which could have taken on much greater dimensions."[48] The effective regulation of bullfights in Sevilla was blocked by a decades-long conflict between the authorities and the Maestranza, which owned the ring. As late as 1895, the Maestranza refused to meet the governor to discuss a set of regulations on the grounds that this was the prerogative of "the promoter, the public, and the ring's owner alone. [Written] regulations are a dead letter, and practice is the only true guide."[49]

The first published set of regulations appeared in Madrid in 1852 over Melchor Ordóñez's name. The forty-one articles were grouped into four sections. The first fifteen outlined the responsibilities of the owner of the bullring, including prohibiting the sale of more tickets than the ring could accommodate. The next ten articles set out the responsibilities of the picadors, including limiting the number of times each could pick a single bull and requiring them to withdraw from the ring if "a horse's guts are hanging out in a manner that is repugnant to the public." Six articles dealt with the responsibilities of the bullfighters, including "fulfilling what the poster advertises" in terms of who would kill the bulls. The final ten were "general rules," among them ones fixing the number of bulls to be fought at eight and requiring the fight to begin at the announced time; requiring the troops present to maintain order to "unfix their bayonets in order to avoid accidental tragedies caused by the large crowds," and prohibiting spectators from "throwing objects into the ring" and from "insulting anyone else for any reason or occupying a seat that belongs to someone else."[50]

Local sets of regulations flourished from this point on, and as time passed they became lengthier and much more detailed.[51] The set issued for Madrid by the conde of Heredia in 1880 had 106 articles, among them three about medical facilities, including a requirement that a doctor attend and that the infirmary be properly supplied, and one that fixed the number of bulls in a corrida at six.[52]

With the Royal Order of October 31, 1882, "On Bullfights," the nature of regulation changed qualitatively: An issue that, to that moment, had been handled by provincial governors, was assumed by the national government.[53] No new bullrings could be opened without permission from the Ministry of the Interior; no local government that had not met all its other obligations, "especially education," would be permitted to use public money to hold bullfights or build bullrings; civil governors were to exercise "prudence" in authorizing bullfights and were especially enjoined to ensure that "all measures to prevent the disasters that repeat themselves with sad frequency" had been taken.[54]

At the same time, the order offered formal recognition that, whatever the preferences of those in power, the bullfight was there to stay:

> The bullfight constitutes a spectacle so deeply rooted in popular custom that it would be reckless to try and eliminate it, thereby yielding thoughtlessly to the hysteria of those who call it barbarous and opposed to culture. But if, out of respect for opinion, the Government can do no less than authorize it, it also has the duty to prepare carefully thought out reforms in the regulations so that its often gory character, especially in small towns and villages, disappears.[55]

This official recognition of the victory of bullfighting over its enemies was all the more striking for its language. Critics of the corrida had always portrayed themselves as the defenders of culture and civilization against the barbarism and irrationality of the bullfight and its defenders, yet here the demands of the critics are described as hysteria to which the authorities must not surrender "thoughtlessly."

Bullfighting and Public Opinion

During the eighteenth century, the debate over the bullfight was limited to a
tiny elite of government officials and local notables, especially the clergy. The
reformers who tried to have the bullfight banned were the standard bearers
of enlightenment and centralized government, but as the cases investigated
by the royal court in Granada show, their prescriptions for improving Spanish life were not always readily accepted by ordinary people or local elites.
During the nineteenth century, the debate over the bullfight took place in
the much wider realm of a modern public opinion, embodied in newspapers,
magazines, pamphlets, and voluntary organizations. This debate was ongoing and diffuse and much less focused than the more limited debate of the
previous century. There were, however, a number of dominant themes: economics, the working class, and the comparison between Spain and other
countries, or what will the foreigners think?

The eighteenth-century economic argument had workers at its center:
The economy would be damaged by workers taking time off to attend bullfights. The nineteenth-century critics continued to conflate concerns about
the workers and economic damage, but they also worried about the workers
themselves. From early in the century, but particularly as the working class
organized into trade unions and class-based political parties, critics
expressed their concern for the moral damage attending bullfights did to
members of the lower classes and its potential political implications. In
short, the bullfight became part of the "social question."[56]

A petition in July 1820 in which the city government of Seville requested
that parliament ban bullfights provides a bridge between the two perspec-
tives. The workers' fondness for the corrida distracted them from "honest
occupations" and led to their families' being subjected to "all types of privations." And when the fights were held on weekdays, workers "abandon[ed]
their workshops and all industry and personal occupations . . . the dangerous
occasions suggested by leisure are repeated, and the propensity to laziness
stimulated."[57] This much was a commonplace of enlightened critique, but
the city councillors went on to add something new. Workers' enthusiasm for
the bullfight not only harmed the economy, it harmed the workers themselves and, above all, their families: "It is considered clever for the father, the
head of the family, to sell his cape and even use other, more reprehensible
methods to be able to attend."[58]

This caricature foreshadowed what later in the century would become the prevailing stereotype of the working class, what Manuel Pérez Ledesma has called "a *moral,* or *cultural,* fear caused by . . . the workers as a group. The new ways of life, the new forms of behavior of this group, their modes of association on and off the job appeared as a threat to the prevailing social and moral norms. . . . The workers had been made into a threat because of their very existence and not because of the ideas they held."[59]

By the last quarter of the century this image of the working class had become one of the clichés of the antibullfight arsenal. In his novel *Ricardo,* Republican politician Emilio Castelar commented that for the working people of Madrid the bullfight began even before the day on which the spectacle took place, with "a visit to the pawn shop, if nothing else is available, so as to procure a few coins to buy a seat in the bleachers out in the sun."[60] Concepción Arenal, the country's foremost advocate for philanthropy, opposed the bullfight in general but was especially concerned about its effect on the working class: The corrida was an irrational entertainment that caused them to squander money their families needed for their subsistence; what was acceptable behavior for the affluent was a vice for the less well off.[61]

An incident in June 1884 produced a flood of such arguments. The crowd at the Madrid bullring's downtown ticket office got out of hand, and the police, sabers drawn, were required to restore order. The crowd then moved to the bullring itself and spent the night waiting for tickets to go on sale there. The press was scandalized and used the occasion to condemn the bullfight as evidence of the country's lack of seriousness. But within the overall critique, the effect on the workers received special attention. The return to holding bullfights on weekdays not only hurt the economy, it also "widened the already deep breach that this barbarous taste has caused in the economy of the workers."[62] Even *La Lidia,* a bullfight periodical, commented on the ill effects of the workers' love of the corrida: "Let our readers judge the sacrifices, losses, sleepless nights, and sorrows made by families with a poor and miserly wage who, drawn by their enthusiasm for this popular fiesta, do not think about the future, slowly going into debt and more often than not losing their wage for the day on which the fight takes place."[63]

At a moment in which food prices were high, workers were displaying their lack of judgment and maturity. *La Epoca,* for one, was moved to reconsider its sympathy for their difficulties:

Recently, we journalists of good faith have complained loudly about the high price of bread and potatoes, and we felt sorry for the people of Madrid, who must live in such an expensive capital . . . we were truly moved and deplored the sad state of the poor; well, they responded by rushing, under the influence of a crazy hysteria, to buy tickets for the bullfight . . . causing riots and spending a cold night in the open, sacrificing their health and the comfort of their homes, everything for a seat at the bullring.[64]

A people that behaved this way, "that forgets its misery and begs in order to buy a ticket . . . that complains about the price of basic necessities, that their wages are too low, that their houses are unhygienic" could only be described as "frivolous, thoughtless; not worthy of respect," and certainly not of the right to vote and "intervene directly in governing the state."[65] Like Concepción Arenal, the paper judged bullfight fans differently according to their social class: "If the rich enjoy it and spend money on it, there is no harm done because they are rich. But what about those who pawn their mattress, or spend their week's pay, who foresake their home and their children to satisfy a vice?"[66]

The pamphlet *Bread and Bulls* had compared Spain's love of the bullfight with what went on in countries such as France and England, but in the nineteenth century—and especially in the second half of the century—the corrida's critics claimed that the popularity of the bullfight kept Spain from being truly European. Writing in *El Heraldo de Madrid* in 1852, Antonio Méndez called the bullfight "a terrible barrier that divides our Spain from the march of modern civilization" and "an anachronism that covers us in ignominy in the eyes of cultivated Europe."[67] Novelist Fernán Caballero congratulated *El Heraldo* for its attack on the corrida, which will

cover it in glory in the eyes of cultured Europe. . . . How surpised the liberal and cultivated fans of the bullfight would be if they knew that enlightened Germany, which has so much admiration for the land of Calderón and Lope [de Vega], simultaneously throws in Spain's face the bullfight and the Inquisition. We only wish that the defenders of this bloody pastime would hear how the most sensible and cultured men of other countries cite the bullfight as evidence of our moral backwardness in European culture.[68]

For some critics, the bullfight belonged to the "Black Spain," to the "nation of the Inquisition, the nation of the Jesuits," as Castelar's hero, Ricardo, put it.[69] Angel Fernández de los Ríos ended an eighteen-page diatribe against the bullfight in his *Guide to Madrid* by predicting that until the corrida was abolished, "Spain will continue to present Europe with the exceptional sight of a people educated by the Inquisition who have no enjoyments other than the auto-da-fé, the gallows, the bulls, and civil wars."[70] For others, the situation was even worse: The true horror of the bullfight was that it turned Spaniards from Europeans into Africans. The article that drew Fernán Caballero's praise had likened the bullfight to what went on in the "courts of some African chief . . . where they sacrifice some miserable slave."[71] The bullring brought Spaniards down to the level of the Moors, and the bullfight was nothing more than an "African ferocity."[72]

Regional nationalists in Catalonia had their own take on this. The bullfight may have been Spanish, but it was certainly not Catalan. Thus in 1884, the regionalist paper *L'Arch de Sant Marti* proclaimed that "the so-called 'national pastime' is far from forming part of our national customs and the Catalan people should be proud of being less than the Spaniards in this respect. It should be replaced by something more suited to our character." For *La Veu de Catalunya*, the voice of Catalan nationalism, the bullfight was "one of the principal elements that do most harm to our fatherland."[73]

The nationalist paper *La Tramontana* expressed its views visually. A cartoon published in August 1885 contained a large image of a triumphant bullfighter at the center, surrounded by smaller drawings of women begging, uneducated children, unemployed men, and a man dying of cholera. The caption read: "While misery advances, surrounding us on all sides, only the *national* spectacle takes root and prospers." In April 1886 it published a more complex cartoon that told the story of a typical Catalan peasant who was in Barcelona for a visit. Fed up after only three days in the big city, he was trying to find the train station when he got caught up in a "torrent" of people that carried him to the bullring. He finds the ticket window, and although he cannot read the posters announcing the corrida featuring Lagartijo and Frascuelo, he decides to buy whatever they are selling. Just as he approaches the window, he is enveloped by a crowd wielding sticks and knives; "frantic and furious," and clinging to the bars of the ticket window, he cries out, "Give me a third-class ticket to Vilassar."[74]

Animal Protection Societies

One of the most characteristic features of the liberal world of the nineteenth century was the emergence of what has been called a civil society, a realm independent of the state in which people came together freely to express opinions and debate. The most distinctive feature of this civil society was the voluntary organization. These were formed by the hundreds and thousands in every country in western Europe, and they were formed for every conceivable purpose, although in Spain philanthropy and welfare were the most numerous. After 1870 a small number of animal protection societies were created, and they took as one of their principal tasks the struggle against the bullfight.

The most active of these organizations was the Cádiz Society for the Protection of Plants and Animals, which was founded in 1872. The society's goal was "to promote by all possible means the conservation of plants and animals," and it committed itself to combat "without truce, but with moderation and much tact, bullfights, cockfights, the mistreatment of useful plants and animals, and any pastime which makes them suffer." The society was keen to involve women but, unusually for any organization at that time, it promised "equal rights to both sexes," and, in fact, women sat with men on the executive committee.[75] A Madrid-based society founded two years later was much more conventional in its approach to women: It had a separate women's section and sought to harness woman's "delicate sentiments and her place of honor as teacher to her children" to achieve the desired "victory over bad instincts."[76]

In its public pronouncements on the bullfight the society combined a number of widely used themes with a marked religious tone. In May 1874 it issued a flyer addressed to the "people of Cádiz" in which it attacked the corrida for its cruelty to bulls and horses but also because they encouraged people to join a dangerous profession and exposed the audience to "acts of cruelty and . . . the sight of blood, which awakens the instincts most opposed to the gift that distinguishes mankind, reason."[77] The next month it published an open letter urging the city's "Catholic Public" not to participate in acts of which God would disapprove and which "reduce Spain's stature in the eyes of other nations." The society also congratulated the city government of Málaga for stopping work on the bullring when schools, hospitals, jails, and cemeteries were more pressing necessities, and called the bullfight "the seal of our smallness and backwardness, the perpetual enemy of religion."[78]

In 1875 the society held a contest for the best essay condemning the bullfight with a prize donated by a French woman. The winning entry was Fernando de Antón's *Memorial written against the Bullfight*. For the most part, this was simply a catalog of the well-worn themes of the antibullfight tradition.

There was the religious argument: The bullfight was opposed to Christian principles. There was the threat to public order: People drank to excess both before and after the corrida and behaved in a "sublimely monstrous fashion." There was economic damage: He estimated that some 40 to 50 million pesetas were spent on the bullfight each year, most of it by workers who also took time off and "left a hole in national production." And raising bulls distracted people from the more useful pursuit of raising cattle for milk. There was the concern for Spain's standing: The bullfight was not fit for a civilized country. He also rejected the claim that the bullfight contributed to Spain's manliness; after all, Prussia and the United States did quite well without it.

Antón concluded by recognizing that since the government would never ban the bullfight, indirect measures were necessary. Here he was at his most original. He appealed above all to the "spirit of association" embodied in the Cádiz society and called for other such organizations to be created under the motto "Morality and Work." The clergy must preach against the bullfight, and essay competitions should be encouraged, especially in the schools. Finally, he proposed the promotion of alternative entertainments directed at the working class. The circus was one, but Sunday outings in the countryside would be the most effective, "separating the worker from the tavern, where they poison themselves, and from the bullfights, where they become brutalized, and from the clubs, where they hear people railing against the constituted powers and where their spirit becomes predisposed to insurrection."[79] The pairing of the bullfight with worker morality and the social question could not be clearer.

Even in parts of the country where they barely existed, bullfights were the target of voluntary organizations. The Antiflamenquista Society, which was founded in Gijón in 1913, and which had its own publication by 1915, drew its support from Republicans and anarchists, who were significant political forces in the city. The Society fought *flamenquismo*, cultural activities emanating from Andalusia that it saw as immoral. The corrida was only one of its targets, but it was also the most significant, even though Asturias had little bullfight tradition. In terms indistinguishable from those used by the clergy, Eleuterio Quintanilla, the best-known of Gijón's anarchists, explained the society's enemies as: "Movies, cabarets, foolish zarzuelas, music hall; foul, obscene, rotten pornography; crime reporting, which feeds criminal morbidity; detective plays, which praise humanity's most bestial instincts; cops-and-robbers books, which destroy the tender imagination of children; the so-called erotic novels, which promote lust beneath the cover of a moralism that would be healthy if it were applied." In this company, the bullfight was flamenquismo's "most graphic representation . . . a macabre poem of baseness, cowardice . . . physical and moral misery." From Quintanilla's anarchist perspective, they all constituted the "foul-smelling bouquet of degradation promoted by the international bourgeoisie to the rank of forces of social conservation."[80]

Defenders

In the eighteenth century the bullfight went virtually undefended; in the nineteenth it found numerous advocates. To a significant extent, their arguments echoed those of the critics while turning them on their heads. Their arguments were also much more forward-looking than those of their opponents and free of their time-worn moralism.

Nowhere did the supporters of the bullfight seem more modern than in their rebuttal of the hoary old argument that the corrida damaged the economy by encouraging working people to stay away from work. Against this moralistic position they offered an emerging realization that entertainment and leisure were economically valuable activities in their own right.

For Francisco Montes the claim that working-class attendance at the bullfight on weekdays hurt industry and reduced economic activity was "specious":

> Whatever the sums that the multitude spend on the bulls, and recognizing, of course, that it is the industrial class that benefits from it, since the money involved merely passed from the hands of one part of this class to another, it is clear that industry as a whole is not hurt at all. . . . We could insist much more in this argument by merely enumerating the branches of industry that the bullfights put in motion and stimulate.[81]

José Sánchez de Neira claimed that the bullfight provided work for "countless laborers and artisans," and Francisco Sicilia de Arenzana emphasized the economic benefits of the bullfight, which created jobs not only for the bullfighters but for contractors and hands on bull ranches and also promoted the economies of the towns where the events were held.[82] *El Toreo* was more explicit: It calculated that in 1893 tickets sales reached 14 million pesetas; in addition, people who traveled from villages and small towns would "buy things that appeal to them," benefiting small merchants to the tune of 70 million pesetas, while innkeepers and restaurant owners owed 46 million to the bullfight, and railway companies another 15 million. The bullfight also generated considerable tax revenues, more than all other public entertainments combined in 1889–1890.[83]

The corrida's defenders were much more inclined to let the working class simply enjoy itself, limitations and all. Francisco Montes argued that working people needed entertainment and that the bullfight was the best form going. It provided precisely the appropriate sort of diversion:

> exciting their senses and moving their spirit through eyes rather than the intellect. They love to see great and surprising events that require valor and ability, but they cannot be moved by sublime sentiments, correct style, or fluid verses. . . . The working public should be offered an entertainment that entertains without tiring the imagination, without hurting morality, and stimulating bravery and valor without basing triumph and glory in the death of another man but in that of a daring, brave and powerful beast.[84]

The bullfight was excellent entertainment, especially when compared to other entertainments available in Spain or in supposedly superior foreign countries. It was better than the circus, cards, and masked balls, which produced injuries and immorality, and it was much preferable to the cancan, "which degrades and debases nations."[85] Theater was the worst of all.

> We say with sadness that this spectacle, the first to attract the attention of the educated public, is full of immoralities: Here a daughter carried away by criminal ardor disobeys the voice of a tender father and secretly delivers herself to a seducer; there an inhuman, despotic father tyrannizes his daughter and offers her the choice of marrying a man she abhors or going into a convent. . . . Enormous crimes, scandalous injustices and cruelties, vengeance, blood, death and horror, this is what the theater offers us today.[86]

If the bullfight offered "instinct, crazy bravery, [and] temerity, the theater offered much worse: "self-abasement, prostration, neurosis, anemia."[87] It was also antipatriotic, or so said *La Lidia* in criticizing the "privileged classes" who monopolized the Teatro Real and "protected foreign music."[88]

When defenders of the bullfight looked abroad, they targeted boxing and horse racing. In 1836, Francisco Montes pointed to the French fondness for races in which horses were often seriously injured and jockeys killed. Antonio Peña y Goñi claimed that horse races were more dangerous than bullfights: Only eight matadors had been killed during the 127 years the old Madrid bullring had been used, but "at least half a dozen jockeys die annually."[89]

But it was boxing that most drew the barbs of Spanish commentators, all the more because it was so popular in England. "Even more ridiculous is the horror that the bullfight inspires in the gloomy Englishman . . . who watches two men assault each other rather than a contest between a man an a beast. Will we tolerate being called barbarous . . . by a people who permit two men to beat each other to death in front of a crowd but prohibits a doctor from studying the structure and organization of a cadaver?"[90] Responding to rumors that the government was going to abolish the corrida, *La Linterna Mágica* suggested that "seeing two men hit and kick each other until their eyes pop out and their mouths and noses bleed would be a diversion much worthier of an enlightened public."[91] José Picón recognized that "other European countries are a half century of progress" ahead of Spain, but he denied that this made the bullfight more barbarous than the entertainments those Europeans enjoyed. "Can there be anything more savage, or more incomprehensible," he asked, "than two men, two brothers . . . beating each other to a pulp, causing serious wounds that sometimes lead to death, justified only by the need to amuse the *respectable*, civilized, public, which attends this repugnant spectacle and attentively follows with refined cruelty all the details so as to know whether they win or lose the bets they have placed?"[92]

This argument was repeated during a parliamentary debate in May 1922. Responding to charges that the bullfight was barbarous and brought Spain into disrepute abroad, Sr. Senra took the position that bullfighting was less barbarous than

> boxing, which draws crowds, not of 13,000, as go to the bullring in Madrid, but of 200,000 in the great capitals of the United States and 200,000 to 300,000 in London and other great English cities. They do not watch a fight between a man and a beast, in which understanding must defeat irrational brute nature, but a fight between two men . . . two rational beings beating each other, and until one is robbed of his reason, man's most precious attribute, the ferocious fight is not over, and then the crowd, drunk with enthusiasm, roars. . . . More barbarous [than bullfighting] are horse races . . . where the accidents of the riders and the fortunes that are lost are overshadowed by the fact that in

the greatest capitals of the most civilized nations it is necessary to create a special man, to degenerate the human race, to fabricate the jockey. . . . And while this goes on in the world, we should not echo ignorant foreigners who would judge us by the bullfight.[93]

This line of argument could also be used in reverse by non-Spaniards disgusted by entertainments popular in their own countries. The growing popularity of college football in the United States during the 1890s provoked a campaign in the press against the sport's excessive violence. The New York *World* contributed a front-page article carrying the headline "'Cruel,' Says a Bull-Fighter" to its coverage of the 1897 edition of the annual Yale-Princeton game. Teodoro Lamadrid attended the game at the invitation of the paper's editor "to tell with justice whether I, a toreador, find it as cruel as bull-fighting." In fact, he found it crueler. The game was a true test of manhood: "If a man can play one season at such a game he must be a hero," but Lamadrid was unimpressed by the gang tackling and the illegal punches that were so common. "Did you see that? There is a Yale man jabbing with his heel at a Princeton man's foot. That is savage. . . . How can Americans call [this] a game? . . . Every time the players rise up from the ground some one is left there groaning. I tell you they are in great pain. Men do not writhe like that for nothing. . . . Never in all my years of bull-fighting have I seen such sights as this. I think the game is cruel because so many men run and throw themselves on one." He was also struck by the primitive nature of the arena, "open to the sky and no roof to protect the ladies from the wind or the rain or the snow" and by the absence of civility with which the game began: "Now the young men are running around the field, rolling a ball and falling down on it. I am informed that these undignified acts are . . . only the preliminary. In my country . . . every fighter first marches around and salutes the crowd."[94]

Bullfighting in Parliament

Critics also took their complaints to the Cortes (parliament), albeit to no effect. In February 1864 a deputy from Valencia presented a petition signed by 150 citizens "of all classes and opinions" that requested the legislature to "copy the Cortes of Valladolid in 1535," which had proposed "the complete abolition of the barbarous, repugnant and anti-Christian fiesta." The petition was sent to the minister of the interior, and nothing more was heard of it.[95] The next debate came in June 1877, when the marquis of San Carlos presented a proposal from the Cádiz Society for the Protection of Plants and Animals that would "lead without violence to or ignoring of any right and with the pasage of time" to the disappearance of bullfighting. The bill, signed by four other deputies, declared that the corrida "exercises a pernicious influence on our customs and constitutes a spectacle unworthy of a cultured people" and called for a ban on the construction of new bullrings or the repair of existing ones as well as for the government to "adopt measures that it considers convenient for the suppression of the bullfight within a prudent period of time." San Carlos denied that it sought to suppress the bullfight, since the 101 bullrings that existed in 1875 were "sufficient for the devotees to render homage to the cult which pleases their chosen deity."[96]

In 1894 seven deputies presented another bill to ban the bullfight. This time the argument was much more fully developed. The corrida was "barbarous, inhuman, and impious [and] excited the people to the grossest instincts of barbarism and cruelty." This was standard rhetoric, but then the defense took a new turn: It was the duty of a "modern state . . . to intervene to reduce the risk" to its citizens, and this was true above all for a "profession that consists of risking one's life, a spectacle whose attractiveness lies precisely in this danger." The bullfight also involved "unnecessary violence against animals, which is punished by law in many countries." Finally, the fact that agents of the state presided at bullfights and thus became "the targets of the gravest and most disgusting insults, delivered under the protection of an immunity sanctioned by custom" was another argument for the ban. The proponent of the bill asked the minister of the interior to provide him with detailed statistics on the number of deaths and woundings that had taken place since 1875, and another deputy urged that the *Boletín Oficial* publish monthly statements of such tragedies as well as of the "riots, fights, fines, disrespect for the authorities, etc."[97]

Less formal village bullfights known as *capeas* became an issue in the first decade of the twentieth century as they came under attack not only from opponents of the bullfight but also from some of its supporters. In November 1907, the bullfight magazine *La Coleta* launched a blistering attack on these village corridas: They were "a parody [and] the real reason that people say that the national fiesta is barbaric, savage, and other similar insults." Real bullfights involved trained professionals and specially bred animals, and produced few accidents, "fewer than those that occur in other sports that are exalted by progress and civilization, such as boxing and automobile racing." Capeas, on the contrary, produced many victims and benefited no one, "undertakers excepted."[98]

Such parliamentary protests had precedents locally. Thus, in March 1889 *El Avanzado* criticized the "boys' bullfight," which was one of four corridas that formed part of the Carnival celebrations in Vitigudino (Salamanca). For the paper, "entertainments of this sort, are less entertainments than something else, which we choose not to dignify with a name."[99]

This attack on the capea was especially ironic because it was a much older form of bull event than the professional bullfight. Still, these complaints found a receptive ear in the minister of the interior, Juan de la Cierva. Ever eager to use the power of the state to improve public morality, on February 6, 1908, he issued a Royal Order "absolutely prohibiting that bulls or cows be permitted to run through village streets or squares." Civil governors were charged to allow bullfights in temporary rings only after an inspection that showed them to meet the standards required of permanent rings, and mayors were required "not to permit that anyone other than those previously approved as participants take part in the fight." *La Coleta* cheered this order, calling it "one of the [the minister's] most just and reasonable actions," but worried that it would not be enforced.[100]

In a replay of the local resistance to the 1785 edict, the ban produced conflict almost immediately. In August 1908, the civil governor of Cáceres refused to allow a capea in the village of Alia. When the villagers ignored the ruling and held the bullfight anyway, he called in the Civil Guard. This led to a riot: "The Civil Guard fired a number of rounds, leaving many wounded and three or four dead."[101] The republican paper *El País* reacted the following day with an unusual show of honesty. Rather than attack the minister for the slaughter, the paper accepted its share of responsibility:

> Mr. de la Cierva has only done what we have asked. Even yesterday, when we reported the events in Alia on the front page, on page three we asked that the royal order on capeas be enforced after a young man was injured in Vicálvaro. Well, it has been enforced and the enforcement horrifies us. . . . Who has not written against the capeas? . . . Finally we got the prohibition and with it riots, wounded, and dead, a much worse barbarism than the one that we, with an imbecilic sensitivity, tried to avoid.

The paper also recognized the truly popular nature of the capea, which gave it a new legitimacy: "The capea is the last honorable, legitimate, noble, and popular manifestation of the so-called national pastime. . . . In it the people fight and so maintain the valor of the race. In the squares of their villages the hicks do what the nobility used to do in the squares of the cities. The capea is purely Spanish. . . . [I]t is a classic . . . Olympian diversion." In contrast, the bullfight, with its professionals, "dressed up like ballet dancers" and fighting for money and not for pleasure, was a "parody, a degenerate detour" from the old noble spectacle, a "decadent spectacle from the Roman circus." The capea "strengthens and ennobles," while the bullfight "weakens and degrades," and there was no logic in banning the former while allowing the latter to continue.[102]

Not everyone agreed. *Los Toros* supported the ban in 1909, and by 1912 *La Coleta* was lamenting that de la Cierva's order against "the barbaric spectacle of the capea" had become a "dead letter: there is a capea in any village whose residents want one."[103] This matter was raised in parliament from time to time. In November 1910 a Sr. Azzati asked that the government "take firm measures to prohibit *corridas de vaquillas* in the villages." He spoke of one that had been held recently in the village of Carlet, in Valencia, even though many local people had petitioned the civil governor to stop it. That event "produced a disturbance of public order . . . and two, three, or four injuries." The "majority" of the people of Valencia were opposed to such "barbarous spectacles," and in their name he requested that they be stopped. The minister of the interior replied that his predecessor had prohibited these bullfights, that the order was still in effect, and that he had been enforcing it. He personally believed that they "should be totally prohibited," and he undertook to remind the civil governors to enforce the ban.[104] This matter was raised again in June 1914: Pablo Iglesias, the leader of the Socialist Party, reported that a capea had been held in a village in Jaén province and asked that the law be enforced. The minister repeated his support for the prohibition, but pointed out that it was often difficult to enforce because "it is the locals who . . . are upset when this tradition is not respected."[105]

Sunday Rest: 1904–1905

All the questions raised by government regulation—and toleration—of the bullfight coalesced in the fall of 1904 around the Social Reform Institute's recommendation that the Sunday Rest Law (Ley de Descanso Dominical) be applied to bullfighters. The law was designed to guarantee workers a day off, but the institute, an advisory body to the minister of the interior that included a number of appointees from the labor movement, appeared to be making a covert attack on the existence of the bullfight. Certainly, prohibiting the corrida on the day on which people were freest to attend did threaten its viability and provoked a protest from the various groups whose interests were affected. But the protests attracted people beyond those directly involved and soon became a political issue seen in distinctly political terms.

About a month after its initial decision, the institute met again to discuss a number of requests for exemptions from the Sunday Rest Law. These included milk stalls, pastry shops, ice dealers, public laundries, and refreshment stands as well as bullfights. After a long and heated discussion, the institute voted 13 to 8 against exempting the corrida, with all six working-class delegates opposing the exemption.[106]

Even before this second meeting, Luís Mazzantini denounced the institute's action in an article in *El Heraldo de Madrid*. The ban was a "knife in the back of a beautiful and virile spectacle on which many families depend and around which many [economic] interests exist." Bullfighters, like actors, were artists, not workers, and should be exempted from the ban. More important, the Social Reform Institute had—or should have had—more important things to worry about. Borrowing the rhetoric of Europeanization usually brandished against the bullfight, Mazzantini declared that "to become Europeans, to acquire the culture we need, to become a powerful and feared nation we require other laws and other measures," and he suggested an imposing list that included better schools, reform of the prison system, a more effective system of taxation, higher wages for agricultural laborers, and less spending on the Church, since "too much thinking about things above has led us to abandon the here and now." Finally, the law was discriminatory; if the goal was Sunday rest, then why not "totally suspend material life"?[107]

Much of the Madrid press saw the decision of the Social Reform Institute as a covert attempt to eliminate the bullfight entirely and argued that if this were the goal, it should be done openly. "Sundays or not at all" declared *El Imparcial* in an article that questioned a prohibition that applied to the bullfight but not to other, more harmful entertainments such as theater and dance. If "the Social Reform Institute feels that bullfights are contrary to the progress of the Spanish race, then it should have the courage to suppress them," but if they cause no harm, then there was no reason not to allow them on Sundays. Moreover, the Sunday ban would hurt business, which was why bullfights were on Sunday in the first place. "Everyone remembers that when the custom in Madrid was to hold bullfights on Mondays, commerce, industry, and the guilds of the city requested that the government move them to Sundays because . . . workers did not show up for work and the number of people in the street declined."[108]

Breeders in Andalusia decided to send a delegation to Madrid and to work with breeders from the rest of the country to defend the bullfight. Then the deputation of Madrid, which administered the city's bullring on behalf of the provincial charity hospital, announced the cancellation of the annual Charity Bullfight because "it will be impossible to produce enough profit on a weekday to cover the hospital's needs." The situation was similar in Valencia, where the bullring was a major source of revenue for the provincial hospital; the deputation sent a delegation to Madrid to protest. On top of this, Pedro Nembo, the promoter who had leased the bullring, was demanding that the contract be voided and his money refunded. The result, according to the president of the deputation, was that the hospital stood to lose 290,000 pesetas, which would mean closing 360 beds.[109]

Nembo did make a formal protest to the minister of the interior and the provincial deputation. Applying the Sunday Rest Law to the corrida was discriminatory, since it prohibited bullfights but not the theater, which operated throughout the week. It also constituted a clear violation of his contract: "It is impossible to permit that a government regulation terminate a contract because this would set a precedent that would make it impossible to securely enter into contracts with the State or its agencies." The ban on bullfights was going to cost him a lot of money, and he demanded that if it remained in force, his contract be revised accordingly or that he be indemnified for "the enormous damages . . . arising from his already having formalized contracts and prepared the season."[110]

By this time a more grassroots protest was already getting underway. The first sign was a letter from a number of fans calling on Pedro Nembo to "organize a solemn act, a mass meeting . . . where the fans of the capital can gather to arrive at an energetic and just decision in the face of this absurd and ridiculous measure." Significantly, the fans blamed the ban on one specific group, the six Socialist members of the institute, conveniently ignoring the seven others who also voted for it.[111] Letters of support arrived, from the retired star Guerrita, from the fans of Córdoba, from the breeders and from politicians. So did petitions from provincial cities such as Bilbao, Valencia, Burgos, Yecla, León, Málaga, Gijón, and Torrenueva.[112]

While the meeting was being organized by a committee that included journalists, fans, bullfighters, and Liberal politicians, a number of bullfighters, organized as the United Bullfighters of Spain, carried out protests of their own. They circulated a petition, addressed to the minister of the interior, signed by people from "among all social classes [and] the Social Reform Institute should take note of the fact that almost all the workers of a majority of the city's workshops have signed."[113] The petition claimed that the Sunday Rest Law represented a covert prohibition on all bullfights and did not take into account the unusual nature of the bullfighters' work: "Because we dedicate ourselves to the recreation of others, our profession demands that other people be at rest . . . otherwise a happy and enjoyable pastime would become a censurable stimulus for hardworking people to become lazy." Bullfights were prohibited, but theater was not; indeed, there were usually two shows on Sunday, even though actors worked the rest of the week, too. The bullfight was more healthful than the theater: "As an eminent doctor wrote in the press not long ago, entertainments offered in the open air and in the sun's light are better for the public health than crowding togther in closed places." Finally, the law seriously hurt the economic interests of the breeders and the bullfighters. But not all bullfighters would suffer equally, and the petition reflected what others had already referred to as bullfighting's "social question":

> The upper classes of the art, the great figures who merit or luck has elevated to the top of the profession, will continue to earn large amounts, fighting in the great festivals, which are exempted from the law . . . as well as in the rings of Portugal, France . . . But the obscure and the unknown . . . will be shut out of the rings where up to now they have earned their daily bread. . . . If the bullrings of Madrid, Barcelona, Valencia, Sevilla, Bilbao, Zaragoza, Valladolid, Córdoba, Cádiz, and Málaga are prevented from holding the Sunday bullfights . . . they will see themselves condemned to poverty and to a change of profession at a stage of life at which age and acquired habits make it impossible for them to learn a new trade.

The petition concluded with a reminder of the bullfighters' great patriotism: Whenever there was "a great national calamity" they "never hesitated to risk their lives by participating without pay in fund-raising activities."[114]

On the day of the rally, a huge crowd gathered early, waiting for the doors to open. According to press reports, as many as ten thousand packed themselves into the theater, while an equal number were left outside. In the orchestra pit were the bullfighters, both active and retired, along with their agents;

in the boxes, "old-time fans"; on the stage, the committee, with journalist Pascual Millán in the chair. The front rows of the boxes were reserved for the ladies, and one woman's entry was highlighted in all the press accounts:

> A beautiful young woman . . . accompanied by her father entered modestly, giving an eminently Spanish note [and] caused a rush of enthusiasm. The entire audience rose to its feet and applauded the beautiful girl who . . . wearing the classic mantilla appeared among thousands and thousands of men who had only one aspiration related to their favorite entertainment and saw in this woman the most perfect embodiment of their ideal.[115]

The start of the meeting was delayed a few minutes to accommodate "a number of famous matadors who were coming on the express train from Seville and Córdoba." Then came the reading of a letter from Canalejas, and speeches by Pascual Millán, by Manuel Aleas, speaking for the breeders, by the former president of the provincial Deputation, by the editor of the *Diario Universal*, and by Tortero, the leader of the United Bullfighters, who also presented a petition with more than one hundred thousand signatures. The meeting ended in "perfect order," the "great precautions" taken by the authorities unneccessary. The next day Millán and Tortero called on the minister of the interior, who expressed his sympathy for their cause but explained that he could promise them nothing.[116] Other meetings took place in Bilbao, Valencia, and Córdoba.[117]

The next day the question was debated in the Cortes. After expressing his personal dislike for the bullfight, "Spain's ignominy and disgrace," Deputy Soriano asked the minister of the interior if he would permit such an attack on the rights of bullfight promoters and referred to a telegram he had received "in the name of twelve thousand people who attended a meeting in Valencia yesterday to protest the application of the Sunday rest regulations." The minister replied a few days later: The government would decide only after receiving advice from the Council of State.[118] The council was a consultative body composed of former cabinet ministers and other such "senior statesmen." It waited until March 1905 before deciding, with only the former Conservative leader Francisco Silvela dissenting, to permit Sunday bullfights.

The leading figure in the campaign against the Sunday ban was Pascual Millán, a bullfight critic and author of numerous books on the corrida. Millán made his case in his weekly column in *Sol y Sombra*, and he did so in language that was nothing if not forceful. The issue was clearly a political one: "The line has been drawn; on one side the *neos* [clericals], disguised or without disguise, with their . . . narrowness of vision and their idiocy; on the other the democrats, with their generous ideals, their law of progress, and their cult of the aesthetic."[119] The Socialists, with whom Millán identified the Sunday ban, were little more than tools of the clergy. "For every protest by the ignorant clerical workers we have presented the signatures of hundreds of true sons of labor, intelligent, educated, patriotic, lovers of knowledge and avid for regeneration and progress." The real danger, however, was the Jesuits: "Oh Jesuits! I know you all too well: strong against the weak, pusillanimous, humble and fearful against anyone who strikes back readily." The Conservative government that was so reluctant to do the right thing was a "reactionary government that wants to turn every dwelling into a cell and every Spaniard into a monk."[120]

Millán's anticlerical rhetoric carried special resonance at that moment. Long an important issue in Spanish politics, anticlericalism had moved into the headlines just a couple of years before. In 1902, Benito Pérez Galdós's play *Electra*, about a young woman who was forced to become a nun, caused riots outside the theater where it was being performed and became a rallying point for people concerned about what they saw as increasing clerical influence in the country. The more progressive Liberals around Canalejas increasingly brandished anticlericalism as an issue.[121]

The Socialist Party (PSOE) and the labor movement were the firmest and most consistent advocates of the ban on Sunday bullfights. The party newspaper, *El Socialista*, quickly voiced its support for the measure and reported that 232 union locals had also done so. It also questioned the validity of the petition in favor of Sunday bullfights allegedly "signed by all the workshops of Madrid" on the grounds that "we know that the signatures from some workshops were obtained through pressure on the workers by their employers and that some who refused to sign were fired."[122] The paper also criticized the liberal and democratic politicians, among them former prime minister the count of Romanones and future prime minister José Canalejas, who supported the probullfight movement and suggested that they might adopt as their slogan "A free horn in a free state."[123] (This was a parody of the famous declaration by Camilo Cavour, the first prime minister of united Italy, that the goal of his religious policy was to create a "free Church in a free state.") And when the Ateneo of Barcelona announced the creation of the Abolitionist Committee to pressure the government to retain the Sunday ban, *El Socialista* urged "all Party groups and all unions to show their support for the [Sunday Rest] Law by writing to the President of the Committee."[124]

When the Council of State recommended that bullfights and taverns be exempted from the law, *El Socialista* denounced the decision in terms that made clear that its goal was the total abolition of the bullfight in the name of the progress of the nation:

> These cultured and capable men who continually talk about the urgent need to make an effort to pull our people out of the ignorance in which they find themselves and make them give up their bad habits have not shown the slightest concern about coming down against a legal measure designed to restrict a barbarous spectacle that morally and materially harms the development of wealth and, above all, contributes to the depravity of much of the working class.
>
> This decision has been applauded by journalists who thunder against the coarseness, ignorance, and bad customs of the proletariat; artists who complain that in Spain there are too few supporters of the arts; and even university types who go on about the fact that "this country is lost."
>
> And who supports the maintenance of that law, who protests against the decision of the Council of State? The uncultured, the ignorant, the coarse, those who rarely talk about regeneration, nor illiteracy nor that Africa begins at the Pyrenees. That law is due first of all to the workers' delegates at the Social Reform Institute, the representatives of the unionized masons, carpenters, locksmiths, miners, bakers, printers, agricultural workers, and laborers. And the more than four hundred telegrams that the Minister of the Interior has received protesting against the report of the Council of State, are also from them and the unions they have created.
>
> In this matter, then, who are cultured and who the uncultured? Who desires instruction and education and who the maintenance of backwardness and barbarism? There can be no doubt: The cultured and the progressive people who want to raise the intellectual level of the people are the organized workers.[125]

Spanish governments had long been concerned with the bullfight, but by the early twentieth century the bullfight had clearly become a political issue in a new way. Not only did government attempt to regulate the corrida; the debates that those efforts provoked, and especially those surrounding Sunday rest, mobilized people along existing political lines and were expressed in explicitly political—and party political—terms. Yet this did not exhaust the corrida's political charge; the bullfight had many other political uses and meanings.

6 *six* The bullfight was a commercialized leisure spectacle, but on certain selected occasions it was deliberately made into a political event. These political bullfights were invested with carefully constructed messages about the glory of the monarch, about imperial rule, about political power, about social prestige and display, and about the nation. In these ways, the corrida became a form of politics in the afternoon.

It had long been so. The first such bullfight took place in the twelfth century, on the occasion of a royal wedding, and these funciones reales have been held on important royal occasions in every century since.[1] Until the sixteenth century such events were rare, but then, in the age of Charles V and Philip II and at the height of Spain's power in Europe, they became a standard part of every type of royal celebration. The most typical occasion was a wedding or the accession of a new monarch, but they also came to be held to celebrate royal births and baptisms, visits by royals from other countries, military triumphs, and peace treaties.

These special bullfights were most numerous in the seventeenth century, when there were ninety-eight. The War of the Spanish Succession brought the French House of Bourbon to the Spanish throne, but the members of the new dynasty turned out to be almost as fond of these spectacles as their Hapsburg predecessors had been, presiding over eighty in the eighteenth century and seventy-three in the nineteenth. Even if the monarch did not like bullfighting, the event was too popular to do away with. Charles III prohibited bullfighting in 1785, but a royal bullfight was held for the accession of his son, Charles IV, when the government decided that it was "convenient to follow previous examples in which the public displayed its pleasure."[2] Madrid had the most elaborate bullfight, but the public's pleasure was clearly not limited to the capital. At least thirty-two other cities and towns celebrated Charles's accession that year, and thirteen of these included a corrida. In the absence of the king himself, his portrait frequently presided over the spectacle.

The last royal bullfight was held in 1906, to celebrate the wedding of King Alfonso XIII to Victoria Eugenia of Battenburg, a granddaughter of Queen Victoria. Some anarchists attempted to assassinate the king by throwing a bomb at his coach as he and his new wife drove through the streets of the capital after the marriage ceremony. The royal couple were not harmed, and the bullfight was held as scheduled.

The great political upheaval that swept across Europe following the French Revolution affected Spain as well. The power of the monarchy, which had gone unchallenged for centuries, was called into question by the new political doctrine of liberalism as well as by the invasion of the country by the French in 1808 and Napoleon's decision to put his brother Joseph on the Spanish throne. These events initiated a period of political upheaval that lasted almost forty years and saw the country racked by military coups, civil wars, foreign intervention, and the proclamation and abolition of constitutions. When it all ended, in 1845, Spain was still a monarchy, but it also had a constitution and an elected parliament.

In this whirlwind of change bullfights were used to celebrate a much wider range of political events. They were still held on royal occasions, such as the marriage of Queen Isabella II in 1846, the birth of her son, the future Alfonso XII, in 1857, or the visit of King Luis of Portugal in 1883, but political bullfights had ceased to be a royal monopoly. The proclamation of constitutions, the abolition of constitutions, the end of civil wars, the suppression of revolutions, and even successful military coups were all moments for rejoicing, and bullfights were often part of the fun.

Monarchy and Social Hierarchy

Royal bullfights were a display of the majesty of the monarch and a carefully crafted portrait of the entire social and political order as seen from above, a "model or map of proper power," to use Greg Dening's phrase, a "representational ritual" to use Jürgen Habermas's.[3] Both the spectacle of the bullfight itself and the seating of the spectators were direct statements about political power and social hierarchy. Seen by vast crowds—as many as fifty thousand people could fit into Madrid's Plaza Mayor—they were visually stunning occasions; Jacinto Benavente, the 1922 Nobel laureate for literature, called them a "splendid gift for the [people's] eyes." Even foreigners who found the bullfight itself barbaric praised the visual magnificence of the occasion. For Edward Clarke, "this spectacle is certainly one of the finest in the world, whether it is considered merely as a coup d'oeil or as an exertion of the bravery and infinite agility of the performers."[4]

The *funciones reales* developed at a time when bullfighting was an aristocratic activity, done on horseback and with a lance. In the eighteenth century, when bullfighting was taken over by plebeian professionals who fought on foot and with cape and sword, the royal bullfight deliberately retained the older, increasingly archaic form. This meant that the stars of the show were the *caballeros en plaza* (knights in the ring). Each caballero, and there were usually four on each day, was sponsored by a member of the high aristocracy, who was called his *padrino*, or godfather. The sponsor supplied the caballero his elegant outfit, provided the horses, accompanied him into the ring in his state coach, and presented him to the monarch. The background was provided by hordes of sponsors' liveried servants. Professional, plebeian bullfighters were present but in a secondary, supporting role. Their official title was *padrinos de campo* (sponsors in the field), but they were frequently referred to as *chulos*—a word more usually applied to the matador's own assistants—or *lacayos* (lackeys). Only rarely was their true role, to protect the caballeros, acknowledged.

The spectacle began with a procession that described an unmistakable hierarchy: monarch, aristocracy, gentry, plebeians, servants. Thus the procession on September 24, 1789:

> Four sumptuous French carriages entered from the Calle de Toledo in which rode the four knights with their respective noble patrons. Each was drawn by six horses and was equipped with lackeys and porters; at the doors stood the assistants to the aristocratic [sic] bullfighters. . . . [Afterward] came the parade in which the knights appeared once more, this time on horseback, each one of the four preceded by a hundred lackeys marching in two rows and headed by a single lackey carrying a staff. At each side of the latter walked one of the chulos and behind him rode six liveried royal grooms mounted on steeds from the royal stables. The first knight's attendants were dressed in the Roman style . . . those of the second knight were attired in the old Spanish style . . . those of the third in green and silver hussar uniforms, and those of the fourth in silver and straw-colored Moorish costumes.[5]

These processions had a certain megahistorical timelessness about them. By October 1846 the face of Spain had changed radically, but to judge from the opening of the bullfights held to celebrate the marriage of Queen Isabel II, none of this had happened. The correspondent of the *Times* of London described a scene with scant differences from the event that had been staged almost sixty years before:

> Then entered four very handsome carriages, each drawn by six horses, covered over with the richest and most massive . . . caparisons. From their lofty crests nodded high plumes of different colours, designating the noble houses to which they belonged. They were the state carriages of four Grandees; namely the Count of Altamira, the Duke of Abrantes, the Duke of Medina Celi and the Duke of Osuna. The horses were of the pure Andalusian breed, and were certainly beautiful creatures. . . .
>
> After the carriages came, led by grooms dressed in the richest livery, twenty-eight horses, at the rate of seven for each carriage. The harness of the horses was of the most gorgeous description. A complete band of *toreros*, bullfighters, engaged to protect the *caballeros en plaza*, accompanied each carriage on foot. All this train made the circuit of the square . . . until they came in front of the Royal balcony, when each *caballero* and his *padrino* descended and made a profound obeisance to Her Majesty. They again entered the carriages, and having once more made the circuit of the place, they disappeared in a different direction from that they entered.[6]

This continuity and disregard for history helped "reproduce in the imagination the memory of the old tournaments and of the Court in the best times of Spain's past," as the Madrid weekly the *Semanario Pintoresco Español,* put it.[7]

The first bulls, usually four, were for the horsemen to "break their lances," as the Spaniards said. Occasionally the lancers would kill the bull, but more frequently this was left to their assistants. Edward Clarke, an Englishman, attended the royal bullfight for the accession of Charles III in 1760 and described it in his *Letters Concerning the Spanish Nation*:

> The King then making the signal for the doors to be opened, the bull appeared, to the sound of martial music, and the loud acclamations of the people: and seeing one of the attendants of the first cavalier spreading his cloak before him, aimed directly at him, and gave his master an opportunity of

breaking his spear in the bull's neck. In the same manner the bull was tempted to engage the other cavaliers, and always with the same success: till having received the honourable wounds from their lances, he was encountered by the other men on foot: who, after playing with him, with an incredible agility, as long as they think proper, easily put an end to him. . . . After this the bull is hurried off by mules, finely adorned and decked with trappings for the occasion.[8]

The role of caballero en plaza demanded superb horsemanship, but even so, it could be dangerous. Clarke saw "two beautiful horses . . . gored; one of which was overthrown with his rider, but fortunately the man escaped any mischief from his fall." While he admired the riders, he marveled at their horses: "The courage of these horses is so great, that they have been often known to advance towards the bull, when their bowels were trailing upon the ground."[9] When the gentlemen had finished with their bulls, the matadors took center stage for the rest of the afternoon.

The seating of the spectators reinforced the message of power and status, and the seating plan was put together with great care and seriousness. In the seventeenth century the arrangements were handled by a high-level committee that included the president of the Council of Castile (the equivalent of the prime minister), the mayor of Madrid, and the king's chief majordomo. By the late eighteenth century, the majordomo was in charge. Rights to the seats, and especially to the balconies, were jealously guarded by those individuals and corporations who had held them in the past; they were equally coveted by those who had not. Once a royal bullfight was announced, the majordomo was inundated by requests and reminders of places previously occupied—often "from time immemorial." Such reminders were not really necessary, since the majordomo usually had a report on the seating plan from the previous royal bullfight to guide him.

Changes from past practice—"novelties" in the language of the eighteenth century—inevitably caused problems. In October 1746, when King Ferdinand VI made his entry into Madrid, the mayor thought that he could dispose of some places that were usually assigned to the royal councils. The bodies affected, the Inquisition and the Council of War, complained, with the result that the king ordered "that there be no innovations in any of the practices from similar occasions in the past." There was also a problem in finding balconies for all the grandees, the highest category of the nobility, as these had increased in number in the eighteenth century. The solution was to assign them a number of balconies previously reserved for the clergy of the royal household and the wives of the members of the Royal council, but this caused "much scandal, as people were denied a balcony without any reason whatsoever."[10]

The correspondence provoked by the royal bullfights, and the ways in which people justified their claims to seats, offer a rare view of how people conceived their society, or at least how they thought that those in power did. June 1833, when Princess Isabella took the oath as heir to the throne and, as it turned out, at the very end of the life of the absolute monarchy, is a particularly interesting moment to explore in detail.

Just as his predecessors as chief majordomo had, the marquis of San Martín received a large number of requests for balconies and other places from many different kinds of people: members of the royal household, the aristocracy, the military, the Church, and, above all, the state administration. On the eve of revolutionary political and social change, virtually all the supplicants made their requests through appeals to past privilege or to a position of personal service to the monarch.

The servants of the royal household were well taken care of: The chamberlain made sure that the majordomo provided them with "the appropriate seats." Others sought to claim the status of royal servant. One Andrés Toribio wrote on behalf of his acting troupe that "the actors consider themselves servants of Your Majesty and hope you would have them present to enjoy the royal bullfights," but the request was annotated that they were not "in the rank of servants of the Royal Household."[11] The employees of the Royal School of Veterinarians tried a similar ploy; they got the duke of Monzón to write on their behalf:

> These people belong to a loyal establishment that has always been worthy of the special protection of the King, Our Lord; they also daily serve the interests of the Royal Patrimony, the professors attend without charge the Royal Menagerie and cure all the animals that are sent by express order of Their Majesties to that establishment, and this really puts the employees [of the School] in the honorable class of servants of our August Sovereigns.[12]

Some aristocrats—the duke of Infantado was one—had the right to a balcony in their own name, but most were present because they held some office or some position in the royal household, such as gentleman-in-waiting.

Those who were in neither category risked being left out unless they could persuade the majordomo to find them room. The countess of Cartagena, for example, wrote that she expected to be treated as "the other ladies of my class," only to be told that "your class as the wife of the Count of Cartagena does not entitle you to a personal seat." (Her letter is also interesting for the gendered terms in which it was written: She apologized for writing to the majordomo without knowing him but excused herself "because of the absence of my husband, the Count of Cartagena, from the Court.")[13]

The duke of Alba claimed a balcony on the basis of his holding the office of chancellor of the Royal Seal of Navarre as well as on his titles. In forwarding this case to the palace, the mayor of Madrid commented that "even with his titles and *grandezas* and being Chancellor of the Royal Seal of Navarre, there is no privilege in his favor," and the majordomo turned him down because of "the necessity of attending to those people who because of the quality and rank of their employments should enjoy [a balcony]."[14]

The largest number of requests came from the state administration. The majordomo wrote to the ministers asking for a "detailed note of all the corporations belonging to the Ministry in your charge so that they may, according to their rank, enjoy balconies."[15] Once the list of ticket holders had been published in the *Diario de Avisos*, the majordomo heard from those who had been left out. Some, such as the Royal China Factory, the Royal Porcelain Factory, the Office of Roads and Posts, and the Commerce and Coinage Committee (Junta de Comercio y Moneda), based their claims on having had seats at the previous royal bullfight, in 1803. Others argued that they were the equal of departments that had been granted tickets. The Royal Superior Pharmacy Council asked to be treated "in the same way as other, analogous corporations in its class." José Rossi, of the Post Office (Administración del Correo General), was more specific. His department, he argued, was the equal of the Gefes de la Renta. Moreover, "if one takes into consideration the delicate and painful work we do and the continual privations we suffer, we must be deemed worthy of sharing in this just leisure, especially when most of the offices of this Court will be going."[16]

Then there were those departments that had not existed when the last royal bullfight was held. Some claimed to be now extinguished bodies under new names and therefore the rightful heirs to their predecessors' privileges, balconies for bullfights included. Marcelo de Ondarza, the president of the Tribunal Mayor de Cuentas, wrote that this office was the successor to the

Tribunal de Contaduría Mayor and that "the President and his ministers preserve the same prerogatives and faculties of the extinguished [office]."[17] In a similar vein the Contaduría General de Valores del Reino claimed the place of the former Oficina de Valores, the Intendencia de la Provincia de Madrid that of the Juzgado de la Regalía del Real Aposento de Corte, and the Ordenación del Ejército de Castilla la Nueva that of an unnamed predecessor.

Other offices were brand-new, especially in the recently created Ministry of Development (Fomento). The minister, the count of Ofalia, replied to the majordomo's letter with a list of the offices created after 1803, "leaving it to Your Excellency's judgment and discretion to determine those that, in accordance with practice, are equal in rank and hierarchy to the offices of other Ministries and should therefore enjoy balconies in the Plaza Mayor." Later he successfully argued the case of the General Inspectorate of Public Education, "a newly created magistracy" that should not be deprived "just for being new."[18]

In this flood of appeals to precedence and past privilege only one stands out for offering an argument of a distinctly more modern cast, which looked to the future instead of the past. Pedro Jiménez de Haro, the editor of the *Comercio Literario Mercantil*, emphasized the importance of publicity for the funciones reales: "It seems natural that the *Correo* inform its subscribers in the provinces of the details of this event, so that the curiosity that all Spaniards have about it can be satisfied. . . . Please provide a ticket so that one of the editors can be present and write a description that will be published in the paper immediately."[19]

What did the final result look like? The royal box was on the north side of the Plaza Mayor, in the middle of the first level of balconies. Closest to it sat the ministers of the Royal Council, the Knights of the Golden Fleece, the cardinal archbishop of Toledo, the cardinal archbishop of Seville, the patriarch of the Indies, the chief majordomo, the captain of the Royal Bodyguard, the ministers of various royal councils—the Council of the Indies, the Council of Orders, the Council of Finance, the Council of War—the Madrid city councillers, the ambassadors, the gentlemen-in-waiting, and the papal nuncio. In the midst of such grandeur were three balconies that were not at the disposition of the palace and were occupied by their owners, the duke of Infantado, the count of Barajas, and Francisco Antonio Bringas, merchant, financier, property owner, and one of the richest men in Madrid. Then, farther away, came other officials of the royal household, the secretaries of numerous government departments, and military commanders.

In the balconies on the second floor sat the wives of the ministers, lesser palace officials such as the royal confessors, the royal chaplains, and the king's preacher, the palace archivist, the secretary of the royal stables, and the music master, the musicians and children's choir of the Royal Chapel, and lesser officials in government departments. Higher up, balconies were occupied by people of even lower status. Clustered together on the third floor were the General Superintendancy of Police, the Post Office, the Spanish Academy, the Royal Library, the High Committee of Medicine and Surgery, the High Commitee of Pharmacy, and the Royal Academy of History. Another group of balconies housed the officers of the royal bodyguard from the various arms of the military and the officers of the Royalist Volunteers. Finally, in the few balconies on the fourth floor there were the administrators of the royal parks in Madrid, the royal watchmaker, the royal painters and sculptors, the royal doctors, the royal dentist, the royal chiropodist, and the royal janitors.

Seating still told a story in the middle of the nineteenth century. Antonio Rubio drew attention to this in his description of the celebrations for the marriage of Queen Isabella II in 1846: "The most notable thing about the [bullfight] was the presence of all the bodies of the State: councils, courts, ministries, directorates, and their location in hierarchical order. It was . . . the very embodiment of the *Guía [de Forasteros]*[20] because all the classes found there were arranged according to the order of their importance."[21] This order was described in verse by Manuel Azcutia:

> With the pretty Queen in her place,
> Beautiful and of rare quality,
> Such a splendorous star,
> Which shows itself dazzling in the sky,
> When the fierce storm has declined,
> And beside her, her husband,
> Luisa Fernanda, Montpensier, Cristina,
> Aumale, and D. Francisco with his children,
> Who show off their grace and beauty;
> With the Court and the Grandees
> Placed in all the balconies

> Of the first level, and the Senate,
> The Ministers, the high councillors,
> Covered with medals, sashes and braids,
> And a thousand other distinctions;
> With the courts in place,
> And the corporations,
> And the people, finally the drums sounded.[22]

The seating plan was flexible and could accommodate changes to the political and social order. After describing the crowd in 1846 as the "embodiment of the *Guía*," Rubio continued: "The royal bullfights of 1846 have had to take into account three new, and what is more, omnipotent, classes: parliament, the capitalists, and the press. . . . It is a reflection of the epoch; society has broken ranks and it is not likely that the old formations will return."[23]

The balconies housed only a small part of the audience of up to fifty thousand people who squeezed into the Plaza Mayor. The bulk of them always sat in wooden bleachers that were set up specially for the occasion. Each householder in the square had the right to build these bleachers in front of his or her property and to sell tickets to the public at prices set by the palace, but most preferred to sell the right to the bleachers to entrepreneurs. Either way, a royal bullfight was a lucrative occasion. A document produced sometime after the 1789 bullfights estimated that the bleachers were worth between 2,500 and 4,000 reales for each householder.

Gathering such immense crowds together was a potentially dangerous matter, and the authorities were always concerned about the possibility of disorder, especially in the presence of the monarch. A few days before the event a royal edict dictating proper behavior for the occasion was published. "The King, Our Lord, and in his Royal Name the Mayor of the City, order," it began. The public was enjoined not to enter the ring or "take out a sword or any other weapon or wound the bulls with clubs or anything else"; not to smoke or use flints or anything similar; not to "whistle, shout, utter any indecent words, or make any rude gestures"; not to throw any objects, including "dogs, cats, the rinds of watermelons or oranges, or anything else."[24] These injunctions were accompanied by a formidable display of troops around the Plaza Mayor.

Such concerns were, it seems, exaggerated. There were no major incidents of disorder, and the biggest problems appear to have come from people without tickets trying to get in. In 1728, Madrid city hall found that some of the orderlies charged with distributing tickets to its guests had given or sold them to others, leading to "many complaints and scandal." The mayor ordered them arrested and their goods seized. Three took refuge in churches, and one presented himself to the king's justice; they were sentenced to four years' forced labor.[25] In September 1789, only some problems surrounding the sale of tickets marred the prevailing good spirits. According to the head of the police watch, there was not "a single rude word or action . . . I even went underneath the bleachers and saw nothing more than many villagers and artisans—but not any women—quietly trying to catch a glimpse of the festival through the cracks. The people have been concerned with nothing more than enjoying the entertainments . . . and there has not been a single blow, wound, or even verbal injury reported here in the entire week."[26] He saw to it that people who had bought tickets but had been unable to get in were reimbursed during the next few days.

Royal bullfights were great statements of the glory of the monarch and the hierarchies of society. For some commentators this was not enough; the bullfights also had to help legitimize social and political realities. Thus, Antonio Rubio likened the spectacle to a kind of election, one in which the people were given a voice they were denied in the real thing:

> If we wanted to imitate those who honor their ancestors by finding a philo-sophical reason for everything, we could say that after the *procuradores* went to the Cortes [the medieval Spanish version of parliament] with their vote or oath of loyalty to their monarch, then the people, gathered in a bullring and wildly cheering their princes, constituted the old-style election, the original modern assembly, which ratified with its cheers—and perhaps with its blood on the field as well—the decision of its representatives.[27]

Did the "people" see these spectacles in the way their creators intended? The available evidence suggests that the royal bullfights were very successful. Certainly, lots of people wanted to attend, and with the exception of one scurrilous letter to the king in 1789, there was nothing that could be called serious dissent. But there were other—less conspicuous and safer—ways of voicing discontent or skepticism.

The royal bullfights certainly offered opportunities for a good joke at the pretensions of the elites. Antonio Rubio suspected as much but tried to claim that some of this was deliberately written into the script so as to permit some harmless laughter at authority, in the person of the *alguaciles*, or mounted constables, who led the procession into the ring.

> The custom of having the six mounted constables in the plaza and looking at the royal box as if they were unaware that a bull was being fought behind their backs is, at once, entertaining and absurd. Thus, in the royal bullfights cowardice entertains as much as valor, and the people take an undisguised satisfaction from seeing someone from whom they are made to flee have to flee from something else. Our forebears no doubt wanted to permit the crowd this innocent and minimal outlet against authority. I am sure that if we had to invent the ceremony today, for this same reason we would put two or three . . . security agents among the constables.[28]

This is a clever argument, but not even Rubio could find a way to construe as scripted entertainment the inexperience, and even downright incompetence, of some of the star performers. The basis on which the caballeros were selected is not clear, but whatever it was, they did not have to have experience in fighting bulls on horseback. Thus, before the 1833 bullfights the corregidor of Madrid reported to the palace that the professional bullfighters wanted the caballeros to practice; the secretary agreed that they should "practice as the bullfighters indicate *so that they will know something when they go out to fight the bulls.*"[29] On the day, it could be very clear that the plebeian bullfighters were more than underlings. One Spaniard said of the 1833 bullfight that "the safety of the horsemen depended very much on their attendants," and by 1846 commentators were openly stating that the role of the bullfighters was to protect and defend the caballeros.[30]

Even the caballeros's horsemanship could be inadequate. The crowd could respect a caballero who was unhorsed in the middle of combat, but it had little patience for someone such as the unfortunate Morales, who, in the first of the 1878 corridas, was unable to get his horse close enough to the bull to place a lance and, "feeling the impatience of the public," decided to withdraw. As the first of the 1846 bullfights was about to begin, the caballero sponsored by the duke of Medinaceli was thrown from his horse and "had to present himself on foot before the royal box." Then, when the first bull came out, the duke of Altamira's protegé "fell with a great thump" and had to withdraw without even picking up a lance.[31] This can have done very little for the prestige of the caballero in question, nor for that of his aristocratic sponsor for that matter, and one can well imagine both the guffaws at the moment and the jokes told in numerous taverns afterward about the uselessness of the so-called gentlemen. Back in 1600 Bernardo de Vargas Machuca had commented that when a caballero performed poorly "there is not a scoundrel or secondhand shoe dealer who does not laugh himself silly."[32]

Imperial Spectacles

Royal bullfights were also held in parts of the empire, especially the viceregal capitals of Mexico City and Lima, where they were part of a larger spectacle complex exalting the viceroys and the "faraway kings" whom they represented.[33]

The new rulers of America wasted little time in introducing this spectacle of power to their recently conquered domains. Beginning in 1529, Mexico City celebrated San Hipólito's Day, the day on which Hernán Cortés had conquered the Aztec capital of Tenochtitlán only ten years before, with a bullfight, and from 1535 on the entry of new viceroys into the capital of New Spain was marked with a series of bullfights. In 1535 the bullfights lasted three days, but by 1789, when the second count of Revillagigedo assumed the office, there were two weeks of corridas. Bullfights were also held to mark accessions to the throne, royal marriages, royal births, and the end of wars. Mexican officials soon designated a special locale, the Plaza del Volador next to the viceregal palace, for these bullfights. Other bullfights had to be held elsewhere.[34]

In the empire, royal and viceregal bullfights bore the additional task of legitimizing "the right of the Spanish conquerors to rule the native peoples."[35] Thus the importance of San Hipólito's Day. The royal bullfight could also be adapted to fit the Indians into its representation of social and political hierarchy. In 1790 Lima, capital of the viceroyalty of Peru, celebrated the accession of Charles IV the previous year with a series of bullfights. The first two, organized by the city, were followed by a number of corridas put on by the guilds, those of the silversmiths and bakers among them. So, too, did the "original Natives . . . of this Kingdom," who showed their "love for the Sovereign" with dances, songs, a masque, and a bullfight in which the bullfighters were themselves Indians. But "separated by custom from the rest of the guilds," they were the "last in order who celebrated the coronation of our Monarch with public demonstrations."[36]

As in Spain, royal bullfights in New Spain were events "in which the hierarchical model of Mexican society was expressed in material form."[37] The viceroy presided from a special box, and the other authorities and corporations of the capital had their own, provided free. And, as in Spain, the allocation of boxes was the source of contention among the elites, especially in the second half of the eighteenth century, as reforms in the administration of the empire led to the creation of numerous new offices. The response of the city council, which organized the bullfights, was to reject such demands because "if out of respect for the equality of the arguments we had to give balconies to everyone, there would not be enough, even if the square measured half a league."[38] As a result, the social hierarchy portrayed in the seating plans for these royal bullfights increasingly "ceased to reflect the essence of the society of New Spain only to be transformed into the symbols of reaction."[39]

The contradictions became glaringly apparent in the aftermath of the War of Independence against Napoleon and the temporary defeat of the Mexican independence movement. The viceroy ordered that bullfights be held to celebrate the restoration of Ferdinand VII and the abolition of the Constitution of 1812, but arranging the seating had become highly problematic, especially as it fell to the constitutionally elected city council to do so. The viceroy insisted that the balconies be distributed as they had always been, but for the city council this was impossible, given how much had changed: "The nobles and officials of the first rank that were once counted by ones and tens now number in the thousands: There are newly created offices and officials; there are a multitude of military men . . . many people worthy of great consideration in the republic who will justly feel that their prestige and services far overshadow those of a clerk of the Royal Treasury and that he should not enjoy such preeminence."[40]

Questions of who got what balcony now also spoke to something much more serious: the very legitimacy of Spanish rule. Even so, the bullfight retained its appeal as a vehicle for political statements even after Spanish rule in Mexico had come to an end. In 1821 Mexico City honored independence and its principal architect, Agustín de Iturbide, with a series of bullfights and forty years later held a special bullfight, with President Benito Juárez in attendance, to celebrate the end of the civil war. The following year, the Committee of Patriotic Ladies, with Juárez's wife as president, organized a corrida to raise money for two military hospitals. Lima did the same in honor of Peru's independence and continued to use bullfights for political purposes, including to raise money for the war against Chile.[41]

From Absolutism to Liberalism

The assault on the absolute monarchy that began with the French invasion of 1808 initiated a period of revolutionary political conflict and unprecedented possibilities: the proclamation of the Constitution of Cádiz in 1812, the restoration of Ferdinand VII in 1814, the Liberal revolution of 1820, the antirevolutionary intervention by France in 1823, the Carlist War of 1833 to 1840, the proclamation of the regency of General Espartero in 1840, and the successful coup against him three years later, the Revolutions of 1854 and 1868, and the Second Carlist War of 1875 to 1876. All were the occasion for celebrations, and more often than not these celebrations included bullfights.

The French invasion and the fluctuating fate of the Constitution of Cádiz provided plenty of opportunities for celebration. King José Bonaparte organized bullfights to celebrate the birth of Napoleon's son in 1811. The next year, the city of Madrid was planning to celebrate the impending entry of Lord Wellington with a bullfight, "a national diversion that will catch their attention."[42]

The town of Noza, in Galicia, followed the proclamation of the Constitution in September 1812 with a bullfight. Two years later, the city of Leon showed its hatred of the Constitution by burning it in the public square—on two occasions!—renaming the square, and holding a bullfight; Talavera de la Reina publicly burned the Constitution, removed the stone monument dedicated to it, and had two bullfights. The Constitution returned for three years following the Revolution of 1820, and in both Jaén and Murviedro the uncovering of the new monument to the Constitution was followed by a bullfight. The city of Badajoz, which had held two bullfights in honor of the return of Ferdinand VII in 1814, had three for the proclamation of the Constitution in 1820.

The liberal triennium was brought to a close by French intervention, the "hundred thousand sons of Saint Louis," as they were called, under the command of the duke of Angoulême. The liberation of King Ferdinand from the Liberals was celebrated across the country, and a number of cities—

Seville, Avila, Huesca, Alcalá de Henares, Córdoba, and Madrid—staged bullfights as part of the festivities. The second of the three corridas in Córdoba taught a very clear political lesson. The bullfighters were all dressed in white and the picadors all rode white horses, while all the bulls were black. The king was in attendance and was presented with a poem that explained this heavy-handed symbolism:

> Even in the bullring,
> This City wanted to display
> the triumph over BLACKNESS
> that its loyalty has achieved:
> Eight great bulls of this color
> Have been run
> And the opposing whiteness
> Of bullfighters and horses,
> Amidst fierce struggles
> Vanquished their ferocity.[43]

The Madrid bullfights did not have this same symbolism, but at the conclusion of the final one there was a large aerostatic balloon, carrying "a figure of Fame with the flag of the union of France and Spain in one hand and a crown of laurels in the other." The real politics here took place behind the scenes. The organizers were reluctant to use bulls from one breeder known for his liberal sympathies. Afraid that "the People might say something in the bullring," they asked whether they could present his bulls "under some other name than that of Arratia and Nephews." Señor Arratia refused to consider this request. The posters bore the names of other breeders "whose political position is at least as disadvantageous as our own" and, in any case, the importance of a breeder's reputation would not permit such a subterfuge: "You know as well as anybody that name means much to breeders because it is always associated with the idea of breeds and their merit, so that if our bulls bore any other name it would only detract from the luster of the event."[44]

The Madrid bullring was a highly political place during the 1820s and 1830s, especially for the matadors. Roque Miranda withdrew from the ring in 1820 to join the National Militia. This cost him later, as he had trouble finding work after the suppression of the Constitution in 1823. (His luck changed when constitutional government was restored in 1835; on one occasion when he was attending a bullfight he gave in to the demand of the crowd and fought a bull while wearing his militia uniform.) On the other side, Antonio Ruiz, "El Sombrerero," was such an extreme royalist that he frequently fought wearing a white suit of lights, "to demonstrate that he belonged to the so-called *servile ones* [as the royalists were called]." On one occasion in 1829, just before killing a bull in the Madrid ring he proclaimed, "This is how to kill those black thieves." The Madrid crowd booed him so roundly for his royalism that King Ferdinand VII issued a royal order prohibiting him from fighting in the capital. Other known royalists suffered under the liberals: Francisco Gutiérrez was removed from his job on the coach line to Andalusia, and in 1837 Manuel Lucas Blanco was executed for killing a Liberal militiaman in a political argument.[45] Even facial hair was employed to make a political statement. Matadors in Spain were traditionally clean shaven, but during the Carlist War (1833–1840), "when barbers drew true political programs on people's faces, some bullfighters kept a moustache in order to make a public display of their liberal ideas."[46]

Both palace and city officials displayed distrust that the crowd would behave properly when the king was present. In 1828 the mayor and the majordomo discussed removing tickets for the bullfights (and the theaters) from sale on those occasions, "so that there is not the slightest breach of the decorum that the presence of the sovereign demands, and this is not easy to achieve at something so eminently free as the bullfight, where anyone can enter merely by purchasing a ticket."[47] They need not have worried. One anonymous diarist noted in August 1828 that even though one bullfighter "was truly awful, he was spared being chased from the arena under a shower of stones only by the great decorum that the people of Madrid display at bullfights attended by the King, Our Lord."[48]

In 1840 Madrid celebrated the arrival of General Espartero, the victorious Liberal commander of the Carlist War, with a series of events including a bullfight. Three years later, the city of Seville held a bullfight to celebrate "the happy outcome of the glorious military rising" against his regency.[49] Espartero returned to power as Prime Minister following the Revolution of July 1854; the following month there was a special benefit bullfight to raise money for those "wounded, widowed and orphaned in the revolutionary streetfighting." The idea originated with two matadors, Julián Casas, "El Salamanquino," and Francisco Arjona, "Cúchares," both of whom offered their services for free. (Cúchares and his assistants had been on the barricades in central Madrid during the revolution itself.) The bullfight raised the significant sum of 85,645 reales, including donations of 500 from José de Salamanca, Spain's leading financier, and 800 each from the French ambassador and General Espartero.[50]

Another revolution, in September 1868, chased Queen Isabella II out of the country and brought to power a coalition of left-wing Liberals. The new regime's constitution was proclaimed in June 1869, and the deputation of the province of Madrid decided to honor the occasion with two bullfights—and the provision of dowries for young women of the province. The bullring was decorated with pennants, banners, flags, "large placards bearing the names of the members of the Constituent Cortes," and, on the presidential box, portraits of Serrano, Prim, and Topete, the leaders of the revolution. From another box hung a large banner with the name of the newspaper *El Imparcial*. Before the bullfight began and during the intervals, the band of the municipal orphanage played "patriotic hymns and national airs."[51] Seville marked the conclusion of the Second Carlist War in 1876 with a bullfight, and the organizers divided the profits among wounded soldiers and the families of those who had been killed.

Changing Rituals of Royalty

Royal bullfights continued under liberalism, but they changed in some subtle yet significant ways. The October 1846 event was more in the hands of Madrid city hall than had been true in the past. The queen's chief majordomo explained that while the palace "took into consideration the changes of the times, the new form of government, and the public rights of the citizens, . . . it *demanded* nothing of any individual or corporation."[52] Even so, that royal bullfight looked little different from those that came before, as we saw earlier.

The visible alterations came on the next important royal occasion, the wedding of King Alfonso XII in January 1878. These changes brought the royal bullfight more up to date but also weakened its impact as a spectacle.

To begin with, the aristocracy was given a much reduced role. They continued to sponsor the caballeros, but did so collectively, through an organization known as the Permanent Committee of the Grandees. Individual nobles made much less of an impression: The entourages of up to a hundred liveried servants from an individual house were replaced by "twenty lackeys from various houses of the Grandees."[53]

The aristocrats also displayed much less interest in the men they sponsored. During the opening procession, they did not "ride in the same carriage as their caballeros, giving them the place of honor," something which, to one commentator at least, "did little honor to the Grandees."[54] Nor did they flaunt the generosity that had been a matter of course in the past, even as recently as 1833, when the duke of Infantado gave both his caballero and Francisco Montes, the professional bullfighter who assisted him, a large cash gift.

The aristocracy's interest in sponsoring the knights had been weakening for some time. In 1833 the palace found itself in the novel situation of having a problem locating enough sponsors. According to the marquis of Belgida, "At past royal bullfights the sponsors volunteered for this role, which produces considerable expense." And the chief equerry reported that while in the past the grandees had volunteered to be sponsors, "perhaps they can no longer sustain the considerable outlay."[55]

To judge from the experience of some of the knights, this was the case. In less than a week Antonio Rodríguez Manzano was rebuffed by the nine aristocrats he asked to be his sponsor. Some had what we could call good reasons: The marquis of Castelar was commanding the royal bodyguard; the duke of Villahermosa was in charge of the tournament that was being put on by the Real Maestranza; the duke of Infantado had already agreed to sponsor someone else with whom he had "more relations," and the count of Villag—lo was suffering from serious eye problems and could not leave his house.[56]

The excuses given by others, including the holders of some of the oldest and most prestigious titles in the country, make it clear that much of the aristocracy was indeed in a "fallen state." The duke of Osuna lacked the necessary "traces, harnesses, and corresponding equipment," the count of Oñate lacked the "equipment needed to make a properly lustrous impression"; and the marquis of Malpica begged off because "the actual state and the previous needs of my household do not permit me to meet, as I would like, the indispensable expenses required." Most forthright of all was the duke of Híjar: "My father had been a sponsor on another, similar occasion and our household had the necessary equipment but it was all lost in the War of Independence . . . and I am not in a position to present myself nor you properly and with sufficient ostentation at an event of such magnificence. . . . Please believe me that this is not an excuse but the truth."[57]

The experience of Juan Nepomuceno Cabrera was, if anything, even worse. He had been designated, at the last minute apparently, as substitute caballero and assigned the duke of Infantado as his sponsor. The duke, however, was not keen: "Without losing any time [I] twice went to present myself, dressed as a *caballero*, as I had been ordered; the first time he did not receive me or let me enter . . . the other, after sweating blood, I managed to speak with him." The duke refused to be his sponsor, and Cabrera went to the Plaza Mayor "alone and alone I remained, dishonored and without anyone to accompany me in the ceremony." Then, when the bullfight was over, he had to "leave alone, on foot, dressed as a caballero, through the busiest streets of Madrid."[58]

But it was not just the nobles who were at fault; King Alfonso also reneged on the monarch's traditional generosity. The caballeros had not been given a formal royal appointment as in the past, and they were not rewarded in the established manner, with the title of equerry and the accompanying salary.

This, too, was subject for criticism. Sánchez Neira pointed out the absence of any reward repeatedly and did so using the language of moral responsibility betrayed. Enrique Morales got no reward from "those who *should* have given him it"; Carlos F. de Florantes was not "rewarded by he who *should* have done so"; and Ramón García del Arenal got nothing from either "the government or the Royal Household, which *failed to respect* the traditional custom." The likely result of all this was that "if this happens again it will not be easy to find real gentlemen to pick up a lance at these joyous events."[59]

The question of payment of the caballeros had been an issue in 1833. Four months before the the installation of his daughter, Isabel, as princess of Asturias, Ferdinand VII had decided that he would give the caballeros the title of equerry but not the salary. A report from the *Veedor* on the payments made in 1789 and 1803 must have had its effect: For the plebeian bullfighters a total of 57,920 reales in the first year and 57,600 in the second,[60] and for the newly minted equerries half salary (6,000 reales) and 200 doubloons each, a total of 48,000 reales. The report concluded with a reminder to Ferdinand that the royal circumstances were much altered from the time of the previous royal bullfight, thirty years before: "Then Your Majesty could dispose freely of the wealth of the General Treasury of the Kingdom, but now you are reduced to a fixed annual appropriation, set by your own Royal will, with which to attend to all the expenses of your Royal household."[61]

After the event, the requests for payment were not long in arriving at the palace. Three of the caballeros, and the wife of a fourth, petitioned for the half salary to accompany the title of equerry. The royal secretary urged the king to accede: "It is very appropriate for your Majesty's sovereign generosity that you deign to grant them the half salary to which they aspire . . . especially when it has always been a practice of your August Ancestors and because the situation of the supplicants is singularly unfortunate."[62]

One thing that did not change was the availability of volunteers to serve as caballeros. There was seemingly no shortage of men prepared to fight the bulls. Richard Ford's claim that there were not enough men "who are willing to expose their lives to imminent dangers" and that one man was allegedly volunteered by his wife, who reasoned that she would get a new husband if he were killed and a pension if he were not, is untrue.[63] The case that most resembled that described by Ford was that of Juan Jacinto Lechuga Fernández de Córdoba: At the end of his request to be a caballero en plaza his wife, María Josefa Salinas, wrote a poem to the queen:

> Beloved Queen and Lady,
> The wife of he who writes
> With a fervent request
> Asks for this grace now
> You are her Mother and Owe
> This grace she asks from you,
> And which is only paid
> Animated by a Yes!!
> That you will put here
> Your Majesty will decide.

He was one of twenty-three aspirants in 1833; most were army officers, but there was also a lawyer and a servant of the royal household "serving in the Wardrobe of the Prince Antonio."[64]

The interest in serving as a caballero en plaza continued through the century. Madrid city hall received five applications for the two places available for the bullfight it sponsored in 1846. And in 1878 there were twenty-seven candidates for the two spots; the selection was done by drawing names.[65]

The most significant change to the royal bullfights was their relocation in 1878 from the Plaza Mayor to the city's bullring. The new venue had a number of disadvantages. The first was simple size: The plaza de toros was much smaller than the Plaza Mayor, and this imposed a much less imposing scale on the spectacle. For one critic, the result was "only a small reminiscence of what this category of event really is and how it was celebrated in not so distant times. The great carriages, the horses, the bullfighting teams, and the retinues that formerly took part in the parade did not do so this time, because the aristocracy does not sponsor the caballeros, as is cutomary, and because the ring does not permit as numerous and splendid entourages."[66] [See photo section.]

There were also far fewer seats available. Between forty thousand and fifty thousand people could view a royal bullfight in the Plaza Mayor, but only sixteen thousand could squeeze into the bullring. This gave rise to complaints about tickets not being available to the general public: "There was no lack of people and newspapers who asked 'Are these celebrations for the councillors, deputies, their friends and families, or are they for the people of Madrid, which is the source of the money which pays for them?'"[67] The daily newspaper *El Imparcial* put these questions in poetic form:

> The bullring was full of women,
> The kind only found in Cádiz,
> In Granada, Seville, or at the Court,
> Where all that which is most noteworthy congregates:
> Marqueses and Counts and Dukes
> Generals, civilians and clergy;
> They were all in the mosque yesterday,
> Those who were worthy of a free ticket.[68]

Finally, and most important of all from the point of view of political symbolism, the Plaza Mayor was a "site of memory" that anchored the royal bullfights in a deep historical continuity that the bullring lacked entirely.[69] Richard Ford, the English traveler, captured this in his description of the 1833 event: "There we beheld Ferdinand VII, presiding at the solemn swearing of allegiance to his daughter. He was seated where Charles I had sat two centuries before; he was guarded by the unchanged halberdiers and was witnessing the unchanging spectacle."[70] Thirteen years later, Antonio Rubio was even more explicit:

Nobody can dispute the historic preeminence of the Plaza Mayor, which has seen so many things! From the canonization of Saint Isidro [the patron saint of Madrid] to yesterday's bullfight, it so lends itself to historic celebrations that only there do they take on life, as the face of an antiques dealer livens up only when he examines a grimy coin of a bygone age. Its earth, so many times torn up because of our discord and on which we passed days and nights, gun in hand, guarding our fatherland, reason enough to disturb it again to celebrate an occasion that should bring our conflicts to an end.[71]

Not surprisingly, many observers found the 1878 royal bullfights far from satisfactory. One leading bullfight critic put it this way: "The Madrid City Council . . . ignoring the opinion of the press and the experts . . . chose not to celebrate them in the Plaza Mayor, and by so doing it took away their luster and their importance." (Apparently, the statue of Phillip III that had been placed in the center of the square in 1848 was not an obstacle.) For another, the 1878 bullfights lacked the spectacle of earlier ones, and provided "only a vague memory and pale imitation . . . a summary idea."[72] On the other hand, to an opponent of the bullfight such as Angel Fernández de los Ríos, the eviction of the funciones reales from the Plaza Mayor could only be good news: "Let it be said in Madrid's honor that it has successively expelled from its heart—the Plaza Mayor—the three spectacles that were staged there: the autos-da-fé, the executions, and the bullfights."[73]

With all these disadvantages, then, why was the change made? And why at this moment? It certainly was not for lack of an alternative venue: Madrid had had a bullring since 1746, yet royal bullfights continued to be held in the Plaza Mayor for another century. The answer lies in the political and social changes that had taken place, so that by the middle of the nineteenth century using the Plaza Mayor had become more trouble than the authorities felt it was worth. The big issue was access to balconies and the growing number of disputes and complaints from property owners, who were increasingly asserting their property rights.

These problems had been around for a long time. In 1765, the residents of the Plaza Mayor complained to the king that the city wanted to deprive them of all their balconies, so that "we will not be able to make use of our homes, which we pay for" and asked him to "grant them the balconies of their homes."[74] Just before the 1789 bullfight one José López Camarra was arrested for having sent the king "an irreverent representation that includes absurd propositions and indiscreet threats against the Sovereign directed at the use and enjoyment of the balconies of the Plaza Mayor at the upcoming royal bullfights by homeowners and tenants."[75] In 1803, one Eugenio de Sanpelayo stood firmly on his property rights, much to the chagrin of the duke of Infantado, who complained to the king's majordomo about "the novelty that . . . the owner of the house" in which the duke had been assigned a balcony "repeatedly denies me the balcony on the pretext that he bought the property after the fire in the Plaza free of any obligation or encumbrance."[76]

Given the obligations imposed upon the tenants on these occasions, such complaints are hardly surprising. They had to "keep the stairways of their houses clean and well lit to the fifth floor, with an eye to the comfort of those who will occupy the balconies . . . put a pleasant glass lantern on each landing . . . [and] leave the balconies and all the adjoining room free for the use of the people who are assigned them . . . so that they can make their family comfortable without the owner or the tenant of the dwelling or anyone else bothering them by putting a bench, stool, or anything else in front of the balcony." They were also forbidden to climb onto the roof.[77]

There were similar problems in the provinces. In 1820, a number of people who owned residences in Salamanca's main square sent a petition to the king that denounced the city government for taking over their balconies and cited the newly reinstated Constitution's respect for private property to bolster their case. The authorities' conduct was a "scandalous usurpation and unprecedented violation of their uncontestable property rights"; beyond "audacious," it was "unconstitutional."[78] When the city chose to celebrate the oath of Princess Isabella in 1833 with a bullfight in the Plaza Mayor, it found that a Sr. Martínez refused to surrender his balcony. As the civil governor described the matter to the minister of the interior, Martínez was insisting on a totally unreasonable respect for private property: "Sensible men can only characterize his opposition as a capricious desire to stand out. [He] uses the argument that his property is being prejudiced but ignores that when it is a matter of honoring the Sovereign, the great dominion of Kings supercedes individual rights."[79]

Logroño, another provincial capital, had two such cases within five years, although these were provoked by the use of squares for regular bullfights and not for funciones reales. In 1845, Diego Ponce de León, an army officer who owned eleven houses in the square in which bullfights were held, complained about "the invasion of his property in the houses he has in the square . . . his property right has been attacked."[80] In the end, the civil governor backed up the city council, which commandeered the balconies. By 1850 the contagion had spread: All the residents were refusing to give up their balconies. The custom that "when the city has held bullfights the householders have ceded their balconies, except for one in each house they keep for their own use" had been throttled by the assertion of absolute property rights.[81]

The royal bullfights of October 1846 generated a lengthy dispute over seating that proved costly to both the palace and the city council. The major-domo had asked city hall for 736 extra seats because a number of the niches and other locations it had traditionally received had been eliminated in a reorganization of the seating plan. The city requisitioned the places from the plaza's householders but did not give them any compensation. Seven months after the bullfight the householders petitioned the palace for the money, but the majordomo claimed that since he had received the tickets from the city council it was they, not the palace, who should pay. The issue reemerged in 1851. The palace continued to say that the city was responsible, but it agreed to pay the city—and not the householders—for the tickets at the prices the city generally applied in such situations, a total of 13,555 reales. (These prices were well below the officially established "box office" prices.) This did not resolve the matter; in 1855 the city was still negotiating with the householders and succeeded in getting them to reduce their demands from 58,000 to 40,000 reales.[82] After this episode, no further royal bullfights were held in the Plaza Mayor.

Political Metaphor

The French invasion of 1808 and the consequent collapse of the absolute monarchy produced an unprecedented opportunity for open commentary on political events. And from the first, one of the favored metaphors for such commentary was the corrida. The first significant defeat inflicted on Napoleon's troops by the Spanish army, at the battle of Bailén in 1808, was quickly celebrated in a humorous fly sheet that copied the form and language of the posters that announced bullfights:

NEWS OF THE BULLFIGHT
held on the fields of Bailén.
NOTICE TO THE PUBLIC.

With the corresponding and superior authority of our August Sovereign, Don Fernando VII (may God protect him) a praiseworthy and desirable performance of French Bulls will be held on July 19, 1808 (God willing) . . . D. Francisco Xavier Castaños will command and preside. The 18 bulls will be: 12 from the herd of Sr. Dupont, Commander in Chief of the Army of Observation of the Gironde, with its black ribbon; 5 from the herd of Sr. Vedel, great Eaglet, with yellow ribbon (a herd which has earned its fame at Austerlitz, Marengo, and Jena); and the final one from the famous breed of Corsica now in Madrid, and new in this ring . . . It is forbidden to throw anything into the ring other than bombs, grenades, bullets, etc., with the warning that anyone who does not do so will be considered a traitor or a coward. . . .

Some days before the fight the cattle will be in the following resting places: Dupont's in Andújar and Vedel's in Despeña-Perros, in case the people of La Mancha want to try out their cape work. . . . Be advised that the famous Bull of Corsica, who was in Madrid to be run with his horns covered [*embolado*] has escaped; even though he is one-eyed he could see well enough what was going to happen. The pursuit has already begun, and when he has been corraled it will be announced with new posters so that the People will not miss such an entertaining time.[83]

The war against the French also produced an abundant crop of comments in the form of engravings and lithographs, some of which employed the bullfight motif.[84] [See photo section.] *The Taurine Allegory of the Spanish Resistance* shows Spaniards, both mounted and on foot, fighting bulls with very human faces before an audience that includes monarchs, generals, and other dignitaries as they would have been seated for a royal corrida in the Plaza Mayor of Madrid. The title proclaims: "To see this event, Portugal, Spain, and England join together in close and firm union," while each episode of the fight has its own caption in verse in which Spaniards proclaim their disdain for Napoleon and his marshals Hugo, Suchet, Massena, and Soult.[85] Another engraving, *The Spanish Bullfight, or the Corsican Matador in Danger*, has Napoleon as a luckless bullfighter being tossed into the air by a powerful beast that has already killed his brother Joseph, while the assembled monarchs of the "royal theater of Europe" cheer it on. The title reads: "The Spanish Bull is so remarkable for Spirit that unless the Matador strikes him Dead at the First Blow the Bull is sure to destroy him."[86]

In two of these three examples, Spain is represented as the matador and the enemy is the bull; only in the last does the bull come to symbolize Spain. This difference derives from the provenance of the documents: The drawing that depicts Spain as a bull was the work of the great English satirist James Gillray, while the other two were produced by Spaniards, for whom a creature with horns, the mark of the cuckold, and one that inevitably died at the matador's hand, could never symbolize them.

When it came to animal allegories, Spaniards inevitably represented their country and themselves as a lion. The Spanish lion overcame the French eagle in many engravings of the period, such as the *Allegory of the Valencian Resistance*, which depicts "a Valencian burning the Frenchmen vomited by the Eagle being devoured by the Spanish lion."[87] Both the symbolism and the very image are strikingly similar to those in the poster for the "patriotic bullfight" of 1898 in Jerez de la Frontera, which was dominated by a picture of a Spanish lion eviscerating an American eagle prostrated on the U.S. flag.[88] The lion originated as a heraldic and royal symbol, part of the crest of the kings of Castile and Leon, but during the Peninsular War it leapt from the royal banner to become a symbol of the Spanish people, and it retained this democratic significance thereafter. Republicans retained the lion in their iconography, often having it accompany Hispania, the Spanish cousin of France's Marianne.

The bullfight was also widely used as a metaphor for domestic politics, especially once the relaxation of the censorship laws in the 1880s made political satire less dangerous. In this context, the usual imagery was inverted: Politicians being skewered became bullfighters, frequently facing the wrath of the Spanish public. [See photo section.] In *The Presentation in the Ring* (*La Filoxera*, June 8, 1879) the matadors at the head of the procession, identifiable as leading politicians of the day, are being pelted with rocklike objects. And in *The Great Corrida* (*Gil Blas*, March 2, 1882) a majestic bull labeled "taxpayer" has driven a cowardly matador against the boards while the crowd hurls oranges and one very visible lady's fan. The caption has the matador telling his teacher, "I can't handle this animal," to which the response is "Then to jail with him."

Bullfight metaphors appeared in less formal settings as well. In his autobiography, anarchist leader Angel Pestaña recounts that while still an adolescent he worked in the machine shops of the Bilbao-Portugalete railroad and got into trouble for making fun of an engine driver: "In this caricature he appeared dressed as a bullfighter, with a banderilla in each hand, calling the bull facing him. And behind him, on the ground, there was a pile of sh—, the product of the fear the bull had caused him."[89]

Nationalism

For centuries the monarchy monopolized the political use of the bullfight. Then, in the nineteenth century, the bullfight was immediately adapted to partisan political purposes in the struggles between absolutism and liberalism and between different strands of liberalism. Spaniards were much slower to use it as a vehicle for assertions of nationalist sentiment. Perhaps this was because there was not much to celebrate. Spain did make some small-scale imperial conquests in Morocco, but over the course of the nineteenth century it lost very much more than it won: most of its American empire to independence between 1810 and 1820, and the rest, as well as the Philippines, to the United States in 1898. Even so, the Spanish state was not especially concerned to create and spread a mass nationalism, by this or any other means. The few examples of nationalistic bullfights were the product of isolated, local initiatives and had limited impact.

In 1866 Spain scored one of its few military victories of the century, bombarding the Peruvian city of Callao in a minor example of gunboat diplomacy. Later that year one of the vessels that took part in the bombardment, the frigate *Villa de Madrid,* visited Cádiz. The local elite organized the celebrations: religious services, a dance, a banquet, a concert and tea at the Casino, a dramatic function at the theater—and bulls. A local chronicler described the scene:

> At two in the afternoon a band received the crew of the *Villa de Madrid* and the troops stationed on her and then, with happiness in their eyes and rejoicing in their souls and in formation they marched through the streets of the city as if to say, "There go the lads who, at the command of their leaders, punished the Chileans and Peruvians."
>
> They entered the bullring in formation and were received with frenetic applause. They did one lap around the ring and sat in the seats beneath the President's box.

. . . The bullring was decorated elegantly, with a multitude of flags with the national colors; in the central box there were three great placards surrounded by laurel leaves: In the center was written Alvar González; on the right, Callao; and on the left, Alstao. These placards bore ribbons with the names of General Méndez Muñoz, Brigadier Topete, and the other commanders of the Pacific campaign.[90]

Spain's next war came in the spring of 1898, against the United States. Novelist Pío Baroja wrote in his memoirs that the people of Madrid learned of the outbreak of war as they were coming out of a bullfight,[91] so perhaps it was only appropriate that bullfights became a prime vehicle for the expression of Spanish nationalism. The most important of these corridas, the Great Patriotic Bullfight, took place in Madrid, but they were also held in Sevilla, Murcia, Valencia, Almería, Jerez de la Frontera, Toledo, and probably elsewhere. These patriotic bullfights offer a valuable counterpoint to the funciones reales: They were "patriotic" and not "royal," and they displayed a nationalism that was strongly independent of the Crown. There was some continuity between the two types of bullfights, but 1898 was the occasion for some striking innovations.

The greatest novelties would have struck the public's eye before they entered the bullring, or even if they did not enter it at all. These were the images used on the posters and tickets. In Jerez de la Frontera the poster announcing the bullfights, which formed part of the annual livestock fair, was dominated by the picture of a lion eviscerating an eagle, beneath which lay the American flag and the U.S. motto, "E pluribus unum." It also bore the words "¡Viva España, Con Honrra [*sic*]!" In Madrid, the new iconography was, if anything, even more striking. The posters had the national colors as their background, and the tickets to the bullfight, which were designed by the great Valencian painter Joaquín Sorolla, portrayed the naked, waist-up figure of a male wearing a crown of laurels and carrying the Spanish flag that bore the word PATRIA and streamers with the names of great military victories of the past: Breda, Lepanto, Bailén, Pavia, San Quentín, and Covadonga. The most unusual aspect of the image is the use of the male figure instead of the female Hispania.

People on their way to Madrid's bullring that May 12 would have seen something else that was new: On the Alcalá Street women of the aristocracy, including the duchess of Bailén, the duchess of la Conquista, the countess of

Agreda, and the marchioness of la Romana, were raising money for the war effort by selling flowers.[92] But the fund-raising efforts were not as innovative as some would have liked. *La Ilustración Española* saw the need for a way of involving large numbers of Spaniards, and their modest donations, and asked:

> Could the Post Office not issue a series of patriotic stamps . . . so that all who want to give themselves some pleasure in their conscience could contribute in silence? . . . These stamps could not be used but they would have value for stamp collectors if they were on first-day covers. Stamp collecting is so popular that such stamps would sell not only in Spain but in all the universe. Let us remember that the stamps issued for the Jubilee of Queen Victoria raised enough money to found a hospital.[93]

This suggestion was not taken up.

The bullfight itself shared some similarities with the funciones reales. The event was sponsored by the deputation of Madrid. There were two caballeros en plaza, one sponsored by the deputation, the other by the city. They each fought one bull and were followed by ten matadors, each of whom fought a bull. The decoration of the ring was also similar, more monarchical than national: the castle and lion of Castile and León, pomegranates and chains "representing the arms of the old kingdoms of Spain." The coats of arms of the provinces were placed on the boxes. On the royal box there was "a magnificent tapestry with the tanto monta of the Catholic Kings," and around it a wreath of the most delicate flowers."[94] Elsewhere the nation was more in evidence. In Sevilla women carried fans and men sported ties in the national colors, flags hung along the boards, and the ring "was covered with colored sawdust that . . . spelled out in large letters 'Viva España.'" One of the bullfighters, El Parrao, used a muleta with "Viva España" printed on it.[95]

But the differences were greater than the similarities. The aristocracy, and especially the women, were prominent in the crowd, but they had no role at all in the corrida, not even as sponsors of the caballeros. The presidency was not held by a member of the royal family but jointly by the mayor of Madrid, the count of Romanones, and the great bullfighter Lagartijo. (He apparently had wanted to fight but was talked out of doing so because of his age. He arrived at the bullring in a carriage, which had been donated for the occasion, pulled by four ponies, "all decorated with the national colors.")[96] The partici-pants also displayed a generosity not found in the royal bullfights: The bullfighters fought for free, and twelve breeders each donated one bull. In addition, two hundred large posters, ten thousand programs, and five thousand flyers were donated. Clearly, where the monarch gave, the nation received.

As always, the matadors dedicated the bulls they were about to fight. Some of these dedications—to Lagartijo, to the memory of Frascuelo (another great bullfighter, who had died not long before)—had nothing to do with the occasion for the corrida. Others dedicated their bull to the nation or to those who were fighting, but two dedications stand out for their exalted nationalism. Cacheta, who fought the first bull, proclaimed: "I dedicate [it] to your excellency, to the public in general, to the Army and the Navy, so that not a single Yankee will remain in all the universe." And Luis Mazzantini dedicated his bull to "the heroic people of May second, [97] to the Mayor, who represents them here, and so that all the money raised in this bullfight be used to buy dynamite to blow that nation of adventurers that calls itself North America to kingdom come."[98]

The bullfight also served as a focus for nationalism in Latin America, but not always in the same way. For nationalists in Spain's Cuban colony, the bullfight was a symbol of Spanish colonialism and backwardness against which they presented baseball as the symbol of modernity and freedom. They "subsumed notions of civilization into baseball and of barbarism into bullfighting and drew a Manichean moral: the contrast between the Old World and the New, Spain and the United States, the past and the future." Thus, for José Martí, the bullfight was "a futile, bloody spectacle . . . and against Cuban sentiment as being intimately linked with our colonial past." The growing popularity of baseball worried the colonial authorities: From 1873 to 1874 they banned it as an "anti-Spanish activity," and one of their first acts after the independence war began again in 1895 was to reimpose the ban. Cubans in Tampa and Key West held baseball games to raise money for the war effort, and for their part, U.S. military authorities quickly banned bullfighting once they were in control of the island.[99]

In Mexico the situation was more complex. Initially the new republic used the bullfight to mark important political occasions, but toward the end of the nineteenth century elite attitudes changed. In his first term as president Porfirio Díaz banned bullfights in the capital and in a number of states. While the ban did not last long, during the 1890s the Mexican elite "rushed to adopt styles, attitudes, and amusements of other modernized, Western nations." This brought "changing attitudes toward bullfighting, the rise of baseball and horse racing, interest in boxing, and the fascination with cycling."[100] This new, more critical attitude to bullfighting did not prevent this same elite from lionizing leading Spanish matadors such as Luis Mazzantini when they performed in Mexico.

Outside the elite things were different. For the lower classes in particular the bullfight was a vehicle for Mexican nationalism, a nationalism that included a strong dose of anti-Spanish sentiment. One day Mazzantini needed a military escort to leave the bullring; on another, angry crowds tried to stone him while they shouted, "Death to the Spaniards." And following a performance by another Spanish matador, Cuatro Dedos, the crowd shouted, "To hell with the gachupines!" [a Mexican insult for Spaniards]. A third Spaniard, who fought in Mexico in 1897, was taunted with cries of "Cuba libre."[101]

Mexicans had their own bullfight idol, Ponciano Díaz, but the role of national icon was a difficult one. He returned from a trip to Spain in 1889 having adopted Spanish dress and signed some Spaniards to his cuadrilla, for which he drew charges of having become a *gachupín*. One thing he did not do was to shave his mustache, for facial hair distinguished Mexican bullfighters from their Spanish colleagues more clearly than anything else. When he was urged to adopt the Spanish style of fighting, he replied that he would do anything except remove his mustache: "Shave my mustache! At the very least they would call me *gachupín* and burn down my bullring."[102] Facial hair was also "a marker of masculinity for [Mexican] bullfighters, a sign of haughty machismo." And not just for bullfighters: Emiliano Zapata "took great pride in his huge mustache; it separated him from 'girlish men, bullfighters, and priests.'"[103]

The Twentieth Century

Politics in the afternoon did not come to an end in 1898. There were two more royal bullfights, in 1902 and 1906, and in September 1921 there was another "patriotic bullfight." This one was organized by the Red Cross in the context of another colonial war, this time in Morocco. But where the 1898 event was part of the euphoria of the early days of a war whose outcome was not yet known, the corrida of 1921 took place two months after the humiliating and disastrous defeat at Anual and with the purpose of raising money for the wounded and the widows and orphans of the dead. The event contained elements of the the traditional fiesta real, such as the presence of caballeros en plaza sponsored by individual members of the nobility. These were combined with a display of nationalism that exceeded that of 1898. In the center of the ring, "done in colored sand, there was a tapestry that included the coat of arms of Spain" surrounded by the inscriptions "Long Live Spain! Long Live the Army!" And Rafael, one of the bullfighters, worked with a "patriotic cape, in the national colors with the mottos 'Long Live Spain' and 'Long Live the Army,' one on each side."[104] There was another novelty. Between the performance of the caballeros en plaza, one of whom was seriously gored, and the regular bullfight there was a kind of intermission that included a "patriotic harangue" given by an actor and "two thousand men of the massed choirs of Infantry and Engineers" singing "The Soldier's Song":

> Soldiers! The entire Fatherland,
> Which is sacred to you,
> Beats in this flag
> Which the nation gives you.
> He who abandons or stains it
> Is a traitor
>
> And the Fatherland does not forgive
> The crime of treason.[105]

The Second Republic did not try to recast this ceremonial form in its own image, but the bullfight did not disappear from political celebrations entirely. When the city of Valencia celebrated the Republic's first anniversary on April 14, 1932, corridas were on the program, although simply as another item alongside the inauguration of a statue to the Republic, the distribution of copies of the Constitution, a military parade, the secularization of the cemetery, and the Miss Republic beauty contest.[106] During the Spanish Civil War both sides held bullfights as fund-raisers. In 1937 there was even one in Republican Alicante to raise money for the Communist Party militias. (The bulls might have come from the Popular Front Ranch [Ganadería del Frente Popular]!) The nationalists celebrated their victory with Liberation or Victory Bullfights. The most important of these took place in Madrid on May 24, 1939. The decoration of the ring matched that of 1921 in nationalist trappings:

There was a huge coat of arms, surrounded by the yoke and arrows and the regime's slogan of "Arriba España" painted on the wooden ring. Before the bullfight began, the crowd and the bullfighters gave the fascist salute. In a new twist, all the gate receipts were given to General Franco. Such Liberation Bullfights continued to be held in Bilbao into the 1950s as part of the annual festivities to commemorate the "liberation" of the city in June 1937. According to a confidential report by the newly arrived British consul, the 1953 celebrations generated "apathy, mingled with ill-humour." Amid a full week of activities, the "only events which really roused public enthusiasm were the completely non-political ones: the 'Corrida de la Liberación' (for those who could afford it) and—the greatest event of all in public opinion—the football final for the Generalisimo's Cup between Bilbao and Barcelona."[107]

When the great idol of the 1940s, Manolete, took his alternativa only a couple of months after the end of the Civil War, he faced a bull whose name had recently been changed: Its original name of Comunista was totally unacceptable in the "New Spain." In October 1940 there was a bullfight, advertised by a striking red poster adorned with the National Movement's yoke and arrows and the Nazi swastika, as part of the official celebrations surrounding the visit of Heinrich Himmler. Bullfighting was a staple of the infant state television in the 1950s, and in 1966 El Cordobés, whose own massive popularity owed much to that medium, played a prominent part in the official campaign for the referendum on Franco's Organic Law of the State.

The corrida could also be used for political statements of another sort. During the 1970s the bullfights held during Pamplona's world-famous San Fermín festival were the occasion for demonstrations by the anti-Franco opposition. The climax came on July 8, 1978, in the midst of the post-Franco transition to democracy, when armed police reacted to a demonstration in the bullring by firing rubber bullets and then live ammunition into the stands.

The democratic Spain that emerged from the transition after Franco's death in 1975 has not employed the corrida for political purposes. For the first time in many centuries a Spanish monarch has not included bullfights in the celebrations for important events in the life of the monarchy. Franco's blatant manipulation of the corrida tainted it, as it tainted so many other national symbols, so that many Spaniards found even the idea of national symbols distastefully reminiscent of the regime. The bullfight was also taken as an anarchronistic emblem of a dark past that they wanted to put far behind them. Long a valuable and versatile voice in the chorus of power, this form of politics in the afternoon has seemingly been silenced.

The Death of Manolete

At 6:42 in the afternoon of August 28, 1947, a Miura bull named Islero gored Manuel Rodríguez, "Manolete," in the ring at Linares. The matador died early the next morning. The death of the undisputed star of the moment shocked the nation and dominated the press for days afterward. Some papers even brought out special editions. His house in Córdoba was surrounded by an immense crowd, and more than twenty thousand people filed through to view the corpse. The family received thousands of telegrams, including one from Generalísimo Franco himself.[1] (Manolete's stature in the early years of the Franco regime had been enhanced by the fuss he raised during his 1946 tour of Mexico over the presence at one of the bullrings of the flag of the Spanish Republic, which Mexico still recognized as the government of Spain.)

Manolete's death was news far beyond Spain, even beyond the orbit of places where bullfighting mattered. The next day, the *New York Times* carried an article, accompanied by a photograph: "Manolete, 30, Dies After Fatal Goring by Bull; All Spain Mourns Her Greatest Matador."[2]

Politics aside, Manolete's visit to Mexico had been a triumph. A fight on Sunday was far from enough to satisfy the demand of the fans in Mexico City, and two more had to be held on weekdays. The great Mexican novelist Carlos Fuentes claims that "people sold their cars and pawned their mattresses" to see him fight. On the fiftieth anniversary of Manolete's death, Fuentes made a pilgrimage to the bullring in Linares and wrote, "The bullfighter was 30 years old, the bull 2,000. . . . If Manolete was the unconscious incarnation of the philosophy of Seneca, he was also the heir . . . to the unmovable appearance of Greco's Spanish gentlemen and the foreshadowing of the mortal poetry of Federico García Lorca."[3]

Novelist's language perhaps, but symptomatic of the essentialist view of the bullfight that reduces it to the permanent symbol of an unchanging Spain and robs it of its history and, therefore, of its interest. And diametrically opposed to the argument I have made in this book: The corrida is a social institution that exists within a broader society; both change over time, as does the relationship between them. At most, the bull would have been two hundred years old, since the fighting bull is a human creation that goes back only that far; or if we take breeds seriously, then one hundred years, since that was the age of the Miura brand when Islero killed Manolete.

The bullfight began in both popular and elite culture. It took its modern form as an activity engaged in by professionals before paying crowds during the eighteenth century, but remained the product of the confluence of these two sources. Even when the nobility withdrew from fighting, it retained a role as breeders of bulls and as sponsors through the Royal Maestranzas. Moreover, the tradition of celebrating the monarchy with special bullfights, in which the nobility continued to have a central place, further tied the elite to the corrida. This connection gave the bullfight a legitimacy that allowed it to survive repeated challenges to its existence.

If elite participation gave it cover, long-standing popular interest provided a ready-made mass audience for the new commercialized bullfight, and its immediate commercial success further strengthened the corrida against its opponents. The corrida's potential as a money spinner was also quickly recognized by cash-strapped religious institutions and local authorities who deluged the Crown with their requests to hold bullfights to raise money for a multitude of public purposes. For their part, royal officials were almost always prepared to accede, even when they felt that bullfights were undesirable. Much like government lotteries today, bullfights constituted a comfortable alternative to taxation that usually trumped any qualms officials had about their less salubrious side effects.

By the 1850s, when a more modern opposition, sometimes organized into animal protection societies, emerged, the bullfight had been established for more than a century. And while many government officials disliked the bullfight, they were not prepared to attempt to ban it once again. Perhaps, as liberals, they were less inclined to use the power of the state in this way than to practice a reluctant toleration and hope that, as Javier de Burgos put it in the foundational document of the liberal state structure, "the progress of public reason will sooner or later eliminate" it.[4] Driven by concerns about public order, officials at the provincial level began to regulate the bullfight in the 1840s, but only in October 1882 did the national government decide to become involved. Yet the very Royal Order that brought it under more central control formally recognized that, whatever the personal preferences of those in power, the bullfight was there to stay.

Through this combination of circumstance and chronology the corrida, alone among the many early modern entertainments in which violence was done to animals, became a modern leisure commodity and a cultural industry. Like any industry, bullfighting had its interest groups, its hierarchical structures, and its power relations. It also had to relate to other groups and institutions in the society within which it was embedded. In both cases, those relations were far from harmonious or unchanging. Spaniards understood and reacted to the bullfight in any number of ways, and the view that the corrida was emblematic of Spain and "Spanishness" was far from universally shared. But even those who held this view did not see the same things when they looked at the bullfight, as the ongoing debate of the eighteenth and nineteenth centuries makes clear.

This is not to say that the bullfight can tell us nothing about Spain. What it tells us, however, is not about permanence and national character but about change and diversity. How Spaniards responded to the business of bullfighting reveals attitudes toward economic change and entrepreneurship, and how they viewed bullfighters displays evolving assessments of respectability and appropriate behavior. Nowhere was this truer than in the realm of gender: The corrida was the forum for expression of concern over the virility of the nation, while the existence of female bullfighters called prevailing gender norms into question. The crowds that the corrida called into existence forced Spaniards to come to terms with a new and, for many, threatening social phenomenon. And where the bullfight changed least, in its use as political representation, it fell increasingly out of step with a political reality that, in the empire as well as within Spain itself, was being revolutionized.

All the businesses in Córdoba closed for Manolete's funeral. It began at five in the afternoon.

Appendix A

Graph 1

**Lease of Seville Bullring
1824–1862
(in reales)**

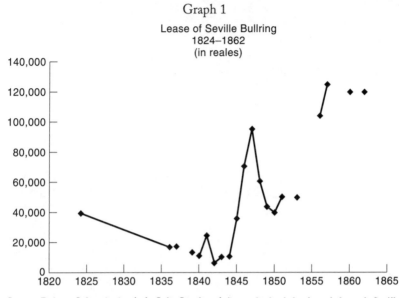

Source: Rojas y Solís, *Anales*; A de Solís Sánchez Arjona, *Anales de la plaza de horos de Sevilla 1836–1934* (Seville, 1942).

Graph 2

**Prices of Fighting Bulls and Wholesale Price Index:
1802–1895
(1869 = 100)**

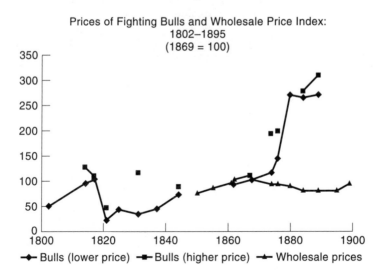

Graph 3

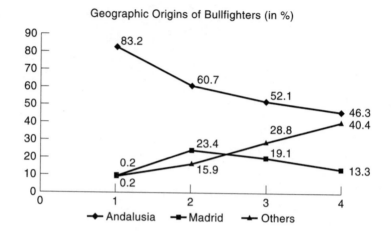

Source: J. M. Cossío, *Los Toros,* vol. 3.

Graph 4

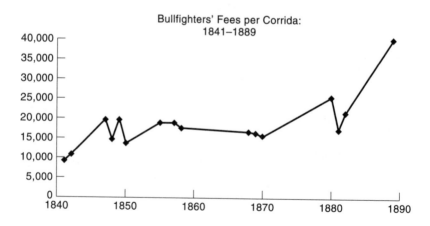

Graph 5

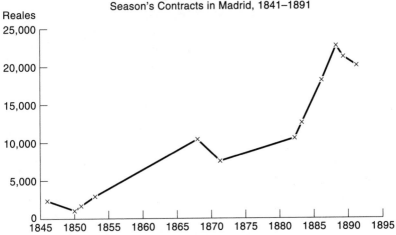

Bullfighters' Fees per Corrida:
Season's Contracts in Madrid, 1841–1891

Appendix B

Geographic Origins of Bullfighters

This table is based on the biographies of the bullfighters, male only, that fill the more than one thousand pages of volume three of J. M. Cossío's *Los toros*. These biographies range in length from two lines to a number of pages, and they do not have a standard format. Some provide the precise date and place of birth; some, only one or the other. Still others mention merely a date at which a bullfighter was active, while some offer no such information at all.

The table is arranged in four columns primarily according to the bull-fighter's date of birth. To compensate for the large number for whom this is not available, date of birth has been estimated based on the date at which a bullfighter began his career, assuming that they typically did so at around fifteen years of age. Thus, column one includes builfighters born before 1815 or who began their careers before 1830; column two, those born between 1815 and 1844 or active between 1830 and 1859; column three, those born between 1845 and 1874 or active between 1860 and 1889, and column four those born between 1875 and 1895 or who started their careers between 1890 and 1910.

The geographic units used are provinces and historic regions, with the exception of Galicia and the Basque provinces, which appear only as regions.

	Before 1815		1815–1844		1845–1874		1875–1895	
	no.	%	no.	%	no.	%	no.	%
Andalusia	154	83	130	60.8	259	52.2	483	46.3
Almería	0	0	0	0	2	0.4	19	1.8
Cádiz	45	24.3	44	20.6	48	9.7	72	6.9
Córdoba	19	10.3	15	7	42	8.5	56	5.4
Granada	2	1	6	2.8	7	1.4	22	2.1
Huelva	4	2	0	0	3	0.6	11	1.1
Jaén	0	0	0	0	3	0.6	12	1.1
Málaga	14	7.6	4	1.9	12	2.4	32	3.1
Sevilla	70	37.8	61	28.5	142	28.6	259	24.8
Aragon	0	0	5	2.4	26	5.2	94	9.1
Huesca	0	0	0	0	1	0.2	6	0.6
Teruel	0	0	1	0.5	5	1	9	0.9
Zaragoza	0	0	4	1.9	20	4	79	7.6

	Before 1815		1815–1844		1845–1874		1875–1895	
	no.	%	no.	%	no.	%	no.	%
Asturias	1	0.5	1	0.5	0	0	7	0.7
Baleares	0	0	0	0	0	0	1	0.1
Basque provinces	3	1.6	2	0.9	9	1.8	52	4.9
Canary Islands	0	0	0	0	0	0	0	0
Catalonia	1	0.5	3	1.4	6	1.2	17	1.6
Barcelona	1	0.5	3	1.4	4	0.8	17	1.6
Gerona	0	0	0	0	0	0	0	0
Lérida	0	0	0	0	1	0.2	0	0
Tarragona	0	0	0	0	1	0.2	0	0
Extremadura	1	0.5	4	1.9	7	2.8	10	1
Badajoz	0	0	3	1.4	7	1.4	6	0.6
Cáceres	1	0.5	1	0.5	0	1.4	4	0.4
Galicia	0	0	0	0	1	0.2	8	0.8
Levante	1	0.5	6	2.8	39	17.8	82	7.8
Alicante	1	0.5	0	0	6	1.2	9	0.9
Castellón	0	0	0	0	0	10	1	
Valencia	0	0	6	2.8	33	6.6	72	6.9
Madrid	16	8.6	50	23.4	95	19.1	138	13.3
Murcia	2	1	1	0.5	10	2	33	3.2
Albacete	0	0	0	0	3	0.6	8	0.8
Murcia	2	1	1	0.5	7	1.4	25	2.4
Navarre	4	2	0	0	2	0.4	4	0.4
New Castile	0	0	5	2.3	23	4.6	32	3.1
Ciudad Real	0	0	3	1.4	6	1.2	9	0.9

	Before 1815		1815–1844		1845–1874		1875–1895	
	no.	%	no.	%	no.	%	no.	%
Cuenca	0	0	0	0	0	0	1	0.1
Guadalajara	0	0	0	0	3	0.6	3	0.3
Toledo	0	0	2	0.9	14	2.8	19	1.8
Old Castile	*2*	*1*	*7*	*3.3*	*20*	*4*	*74*	*7.2*
Avila	0	0	0	0	1	0.2	1	0.1
Burgos	1	0.5	1	0.5	0	0	4	0.4
Leon	0	0	0	0	0	0	0	0
Logroño	0	0	0	0	2	0.4	0	0
Palencia	0	0	0	0	0	0	7	0.7
Salamanca	0	0	2	0.9	1	0.2	8	0.8
Santander	0	0	2	0.9	2	0.4	17	1.6
Segovia	0	0	1	0.5	0	0	6	0.6
Soria	0	0	0	0	2	0.4	0	0
Valladolid	0	0	1	0.5	10	2	28	2.7
Zamora	1	0.5	0	0	2	0.4	3	0.3
Totals	*185*		*214*		*497*		*1044*	

Abbreviations

AHN   Archivo Histórico Nacional, Madrid

AMS   Archivo Municipal, Seville

AMV   Archivo Municipal de la Villa, Madrid

APM   Archivo de Protocolos, Madrid

APR   Archivo del Palacio Real, Madrid

ARCG   Archivo de Ia Real Cancillería de Granada

ARMS   Archivo de la Real Maestranza, Seville

CACM   Centro de Archivos de la Comunidad de Madrid

DSCD   Diario de Sesiones del Congreso de los Diputados

Notes to the Introduction

1. Cited in Ian Gibson, *Federico García Lorca: A Life* (New York, 1989), p. 391.

2. César Graña, "The Bullfight and Spanish National Decadence," *Society*, 1987, pp. 36–37.

3. Cited in Rosario Cambria, *Los toros: tema polémico en el ensayo español del siglo XX* (Madrid, 1974), pp. 24–25.

4. I use the Spanish word *corrida* as a synonym for the English *bullfight* throughout the book.

5. Cambria, *Los toros*, p. 49.

6. Ibid., pp. 85–88.

7. Ibid., pp. 51–59.

8. Ibid., pp. 59–67.

9. Cited in David Damrosch, *We Scholars* (Cambridge, 1995), p. 84.

10. Cited in Rosario Cambria, "Bullfighting and the Intellectuals," in Timothy Mitchell, *Blood Sport: A Social History of Bullfighting* (Philadelphia, 1991), p. 209.

11. José Ortega y Gasset, *Una interpretación de la historia universal* (Madrid, 1960), pp. 178, 193.

12. Carmen Martín Gaite, *Usos amorosos del dieciocho en España*, (Madrid, 1977); Timothy Mitchell, *Blood Sport* (Philadelphia, 1991), xiv; Mitchell, *Violence and Piety in Spanish Folklore* (Philadelphia, 1988), p. 158.

13. Garry Marvin, *Bullfight* (Oxford, 1988), p. 135.

14. Carrie Douglass, "*Toro muerto vaca es*: An Interpretation of the Spanish Bullfight," *American Ethnologist*, 1984, p. 243.

15. Winslow Hunt, "On Bullfighting," *American Imago*, 1955, p. 343.

16. Manuel Delgado Ruiz, *De la muerte de un Dios* (Barcelona, 1986), pp. 167–191, 252–259.

17. L. A. Zurcher and A. Meadow, "On Bullfights and Baseball," *International Journal of Comparative Sociology*, 1967, pp. 99–117. The bullfight contrasts with baseball, its American analogue, which, like the American family, is egalitarian.

18. Julian Pitt-Rivers, "El sacrificio del toro," *Revista de Occidente*, 1984, pp. 23–24.

19. Raphael Pollock, "Some Psychoanalytic Considerations of Bull Fighting and Bull Worship," *Israel Annals of Psychiatry and Related Disciplines*, 1974, cited in Cambria, "Bullfighting and the Intellectuals," p. 206.

20. Julian Pitt-Rivers, "The Spanish Bullfight and Kindred Activities," *Anthropology Today*, August 1993, p. 14.

21. Kate Field, *Ten Days in Spain* (Boston, 1875), p. 108.

22. Ian Tyrrell, *Woman's World, Woman's Empire* (Chapel Hill, 1991), pp. 175–176.

23. Katherine L. Bates, *Spanish Highways and Byways* (New York, 1900), p. 114.

24. Jane Addams, *Twenty Years at Hull House* (New York, 1938), p. 73.

25. Richard Wright, *Pagan Spain* (London, 1951), p. 111. French intellectuals have also been prolific in this respect. See E. Bayarat, "Comment se construit un mythe: La Corrida en France au XXe Siècle" in *Revue d'histoire moderne et contemporaine*, 1997, pp. 307–330.

26. This discussion is based on A. Alvarez de Miranda, *Ritos y juegos del toro* (Madrid, 1962), pp. 33–38.

27. Johan Huizinga, *Homo Ludens* (Boston, 1950), p. 178.

28. Cited in Alvarez de Miranda, *Ritos y juegos*, p. 40.

29. Alvarez de Miranda, *Ritos y juegos*, pp. 41–56.

30. See chapter 6.

31. I. Gómez Quintana, *Apuntes históricos acerca de la fiesta de toros en España* (Córdoba, 1897), pp. 79, 81.

32. See chapter 5.

33. José Francisco de Isla, *Descripción de la máscara* (Madrid, 1787), p. 188.

34. Charles Kany, *Life and Manners in Madrid, 1750-1800* (Berkeley, 1932), p. 345.

35. Alvarez de Miranda, *Ritos y juegos*, pp. 89–95.

36. Ibid., pp. 94, 113.

37. Ibid., p. 109.

38. Ibid., p. 131. Allan Guttman has found a similar origin for other sports. See his *From Ritual to Record* (New York, 1978).

39. Araceli Guillaume-Alonso, *La tauromaquia y su génesis* (Bilbao, 1994), p. 19.

40. Ibid., p. 167. This "antisacrificial" position, which holds that the death of the bull was not an essential part of the corrida, is advanced by a number of French scholars who are known as the New French School. See Pedro Romero de Solís's review of Guillaume-Alonso's book in *Revista de Estudios Taurinos*, 1995, p. 194.

41. Guillaume-Alonso, *Tauromaquia*, p. 173.

42. Pedro de Campomanes, *Discurso sobre la educación popular* (Madrid, 1775), pp. 129–30.

43. *Semanario Pintoresco Español*, 1846, p. 232. Emphasis in the original.

44. Concepción Arenal, *El pauperismo* (Madrid, 1897), vol. 1, p. 286; *El Toreo*, 22 December 1884; Marqués de Boyarga to Diputación, 14 February 1885, Archivo de la Diputación de Madrid, Legajo 5069.

45. See below, chapter 5.

46. P. Antón Solé, "Prohibición de las corridas de toros en días festivos y los Obispos de Cádiz," in *Archivo Hispalense*, 1971, pp. 108–11; Sección 205, Archivo de la Maestranza de Seville.

47. Expediente 117, Legajo 11388, Consejos, Archivo Histórico Nacional, Madrid (AHN).

48. Ibid.

49. F. Bleu, *Antes y después del Guerra* (Madrid, 1983), pp. 175–177.

50. A. Ariño Villaroya, *El calendari festiu a la València contemporánea* (Valencia, 1993), pp. 16–20.

51. J. Keiger, *Raymond Poincaré* (Cambridge, 1997), pp. 11–13.

52. Richard Holt, *Sport and Society in Modern France* (Hamden, 1981), pp. 109–116; Charles Rearick, *Pleasures of the Belle Epoque* (New Haven, 1985), p. 114.

53. Robert Malcolmson, *Popular Recreations in English Society* (Cambridge, 1973), pp. 47, 126–135; Peter Bailey, *Leisure and Class in Victorian England* (London, 1987), p. 38.

54. Keith Thomas, *Man and the Natural World* (London, 1983), p. 159.

55. *Times* (London), 29 March 1870; *Illustrated London News*, 2 April 1870.

56. St. Louis *Post-Dispatch*, 6 June 1904; St. Louis *Globe Democrat*, 4, 6 June 1904.

57. Keith Sandiford and Wray Vamplew, "The Peculiar Economics of English Cricket Before 1914," *British Journal of Sports History*, December 1986, p. 311. See also B. J. Rader, "Modern Sports: In Search of Interpretations," *Journal of Social History*, Winter 1979, p. 311, for an identical explanation from a historian of baseball.

58. David Nasaw, *Going Out: The Rise and Fall of Public Amusements* (New York, 1993), pp. 1–6.

Notes to Chapter One

1. *Censo de la ganadería de España* (Madrid, 1869), p. xvi; *El Enano*, 3 November 1895; *La Coleta*, 20 June 1912.

2. Scruples did sometimes win out: In 1816 the Council of Castile rejected a request from Astorga because "the Council . . . does not find in the concession of bullfights as requested by the city government of Astorga all the advantages and beneficial effects that are proposed; this class of diversion always produces certain moral and political evils that can be overlooked only in populous cities and in those where not to permit them would cause even greater evils." Consejos, Exp. 21, Leg. 11412, AHN.

3. Cited in Gómez Quintana, *Apuntes históricos,* pp. 91-92. On the Maestranza of Granada see I. Arias de Saavedra, *La Maestranza de Granada en el Siglo XVIII* (Granada, 1988).

4. Pedro Romero de Solís, "La Plaza de toros de Sevilla y Las ruinas de Pompeya," *Revista de Estudios Taurinos,* 1996, pp. 26-28.

5. Consejos, Exp. 56, Leg. 11406, AHN; cited in G. Díaz-Y Recaséns and G. Vázquez Consuegra, "Plazas de toros," in *Plazas de toros* (Seville, 1995), p. 66.

6. Sección 205, Archivo de la Maestranza de Sevilla.

7. Consejos, Exp. 96, Leg. 11387, AHN.

8. On official Church attitudes to the bullfight, see chapter 5.

9. Díaz-Y Recaséns and Vázquez Consuegra, "Plazas de toros," pp. 31-35.

10. Consejos, Exp. 70, Leg. 11412, AHN.

11. Consejos, Exp. 60, Leg. 11406, AHN.

12. Consejos, Exp. 3, 57, Leg. 11412, AHN.

13. Consejos, Exp. 63, Leg. 11412, AHN.

14. Consejos, Exp. 12, Leg. 11412, AHN.

15. R. Cabrera Bonet and M. T. Artigas, *Los toros en la prensa madrileña del siglo XVIII* (Madrid, 1991), p. 32.

16. Consejos, Exp. 4, 58, Leg. 11412, AHN.

17. Consejos, Exp. 57, Leg. 11406, AHN.

18. Consejos, Exp. 1, Leg. 11414, AHN.

19. Consejos, Exp. 45, Leg. 11412; Exp. 50, Leg. 11413, AHN.

20. Consejos, Exp. 51, Leg. 11413, AHN.

21. Consejos, Exp. 55, Leg. 11412, AHN.

22. F. Iawasaki Canti, "Toros y sociedad en Lima colonial," *Anuario de Estudios Americanos,* 1992, pp. 326-327.

23. Consejos, Exp. 75, Leg. 11412, AHN.

24. Consejos, Exp. 37, Leg. 11412; Exp. 24, Leg. 11413, AHN.

25. Consejos, Exp. 11, 94, 115, Leg. 11387, AHN; Exp. 55, Leg. 11412; Exp. 9, Leg. 11413, AHN.

26. Consejos, Exp. 2, Leg. 11413; Exp. 21, Leg. 11412; Exp. 20, Leg. 11413, AHN.

27. Consejos, Exp. 9, Leg. 11413; Exp. 43, Leg. 11412; Exp. 62, Leg. 11413.

28. Consejos, Exp. 63, Leg. 11413, AHN.

29. Leg. 768/1, Archivo Municipal, Alcalá de Henares.

30. Consejos, Exp. 15, Leg. 11389, AHN.

31. Consejos, Exp. 69, 129, Leg. 11389, AHN.

32. Leg. 19/85, Serie General, Archivo del Congreso de los Diputados, Madrid.

33. Consejos, Exp. 117, Leg. 11415, AHN. On the symbolism of political bullfights, see chapter 6.

34. Consejos, Exp. 78 and 79, Leg. 11412, AHN.

35. Consejos, Exp. 77, Leg. 11412, AHN.

36. Consejos, Exp. 38, Leg. 11387; Exp. 41, Leg. 11386, AHN.

37. Consejos, Exp. 28 and 37, Leg. 11412, AHN.

38. Political fund-raisers did not disappear entirely; see chapter 6.

39. The bullfight turned a profit of 23,879 reales in 1873, and 57,873 in 1875. Leg. 5065 and 5070, Centro de Archivos de la Comunidad de Madrid (CCM). From 1881 to 1891 the total profit for the hospitals was 623,343 pesetas. *El Toreo,* 29 June 1891.

40. Consejos, Exp. 17, Leg. 11412, AHN.

41. *La Lidia,* 21 July 1884.

42. In December 1885 a committee was formed to organize a bullfight to raise money to build a ship for the navy. *La Lidia,* 12 December 1885.

43. Leg. 5071, ACM.

44. Ibid., Leg. 5072.

45. Ibid.

46. Cited in Nieto Manjón, L. *"La Lidia," modelo de periodismo* (Madrid, 1993), pp. 333–334.

47. *La Coleta,* 8, 15 July 1907.

48. Ibid., 16 September 1907.

49. *El País,* 6, 16, 21, 28 August 1908.

50. *La Coleta,* 16 September 1906.

51. See A. Shubert, *Social History of Modern Spain* (London, 1990), pp. 36-38; Mary Nash, *Defying Male Civilization* (Denver, 1995). On women, see chapter 3.

52. *El País,* 16 August 1908.

53. Leg. 5065, ACM.

54. Ibid., Leg. 5070.

55. *La Lidia,* 21 July 1884; *El País,* 6 August 1908.

56. M. Bowden, "Soccer," in K. B. Raitz, ed., *The Theater of Sport* (Baltimore, 1995), p. 110; B. J. Neilson, "Baseball," in ibid., p. 33.

57. F. Halcón Alvarez Ossorio, "Evolución de las formas arquitectónicas de una plaza de toros," *Revista de Estudios Taurinos,* 1995, p. 113.

58. Pedro Romero de Solís, "La plaza de toros de Sevilla y las ruinas de Pompeya," *Revista de Estudios Taurinos,* 1996, pp. 74-89.

59. Cited in Díaz-Y Recaséns and Vázquez Consuegra, "Plazas de toros," p. 96.

60. Hospital Provincial de Valencia, *Plaza de toros de Valencia* (Valencia, 1947).

61. Exp. 108, Leg. 11405, Consejos, AHN. (This list was later published in the *Gaceta de Madrid*, on 12 November 1862.); J. Sánchez de Neira, *El toreo* (Madrid, 1879), vol. 1, pp. 462-478. Writing in the 1830s, Francisco Montes urged that bullrings be built "with the greatest solidity and most exquisite taste possible . . . for they are public buildings deserving the most brilliant architecture and should display to all the splendor of the arts in Spain." *Tauromaquia* (Madrid, 1836), p. 262. In contrast, until 1908, major-league ballparks were "temporary, cramped wooden structures." G. E. White, *Creating the National Pastime* (Princeton, 1996), p. 20.

62. Consejos, Exp. 129, Leg. 11389, AHN.

63. Consejos, Exp. 93, Leg. 11417, AHN.

64. F. Martínez García, *Construcción de la plaza de toros de Calatayud, 1877* (Calatayud, 1995), pp. 38-43.

65. Cited in J. M. Sergo Díaz, *Plaza de toros de Gijón* (Gijón, 1988), pp. 31, 38.

66. J. K. Walton and J. Smith, "The First Century of Beach Tourism in Spain: San Sebastián and the *Playas del Norte* from the 1880s to the 1930s," in M. Barke, J. Towner, and M. T. Newton, eds., *Tourism in Spain: Critical Issues* (Wallingford, 1996), pp. 42-43. In 1912, a summer bullfight drew three thousand people from Oviedo, the provincial capital, alone. J. Uria, *Historia social del ocio* (Oviedo, 1996), p. 48.

67. Uria, *Historia social*, p. 40.

68. A. Castañedo, *Torerías de la tierra* (Almería, 1911), pp. 55-57, 79-80.

69. P. Flores Guevara, *Guijuelo: Ochenta y cuatro años de historia del toreo* (Guijuelo, 1993), p. 29.

70. *La Crónica de Salamanca, Suplemento,* 24 June 1861.

71. Consejos, Exp. 96, Leg. 11389, AHN.

72. E. de Sena, *Fiestas de Salamanca en fotografías de Venancio Gombau* (Salamanca, 1993), pp. 61-68.

73. Cited in ibid., pp. 71-72.

74. Hospital Provincial, *Plaza de toros,* pp. 16-18.

75. Ariño Villarroya, *El calendari festiu,* p. 152.

76. *Diario Mercantil,* 26 July 1859, cited in ibid., p. 153.

77. *El País,* 13 July 1908.

78. Cossío, *Los toros* (Madrid, 1847-1852), vol. 4, pp. 100-104; *Plazas de toros,* p. 96. Modifications were made to suit French sensibilities: the picadors' horses wore protective padding, the bulls' horns were capped, and the bulls were not killed.

79. C. Rearick, *Pleasures of the Belle-Epoque: Entertainment and Festivity in Turn-of-the-Century France* (New Haven, 1985), p. 139.

80. R. Holt, *Sport and Society in Modern France* (Hamden, 1981), pp. 112-113.

81. Leg. 5005, 5064, ACM; Sección 205, Archivo Municipal, Seville.

82. Leg. 5069, ACM; Nieto Manjón, *La Lidia,* p. 292. In 1912 there were only fourteen bids, but they ranged from 21,700 pesetas to 265,228. *La Coleta,* 10 November 1912.

83. R. de Rojas y Solís, *Anales de la plaza de toros de Sevilla, 1730-1835* (Seville, 1907), pp. 209-214.

84. Rojas y Solís, *Anales,* pp. 105-106. This was true in Madrid as late as 1841. See the posters in ACM, Leg. 5068.

85. P. Romero de Solís, "El papel de la nobleza en la invención de las ganaderías de reses bravas," in *Arte y tauromaquia* (Madrid, 1983), p. 41; E. Ucelay da Cal, "The Influence of Animal Breeding on Political Racism," *History of European Ideas,* 1992, p. 718.

86. M. López Martínez, *Diccionario enciclopédico de agricultura, ganadería e industrias rurales* (Madrid, 1889), vol. 8, p. 387.

87. Ibid., p. 389.

88. Romero de Solís, "El papel," p. 56.

89. Cabrera Bonet and Artigas, *Los toros,* pp. 249-263.

90. Shubert, *Social History,* pp. 60-77.

91. L. Fernández Salcedo, *Trece ganaderos románticos* (Madrid, 1987), pp. 26-28.

92. J. M. Sotomayor, *Miura: Siglo y medio de casta, 1842–1992* (Madrid, 1992), pp. 33-38.

93. Jesús Cruz, *Gentlemen, Bourgeois and Revolutionaries* (Cambridge, 1996).

94. Fernández Torres, "Recuerdos," in *La Tauromaquia en Colmenar el Viejo* (Colmenar, 1994), pp. 104-105.

95. Rojas y Solís, *Anales,* pp. 75-214.

96. Leg. 5052, 5056, 5061, 5062, ACM; *Los grandes sucesos de la vida tauromaca de Lagartijo* (Madrid, nd), p. 165.

97. *Los grandes sucesos,* pp. 76-77; Leg. 339, Diversas colecciones, AHN.

98. The articulation of a fully national market has been much debated in Spanish economic history. See, for example, the sources listed in the following note.

99. J. Simpson, "Los límites del crecimiento agrario: España, 1860-1936," in V. Zamagni and L. Prados de la Escosura, eds., *El desarrollo económico en la Europa del sur* (Madrid, 1992), p. 113; R. Garrabou, "La crisis agraria española de finales del siglo XIX," in R. Garrabou and J. Sanz, eds., *Historia agraria de la España contemporánea* (Madrid, 1985), vol. 2, pp. 477-542.

100. M. Serrano García-Vao, *Toros y toreros en 1910* (Madrid, 1910), p. 253.

101. *El Toreo,* 19 February 1894. There were another fifty-eight ranches whose bulls had yet to appear in Madrid. Ibid., 26 February 1894.

102. *Datos para escribir la historia de las ganaderías bravas de España, por un aficionado* (Madrid, 1876), p. 64.

103. *El Toreo,* 6 February 1893. See chapter 4.

104. Archivo Municipal de la Villa AMV, 3-III-36, Secretaría.

105. *Datos para escribir,* pp. 59, 24-25.

106. *Divisas y coletas* (Madrid, 1908), pp. 25-26, 49-50, 35-36.

107. Fernández Torres, "Recuerdos," pp. 101-110.

108. Cited in ibid., p. 112.

109. Ibid., pp. 112-114.

110. *Divisas y coletas.*

111. Cabrera Bonet and Artigas, *Los toros,* p. 210.

112. F. Pontes, *Reseña general de las corridas de toros verificadas en la Plaza de Madrid en el año 1851* (Madrid, 1851), p. 11; *Estado general de todas las suertes ejecutadas en las corridas de toros que se han celebrado en esta Corte* (Madrid, 1865).

113. A. Moreno de la Cova, "La tauromaquia colmenareña vista por un ganadero andaluz," in *La tauromaquia en Colmenar,* pp. 235-236.

114. *Los toros de bandera* (Madrid, 1910).

115. Cossío, *Los toros,* vol. 1, pp. 351-352.

116. See chapter 2.

117. V. Pérez de Laborda Villanueva, *Historia de una ganadería navarra de toros bravos en el siglo XIX* (Tudela, 1982), pp. 219-220.

118. Ibid., p. 222.

119. Fernández Torres, "Recuerdos," p. 122.

120. J. de la Loma, *Desde la barrera* (Madrid, 1910), p. 68. J. M. Sánchez Vigil and M. Durán Blázquez, *Luis Mazantini, el señorito loco* (Madrid, 1993), pp. 196-201; Nieto Manjón, *La Lidia,* pp. 39-40.

121. Nieto Manjón, *La Lidia.,* pp. 112-113.

122. J. Carrelero y Burgos, *Los toros de la muerte* (Madrid, 1909), p. 22; Diversas colecciones, Autógrafos toreros, AHN; Manjón, *La Lidia,* p. 87.

123. *Estatutos de la Sociedad Unión de Criadores de Toros de Lidia* (Madrid, 1920).

124. *Divisas y coletas* (Madrid, 1908), pp. 25-26; Carralero y Burgos, *Los toros de la muerte,* pp. 18-19.

125. Carrelero y Burgos, *Los toros,* pp. 18-19.

126. Cited in ibid., pp. 61-63.

127. The number of Miura bulls that were fought did decline a bit, to 86 in 1909 and 62 in 1910, but in 1911 and 1912 they were at record highs of 118 and 110. Sotomayor, *Miura,* p. 410.

128. Ruiz Morales, D., *Documentos historicos taurinos* (Madrid, 1971), pp. 132-136.

129. Leg. 339, Diversas colecciones, Autógrafos toreros, AHN. Emphasis added.

130. Leg. 339, Diversas colecciones, AHN.

131. *La Correspondencia de España,* 7, 9, 12 June 1875.

132. J. Francos Rodríguez, *De las memorias de un gacetillero* (Madrid, 1895), vol. 1, p. 114. He describes García as "having disappeared many years ago, leaving no memory other than that of having thrown himself into killing with extraordinary valor and violence."

133. Protocolo 25507, fol. 98-100 (9 July 1847); Protocolo 24526, fol. 225-227, (17 August 1841), APM.

134. Cossío, *Los toros,* vol. 1, p. 594.

135. Manjón, *La Lidia,* pp. 297-298.

136. Cossío, *Los toros,* vol. 1, pp. 594–595. On 27 December 1902, *El Toreo Chico* reported that there was talk of "the most important promoters getting together to strengthen themselves against the demands of certain bullfighters." Its comment took verse form: "I say, gentlemen /Do matadors still exist / Who dare to make demands? / Should they not meet their obligations? / Would they not be better for it?"

137. F. López Izquierdo, *Plazas de toros de Madrid* (Madrid, 1985), pp. 146–149.

138. Juan Belmonte, *Juan Belmonte, Killer of Bulls* (New York, 1937), pp. 306, 323.

139. J. Alvarez Junco, *El Emperador del Paralelo* (Madrid, 1990), p. 63.

140. L. Díaz, *La radio en España* (Madrid, 1997), p. 129.

141. Cabrera Bonet and Artigas, *Los toros,* annex 65, pp. 209–211.

142. Luis Carmena y Millán, "El periodismo taurino," in *Homenaje a Menéndez y Pelayo* (Madrid, 1899), pp. 309–361. There were also twenty published in Mexico City, fifteen in Lisbon, six in Nîmes, and three in Paris.

143. Cesar Jalón, *Memorias de Clarito* (Madrid, 1972), p. 345.

144. Antonio Viérgol, *La matadora* (Madrid, 1903), p. 9.

145. *El Toreo,* 27 October 1874. The following March the case was bogged down in the courts. Ibid., 13 March 1875.

146. *La Lidia,* 7 May 1888. *El Toreo Chico,* 5 July 1902.

147. *El Toreo Chico,* 11 June 1904.

148. *El Toreo Chico,* 7 June 1902. Emphasis in the original.

149. Manjón, *La Lidia,* pp. 311–312.

150. Alvarez Junco, *El Emperador,* pp. 61–63.

151. *El Alabardero,* 12, 19 April 1879.

152. *Don Jacinto,* 25 September, 9 October 1905. Emphasis in the original.

153. Manjón, *La Lidia,* p. 293.

154. M. Serrano García-Vao, *Toros y toreros en 1910* (Madrid, 1910), p. 235.

155. *El Toreo Chico,* 22 November 1902. See also Serrano García-Vao, *Toros y toreros,* p. 8.

156. *El Enano,* 21 November 1897.

157. *El Toreo,* 23 March 1885; *El Toreo Chico,* 12, 19 March 1903.

158. *Censo de la ganadería de España* (Madrid, 1868), p. xvi.

Notes to Chapter Two

1. Cited in Manjón, *La Lidia,* p. 165.

2. Guillaume-Alonso, *Tauromaquia,* pp. 161–165.

3. Ibid., p. 77; DFSA, *Corridas,* p. 58.

4. On *funciones reales,* see chapter 6.

5. Rojas y Solís, *Anales,* pp. 117, 224.

6. Ibid., p. 224.

7. Ibid., pp. 82–148; Toro Buiza, *Sevilla en la historia del toreo* (Seville, 1947), p. 183.

8. Herranz Estoduto, *Orígenes de la plaza de toros de Zaragoza (1764-1818)* (Zaragoza, 1978), pp. 59–61.

9. Rojas y Solís, *Anales*, pp. 114, 152.

10. DFSA, *Corridas*, p. 99; Sánchez Neira, *El toreo*, p. 220.

11. Leg. 339, Diversas colecciones, AHN.

12. Po 28502, fol 30ff, AHPM.

13. Cossío, *Los toros*, vol. 1, pp. 583–585.

14. Leg. 339, Diversas colecciones, AHN.

15. Cossío, *Los toros*, vol. 1, p. 485.

16. Sánchez Neira, *El toreo*, vol. 2, p. 36; M. Ortiz Blasco, *Tauromaquia A-Z* (Madrid, 1991), vol. 1, p. 467; *El Tendido,* 29 October 1882.

17. Po 36620, fol. 3404–7, AHPM.

18. Cossío, *Los toros*, vol. 1, pp. 586–587.

19. Montes, *Tauromaquia,* pp. 271–272; Cossío, *Los toros,* vol. 1, p. 580; Sánchez Neira, *El toreo,* pp. 295–297.

20. Sánchez Vigil and Duán Blázquez, *Luis Mazzantini,* pp. 33–35.

21. Bleu, *Antes y después,* pp. 226–226.

22. Belmonte, *Juan Belmonte,* pp. 117–120.

23. Ibid., pp. 121–122.

24. Ibid., pp. 154–164.

25. Angel Carmona, *Temperamento* (Madrid, nd), pp. 81–85, 57–59, 71–72.

26. Manjón, *La Lidia,* pp. 216, 236, 202.

27. Diversas colecciones, Autógrafos toreros, AHN.

28. *La Lidia,* 10, 17, 31 December 1883. Emphasis in the original.

29. *El Enano,* 9, 12, 16 May 1901.

30. J. del Río del Val, *Los banderilleros y el sindicalismo* (Madrid, 1923).

31. *Estatutos del Centro Taurino de Sevilla* (Seville, 1899), p. 11; Jalón, *Memorias,* pp. 27, 19.

32. J. de Bonifaz, *Víctimas de la fiesta* (Madrid, 1991). Using somewhat different numbers, Bayarat has calculated that between 1814 and 1911 there was one matador killed every 4.9 years compared to one every 2.4 years for the period 1912–1947 and one every 11.75 years for 1948–1994. By calculating the number of deaths in terms of the number of bulls fought, he comes up with one per 4,467 between 1901 and 1947 and one per 37,033 from 1948 to 1993. Bayarat, "Comme se construit un mythe," pp. 323–324.

33. Cossío, *Los toros,* vol. 1, p. 580.

34. Bayarat, "Comme se construit un mythe," pp. 323–324.

35. See the Appendix for the data on which these observations are based and how they were derived.

36. See below, p. 80.

37. Cossío, *Los toros,* pp. 486–487, 380–381.

38. Information taken from Sánchez Neira, *El toreo.*

39. Cited in Cossío, *Los toros,* vol. 1, p. 588.

40. Cossío, *Los toros,* vol. 3, pp. 362–389, 690–695; Bennassar, *La tauromachie* (Paris, 1993), pp. 142–143.

41. Carmona, *Temperamento,* p. 30. Emphasis in the original.

42. Belmonte, *Juan Belmonte,* p. 155.

43. Sánchez Vigil and Durán Blázquez, *Luis Mazzantini,* p. 31. Emphasis added.

44. Leg. 5021, 5033, 5049, ACM; Sección 205, ARMS; D. Ringrose, *Madrid and the Spanish Economy* (Berkeley, 1983), pp. 80–82. With the exception of that for royal councilors, the incomes mentioned are from 1757; by 1790 some inflation had set in, but the earlier figures remain a good basis for comparison. Personal communication from David Ringrose.

45. Leg. 339, Diversas colecciones, AHN.

46. Leg. 5033, ACM; Rojas y Solís, *Anales,* pp. 157, 181.

47. Leg. 5057, 5059, 5061, ACM.

48. The graph is based on the following contracts found in the notarial archive of Madrid (AHPM). Francisco Arjona Herrera: Po 24526, fol. 214–7, 284–5, Po 25507, fol. 98–100, 355–6, 539–40, 685–6; Francisco Montes, Po 24526, fol. 305–8; Cayetano Sanz, Po 26696, fol. 66; Antonio Sánchez, "El Tato," Po 26696, fol. 502, 761, Po 28502, fol. 36–9; Francisco Arjona Reyes, Po 28502, fol. 68–71; Rafael Molina, "Lagartijo," Po 28502, fol. 304–7; J. Sánchez del Campo, "Cara Ancha," Po 34837, fol. 1531–9, Po 34839, fol. 960–8; Angel Pastor, Po 34714, fol. 2310–6; Luis Mazzantini, Po 36276, fol. 993–8.

49. Based on contracts for: Juan Yust, Po 24526, fol. 271–2; El Chiclanero, Po 25328, fol. 747–9; Cayetano Sanz, Po 26042, fol. 38–41, Po 26694, fol. 70–1, Po 26695, fol. 43–6; Antonio Sánchez, "el Tato," Po 28502, f. 201; Antonio Carmona, Po 28502, fol. 191–9; Rafael Molina, "Lagartijo," Po 31223, fol. 21–32 Po 36020, fol. 3538–94; J. Sánchez del Campo, Po 34842, fol. 3–14, Po 38730, fol. 173–88; Francisco Arjona Reyes, Po 35116, fol. 9–19; Salvador Sánchez, "Frascuelo," Po 35730, fol. 413, Po 36020, fol. 3410–4; Luis Mazzantini, Po 36667, fol. 2841–7, AHPM.

50. Po 36020, fol. 3538–94, AHPM.

51. Castañedo, *Torerías de la tierra,* pp. 93–4, 109.

52. *El Tendido,* 20 September 1882.

53. *El Toreo,* 16 March 1896; Po 36276 fol. 993–98, AHPM.

54. H. Cunningham, "Leisure and Culture," in *Cambridge Social History of Britain* (Cambridge, 1990), vol. 2, p. 334; R. Bidwell, *Currency Conversion Tables* (London, 1970), p. 45. The exchange rate was 25 pesetas to the pound.

55. H. Seymour, *Baseball. The Golden Age* (New York, 1981), p. 428; Belmonte, *Juan Belmonte,* p. 306. Before World War I, the prevailing rate of exchange was around 5 pesetas to the dollar, but the peseta lost value consistently through the 1920s, reaching 7.5 in January 1930.

56. Doctor Thebussem (pseud), *Un triste capeo* (Madrid, 1892), pp. 95–99; Cruz, *Gentlemen, Bourgeois and Revolutionaries,* Appendix B, pp. 294–315.

57. Sig. 2, fol. 293–307, Protocolos, Chiclana, Archivo Histórico Provincial de Cádiz. A document from 1861 put the value of the son's inheritance at 574,214 reales.

58. Cruz, *Gentlemen, Bourgeois and Revolutionaries*, Appendix B, pp. 294–315.

59. *El Liberal,* 10 March 1898; M. J. González, *El universo conservador de Antonio Maura* (Madrid, 1997), p. 29.

60. Sánchez Neira, *El Toreo,* vol. 2, pp. 283–284.

61. A. Carmona, *Directorio taurino y anécdotas con . . . mucho tomate* (Madrid, 1945), p. 29; Sánchez Neira, *El toreo,* vol. 2, pp. 275–276; 263–267.

62. Cossío, *Los toros,* vol. 1, pp. 930–931; *El Imparcial,* 14 October 1904.

63. A. de María y Campos, *Ponciano: El torero con bigotes* (Mexico City, 1943), pp. 27–38.

64. *Historia de la plaza de toros de Madrid* (Madrid, 1879), p. 19; Bleu, *Antes y después,* p. 131; Belmonte, *Juan Belmonte.*

65. de María y Campos, *Ponciano,* p. 122; Belmonte, *Juan Belmonte,* pp. 202, 214; W. Beezley, *Judas at the Jockey Club* (Lincoln, 1987), pp. 13–66. Not all Mexicans joined in the adulation of Mazzantini; see chapter 6.

66. Sánchez Neira, *El toreo,* pp. 503–508.

67. Ibid., pp. 377–386, 463–471.

68. Ibid., pp. 17–19, 455–462.

69. Ibid., pp. 327–339.

70. Ibid., pp. 371–376.

71. V. Bagüés, *Siluetas taurinas* (Barcelona, 1924), pp. 7–13.

72. Serrano García-Vao, *Toros y toreros en 1905* (Madrid, 1905), p. 9.

73. Manjón, *La Lidia,* p. 130.

74. Bagüés, *Siluetas,* pp. 86–91, 48–58, 14–19.

75. Ibid., pp. 25–30, 7–13.

76. Carmona, *Temperamento,* pp. 103, 137, 153–54, 163.

77. Ibid., pp. 164–66, 185, 196.

78. Manjón, *La Lidia,* pp. 130–131, 135.

79. Edmondo de Amicis, *Spain and the Spaniards* (Philadelphia, 1895), pp. 239–241.

80. *Los Toros,* 25 November 1909; Uría, *Una historia social del ocio,* p. 126.

81. See chapter 1.

82. A. Broajos Garrido, "La fotografía de prensa como fuente histórica," *Ayer,* 1996, p. 74.

83. Bleu, *Antes y después,* pp. 175–177.

84. *Los grandes sucesos,* pp. 276–277.

85. *La Correspondencia de España,* 9 June 1869.

86. Fernández Torres, "Recuerdos de una familia ganadera," p. 106.

87. Bleu, *Antes y después,* p. 89; Sánchez Neira, *El Toreo,* p. 385. See also *La Nueva Lidia,* 31 October 1884.

88. Carmona González, *Temperamento*, p. 36.

89. Andrés Amorós, *Lenguaje taurino y sociedad* (Madrid, 1990), p. 177. *El Tendido*, 24 November 1882; *La Lidia*, 10 November 1884. The Virgin of the Pillar is one of the most important in Spain, and her feast day, October 12, has long been a major religious holiday.

90. L. Redondo, *Guerrita. Su tiempo y su retirada* (Madrid, 1899), pp. 285–287; J. de la Loma, *Desde la barrera* (Madrid, 1910), p. 45. Camisero cut his coleta without ceremony and without witnesses. He sent it to his mother.

91. Amorós, *Lenguaje*, pp. 177–178. "Hacer coleo" is a humorous jab that equates the pigtail with the penis.

92. This, and the following paragraph, are based on A. González Troyano, *El torero, héroe literario* (Madrid, 1988).

93. Ibid., pp. 142–143, 201, 267, 248.

94. S. Salaün, *El cuplé, 1900–1936* (Madrid, 1990), pp. 170, 177.

95. Pío Baroja, *Obras completas* (Madrid, 1944), vol. 7, pp. 664–668.

96. A. Gallego, "Imagen pública de la zarzuela a finales del siglo XIX," in *Actualidad y futuro de la Zarzuela* (Madrid, 1994), pp. 195–196.

97. Carmena y Millán, *Catálogo de la biblioteca taurina de Luis Carmena y Millán* (Madrid, 1903), pp. 138–152.

98. Cited in B. Gil, *Muerte de toreros (según el romancero popular)* (Madrid, 1964), p. 13. See also Gómez Quintana, *Apuntes históricos*, pp. 120–124.

99. Gil, *Muerte de toreros*, p. 11.

100. J. E. Varey, "Los títeres en Cataluña en el siglo XIX," *Estudios escénicos*, 1960, pp. 59–62.

101. *El Heraldo de Madrid*, 1 April 1853.

102. *El Liberal*, 9, 10, 11 March 1898; *El Heraldo de Madrid*, 11 March 1898.

103. *El Heraldo de Madrid* 12 March 1898.

104. Belmonte, *Juan Belmonte*, p. 283. *Mozo de espadas* is literally the "sword boy," but the term would probably be translated as "traveling secretary."

105. Belmonte, *Juan Belmonte*, pp. 283–284.

106. See chapter 1.

107. *El Tío Jindama*, 9 July 1882. Given the venality of the bullfight press, one has to wonder whether Frascuelo's agent paid to have these two notices published. See chapter 1.

108. Bilbao, *Rafael Guerra*, pp. 85–86.

109. Leg. 339, Diversas colecciones, AHN.

110. See chapter 6.

111. Manjón, *La Lidia*, p. 296.

112. E. Otañon, *Frascuelo, o el toreador* (Madrid, 1936); Díaz-Y Recasens and Vázquez Consuegra, "Plazas de toros," p. 144.

113. *La Coleta*, 18 November 1906.

114. *El Toreo Cómico*, 15 December 1890; diversas colecciones, Autógrafos toreros, AHN.

115. Jalón, *Memorias*, pp. 34–35.

116. Cossío, *Los toros*, vol. 4, p. 881.

117. Cited in González Troyano, *El torero, heroe literario*, p. 157; *Los españoles pintados por sí mismos* (Madrid, 1851), p. 3.

118. Sánchez Neira, *El toreo*, pp. 324, 170–174.

119. *El Tendido*, 1 October 1882.

120. *Ilustración Española y Americana*, 24 April 1873.

121. F. Pérez Mateos, *La villa y la corte de Madrid en 1850* (Madrid, 1927), p. 120.

122. Sánchez Vigil and Durán Blázquez, *Luis Mazzantini*, p. 25.

123. Francos Rodríguez, *De las memorias*, vol. 2, p. 92; *La Lidia*, 10 April 1887; Bilbao, *Rafael Guerra*, p. 9.

124. Carmona, *Temperamento*, pp. 109–111.

125. del Río del Val, *Los banderilleros*, p. 9. Emphasis in the original.

126. *El Toreo*, 5 December 1901.

127. *La Coleta*, 14 October, 16 September 1907.

128. Cossío, *Los toros*, vol. 1, pp. 605–606.

129. *El Liberal*, 20 June 1902.

130. Bleu, *Antes y después*, p. 52; Francos Rodríguez, *De las memorias*, vol. 3, p. 221.

131. de la Loma, *Desde la barrera*, p. 11.

132. Bleu, *Antes y después*, p. 215.

133. *El Toreo*, 5 December 1901; *La Coleta*, 16 September 1907. The line about receiving bulls, not pesetas, plays with "receive" as a form of killing the bull.

134. *La Lidia*, 6 May 1889.

135. *El Toreo Chico*, 22 November 1902. For critiques of breeders and promoters, see chapter 1.

136. Cited in Tablantes, *Anales*, p. 246. This degeneration was also expressed in terms of gender. See chapter 3.

137. Ibid., p. 246.

138. B. Gil, *Cancionero taurino (popular y profesional)* (Madrid, 1964), vol. 2, p. 183.

139. *El Liberal Arriacense*, 6 December 1919; Romanones Archive (Madrid) Legajo 82/48.

Notes to Chapter Three

1. Cossío, *Los toros*, vol. 1, p. 747.

2. Shubert, *A Social History*, pp. 30–37.

3. *El Enano*, 21 August 1898; *El Toreo*, 22 August 1898. Sarah Pink, *Women and Bullfighting* (Oxford, 1997), discusses how these concerns played out in the 1990s.

4. Emilio Castelar, *Ricardo* (Madrid, nd), p. 133; López Martínez, *Observaciones*, p. 19.

5. Cited in J. Varela, "El Desastre de la literatura o la literatura del Desastre," *Intelectuales y nacionalismo,* working paper, Instituto Universitario Ortega y Gasset, p. 13.

6. Cited in H. Ciria y Nasarre, *Los toros de Bonaparte* (Madrid, 1903), p. 54.

7. *El Toreo Chico,* 25 October 1902, 21 March 1903.

8. *El Toreo,* 7 May 1904.

9. *La Coleta,* 15 May 1907.

10. Sobaquillo, *Las fiestas de toros defendidas* (Madrid, 1886), p. 46.

11. *El respingo* (Barcelona, 1877), p. 11; *El Toreo Chico,* 21 March 1903.

12. *La Coleta,* 6 June 1907.

13. *El Toreo,* 7 November 1904; *Respetable Público,* 21 June 1908. Emphasis in original.

14. Carmona González, *Temperamento,* p. 56.

15. *Sol y Sombra,* 13 April 1905.

16. Rueda, "Elogio," p. 400; H. A. Franck, *Four Months Afoot in Spain* (Garden City, 1926), p. 112.

17. Juan Belmonte, *Juan Belmonte,* p. 46.

18. Navas, *El espectáculo,* pp. 234–235.

19. Rafael Alberti, *The Lost Grove* (Berkeley, 1976), pp. 47–49.

20. Castañedo, *Torerías de la tierra,* pp. 70–71.

21. M. Kimmel, *Manhood in America* (New York, 1995), p. 137.

22. Carlos Roure, *Recuerdos de mi larga vida* (Barcelona, 1925), p. 195.

23. F. Bleu, *Antes y después,* pp. 74, 331.

24. Ibid., p. 74.

25. *Diario de Sesiones del Congreso de los Diputados,* 1922–1923, p. 1239.

26. Cited in Cossío, *Los toros,* vol. 1, p. 750.

27. José Daza, *Arte del toreo* (Madrid, 1959), p. 127.

28. Cited in M. Feiner, *La mujer en el mundo del toreo* (Madrid, 1995), p. 43.

29. Cited in Cossío, *Los toros,* p. 753.

30. Pascual Millán, *Los novillos* (Madrid, 1892), p. 113.

31. Ibid., p. 245.

32. Feiner, *La mujer,* pp. 56–58.

33. Mariano Armengol, "Las mujeres toreras," in *Respetable Público,* 7 December 1910, pp. 11–14.

34. Cited in E. Boado and F. Cebolla, *Señoritas toreras* (Madrid, 1976), p. 111.

35. Armengol, "Las mujeres," p. 14.

36. Cited in Boado, *Señoritas,* p. 133.

37. Cited in Cossío, *Los toros,* vol. 1, p. 751.

38. Daza, *Arte del toreo,* p. 130.

39. *El Clamor Público,* 6 February 1849.

40. *La Lidia,* 25 October 1886.

41. *La Nueva Lidia,* 2 November 1886.

42. Cited in Boada, *Señoritas,* p. 115. The verse's humor comes from a play on words between La Fragosa and the word for washing dishes, *fregando.*

43. *El Toreo Cómico,* 16 May 1880.

44. *El Motín,* 5 October 1895.

45. Cited in ibid., p. 60.

46. Cited in Millán, *Los novillos,* p. 105.

47. P. L. Imbert, *L'Espagne: Splendeurs et misères* (Paris, 1876), p. 258; Castañedo, *Torerías,* p. 188.

48. *El Enano,* 21 August 1898.

49. Cited in Cossío, *Los toros,* vol. 1, p. 752.

50. Cited in Boada and Cebolla, *Las señoritas toreras* (Madrid, 1976), pp. 55–56.

51. José Solana, *Madrid, Escenas y costumbres* (Madrid, 1984), p. 261.

52. *La Nueva Lidia,* 13 October 1884.

53. *Heraldo de Madrid,* 25 January, 3 February 1851.

54. *Historia de la plaza de toros de Madrid,* pp. 70–71.

55. *El Toreo,* 20 January 1896; *El Enano,* 21 August 1898.

56. *El Enano,* 20 March 1899.

57. Salaün, *El cuplé,* pp. 125–131.

58. Cited in T. Kaplan, *Red City, Blue Period* (Berkeley, 1992), p. 218, n. 22; Uría, *Historia social,* pp. 112–113.

59. Sánchez Arjona, *Anales,* p. 67.

60. See below, chapter 5.

61. Cited in Feiner, *La mujer,* pp. 41–42.

62. Ibid., pp. 72–73.

63. *El Tío Jindama,* 5 December 1880. This bullfight weekly "applaud[ed] this initiative."

64. *El País,* 5 July 1908.

65. *ABC,* 25 June 1908.

66. *El Heraldo de Madrid,* 26 June 1908.

67. *El País,* 26, 28 June 1908.

68. Ibid., 10 July 1908.

69. *El Imparcial,* 8 July 1908. Emphasis in the original.

70. *El País,* 5 July 1908.

71. Boada, *Señoritas,* pp. 133–146.

72. Edward Clarke, *Letters Concerning the Spanish Nation* (London, 1763), p. 113; J. García Mercadal, *Viajes de extranjeros por España y Portugal* (Madrid, 1962), vol. 3, p. 624.

73. J. Delgado, *Tauromaquia,* p. 20.

74. William G. Clark, *Gazpacho, or Summer Months in Spain* (London, 1850), p. 51; Théophile Gautier, *Wanderings in Spain* (London, 1853), p. 222; H. J. Rose, *Untrodden Spain and her Black Country* (London, 1875), p. 371.

75. Richard Twiss, *Travels Through Spain and Portugal in 1772 and 1773* (London, 1775), p. 289.

76. L. N. Godard, *L'Espagne* (Tours, 1865), p. 227.

77. Gautier, *Wanderings in Spain*, pp. 221–222.

78. J. W. Clayton, *The Sunny South* (London, 1869), pp. 161, 164–165.

79. Rubén Darío, *España contemporanea* (Paris, 1907), p. 118.

80. Mary Elizabeth Herbert, *Impressions of Spain in 1866* (London, 1867), pp. 145, 150.

81. John Lomas, *Sketches in Spain* (Edinburgh, 1884), p. 103.

82. Clarke, *Letters*, p. 113.

83. Richard Ford, *Gatherings in Spain* (London, nd), pp. 342–343.

84. Hugh James Rose, *Untrodden Spain* (London, 1875), pp. 371, 382.

85. T. M. Hughes, *Revelations of Spain in 1845* (London, 1845), vol. 2, p. 330.

86. *Madrid in 1835* (London, 1836), pp. 320–322.

87. Cited in Boada, *Las señoritas toreras*, pp. 68–69.

88. Antonio Guerola, *Memoria* (Madrid, 1882).

89. Cited in Boada, *Las señoritas toreras*, p. 68.

90. J. de Navarrete, *División de plaza* (Madrid, 1885), pp. 27, 21. This last remark contains a play on words that cannot be translated: "una mujer puede, gustando mucho, tener un gusto perverso."

91. Solana, *Madrid, Escenas y costumbres*, pp. 259–260.

92. Carolina Coronado, *Poesías completas* (Madrid, 1884), p. 411. Emphasis in the original.

93. *El Heraldo de Madrid*, 8 August 1852.

94. Concepción Arenal, *La emancipación de la mujer en España* (Madrid, 1974), p. 69.

95. Charles R. Scott, *Excursions in the Mountains of Ronda and Granada* (London, 1838), p. 131.

96. *Boletín de Loterías y de Toros*, 11 October 1869.

97. Mary Lou LeCompte, *Cowgirls of the Rodeo* (Urbana, 1993), p. 2.

Notes to Chapter Four

1. Mark Harrison, *Crowds and History* (New York, 1988), pp. 168–169; p. 319.

2. Susanna Barrows, *Distorting Mirrors* (New Haven, 1981), p. 44. For the details, see Louis Chevalier, *Laboring Classes and Dangerous Classes in Paris During the First Half of the Nineteenth Century* (New York, 1973).

3. Ibid., p. 5.

4. B. Gil, *Cancionero taurino (popular y profesional)*, vol. 2, p. 105.

5. M. Ollé Romeu, *Les bullangues de Barcelona durant la Primera Guerra Carlina* (Tarragona, 1992), vol. 1, pp. 86–89.

6. Marshall Berman, *All That's Solid Melts Into Air* (New York, 1988), pp. 158–160.

7. Tablantes, *Anales,* pp. 101–103; R. Zaldívar, *El Cartel taurino* (Madrid, 1990); Cossío, *Los toros,* vol. 2, pp. 687–700.

8. Alexander S. Mackenzie, *Spain Revisited* (London, 1836) p. 234; Clark, *Gazpacho,* p. 49.

9. Leg. 5070, 5065, CACM.

10. *Adelante* (Salamanca), 5 May 1861.

11. *El Heraldo de Madrid,* 31 July 1852.

12. Pérez Laborda Villanueva, *Historia,* p. 201; *Boletín de Loterías y de Toros,* 31 August 1874.

13. Flores Guevara, *Guijuelo,* p. 45.

14. *Heraldo de Madrid,* 6 August 1852; Jacinto Benvante, *Memorias,* p. 777. See J. Walton and J. Smith, "The First Century of Beach Tourism in Spain," in Michael Barke and John Towner, *Tourism in Spain* (Tucson, 1996).

15. AMV, Leg. 3–92–121, 3–92–78, Secretaría.

16. Henry Blackburn, *Travelling in Spain in the Present Day* (London, 1866), pp. 67–68.

17. de Amicis, *Spain and the Spaniards,* p. 209; Italian edition 1873.

18. Sánchez Neira, *El toreo,* p. 153.

19. Leg. 5065, Diputación de Madrid, CACM.

20. *Semanario Pintoresco Español,* 1 May 1853.

21. Hospital Provincial de Valencia, *Plaza de toros,* p. 124.

22. AMV, 1–97–14, Corregimiento; 3–121–152, 154, Secretaría; *El Toreo,* 4 October 1880.

23. Sección alfabética, Exp. 790, AMSE.

24. AMV, 4–412–19, Secretaría; 2–222–55, Corregimiento.

25. Blackburn, *Travelling,* pp. 67–68. See also Navarrete, *División de plaza,* p. 11.

26. Bleu, *Antes y después,* p. 117.

27. Leg. 5065, Diputación de Madrid, CACM.

28. Ibid., Leg. 5072.

29. *Diario de Avisos,* 1 June 1858.

30. *El Globo,* 9, 18 June 1884.

31. Cited in *El Tío Jindama,* 16 July, 6 August 1882.

32. Leg. 1325, Gobernación, AHN.

33. *Relación exacta de lo más notable* (Jerez, 1794), p. 13.

34. *Toros: Descripción poética* (Madrid, 1846), p. 8.

35. Ibid., pp. 25–26.

36. *Madrid en la mano* (Madrid, 1850), p. 322; *Ilustración Española y Americana,* 22 September 1888.

37. Cited in Lake Price, *Tauromachia* (London, 1852), p. 45.

38. Mackenzie, *Spain Revisited,* p. 235; Lucien Boileau, *Voyage pratique* (Paris, 189?), p. 71.

39. J. Enoch Thompson, *Seven Weeks in Sunny Spain* (Toronto, 1923), pp. 51–52.

40. R. M. McBride, *Spanish Towns and People* (New York, 1931), pp. 83–84.

41. Madge Macbeth, *Over the Gangplank to Spain* (Ottawa, 1931), p. 301.

42. Philip Marsden, *Travels in Spain* (Boston, 1909), p. 198; De Amicis, *Spain,* p. 210.

43. *El Clamor Público*, 10 April 1849.

44. Leg. 5069, Diputación, CACM.

45. Sánchez Arjona, *Anales*, p. 49.

46. Cited in *El siglo de oro de las tauromaquias* (Madrid, 1989), p. 144.

47. Darío, *España contemporánea*, pp. 116–117.

48. Edward Hutton, *Cities of Spain* (New York, 1924), p. 213.

49. José María Salaverría, *Vieja España* (Madrid, 1907), pp. 103–104.

50. Hugh James Rose, *Untrodden Spain and Her Black Country* (London, 1875), vol. 1, p. 383.

51. Katherine Bates, *Spanish Highways and Byways* (New York, 1900), p. 121.

52. McBride, *Spanish Towns*, p. 85; Bates, *Spanish Highways*, p. 121; Edward Hutton, *Cities of Spain* (New York, 1924), p. 213; De Amicis, *Spain*, p. 211. For scoresheets, see also Cossío, *Los toros*, vol. 2, p. 545.

53. Macbeth, *Over the Gangplank*, pp. 301–302.

54. Montes, *Tauromaquia*, pp. 263–264.

55. *Boletín de Loterías y Toros*, 24 June 1881.

56. De Amicis, *Spain*, pp. 212–213.

57. Marc Baer, *Theater and Disorder in Late Georgian London* (Oxford, 1992), p. 185.

58. Cited in Cossío, *Los toros*, vol. 2, p. 689.

59. Leg. 3–466–4, Secretaría, AMV.

60. Gómez Quintana, I. *Apuntes históricos*.

61. Benito Pérez Galdós, *Crónica de Madrid, 1865–1866* (Madrid, 1933), p. 71.

62. Charles Davilliers, *Spain* (London, 1888), p. 49.

63. Mackenzie, *Spain Revisited*, pp. 238–239. For more on this, see chapter 6.

64. Rose, *Untrodden*, p. 388.

65. Mackenzie, *Spain Revisited*, pp. 244–245.

66. Gautier, *Wanderings*, p. 228; De Amicis, *Spain*, pp. 224–225.

67. Gil, *Cancionero taurino*, vol. 2, p. 180.

68. 3–27–40, Corregimiento, AMV.

69. 1–164–12, Secretaría, AMV; *El Tío Jindama*, 3 September 1882.

70. M. Ortiz Blasco, *Tauromaquia A–Z* (Madrid, 1991), p. 1216.

71. Ibid.

72. 3–466–4, 4–28–13, Secretaría, AMV; Gautier, *Wanderings*, p. 228; De Amicis, *Spain*, pp. 224–225; Imbert, *L'Espagne*, p. 256.

73. *Los grandes sucesos*, p. 32; *Historia de la plaza de toros de Madrid*, p. 46; L. Vázquez y Rodríguez, *Curiosidades tauromacas* (Madrid, 1881), pp. 9–10.

74. *Rochefort*, 18 September 1870.

75. *ABC*, 22 June 1908.

76. *El Toreo Chico*, 2 August 1902.

77. *Sol y Sombra*, 23 July 1908.

78. See chapter 1.

79. Sánchez Arjona, *Anales,* p. 45.

80. *ABC,* 6 July 1908.

81. *El Clamor Público,* 21 August 1852.

82. Leg. 1–97–14, Leg. 3–27–40, Leg. 2–228–21, Leg. 2–269–109, Leg. 2–226–3, Leg. 2–228–62, Leg. 2–43–22, Leg. 4–139–2, 4–131–29, 3–25–1, 5–332–15, Corregimiento, AMV.

83. J. F. Bourgoing, *Modern State of Spain* (London, 1808), pp. 356–357.

84. Sánchez Neira, *El toreo,* pp. 405–406; Francos Rodríguez, *En tiempos de,* vol. 2, pp. 149–150. On the "royalists," see chapter 6.

85. Montes, *Tauromaquia,* p. 273.

86. AMV, 1–97–14, Corregimiento.

87. *La Nueva Lidia,* 20 July 1885.

88. J. Johnson, *Listening in Paris* (Berkeley, 1995), pp. 195, 232–233.

89. *Relación de la venida del Rey* (San Sebastián, 1828), p. 29.

90. "Relación de las corridas de toros celebradas en Madrid en los años 1827 a 1831," Biblioteca Nacional, MSS 9505, fol. 24, 94v. See also fol. 30, 42, 45v, 48v, 65v, 71v, 77v, 87, 105v.

91. Montes, *Tauromaquia,* p. 274.

92. Sobaquillo, *Las fiestas de toros defendidas,* p. 37.

93. *La Nueva Lidia,* 25 May 1885; 28 September 1885.

94. de la Loma, *Desde la barrera,* p. 68.

95. Bourgoing, *Modern State,* pp. 350–351. See also Twiss, *Travels through Portugal and Spain,* p. 296.

96. Leg. 1–235–29, Secretaría, AMV.

97. Ibid.

98. Cited in V. Pérez de Laborda Villanueva, *Historia de una ganadería navarra de toros bravos en el siglo XIX* (Tudela, 1982).

99. Exp. 133, Leg. 11.388, Consejos, AHN; Leg. 3–27–40, Corregimiento, AMV.

100. Leg. 3–111–36, Secretaría, AMV.

101. J. Maguire, "The Emergence of Football Spectating as a Social Problem, 1880–1985," *Sociology of Sport Journal,* 1986, pp. 219–220; M. Kimmel, *Manhood in America* (New York, 1995), pp. 170, 140.

102. S. Haine, *The World of the Paris Café* (Baltimore, 1996), pp. 153–154.

103. Ruiz Morales, *Documentos,* pp. 75–77.

104. Fernando de Antón, *Memoria contra las coridas de toros* (Cádiz, 1876).

105. Antonio Guerola, *Memoria sobre las medidas que convendría adoptar para la desaparición de las corridas de toros* (Madrid, 1882), pp. 8–9.

106. Navarrete, *División de plaza,* p. 51.

107. Montes, *Tauromaquia,* pp. 58–59; 264–267.

108. *El Tendido,* 8 October 1882.

109. *El Toreo Chico,* 1, 8, 15 November 1902.

110. Salaverría, *Vieja España*, p. 112.

111. Navarrete, *División de plaza*, p. 23.

112. Sobaquillo, *Las fiestas de toros defendedas* (Madrid, 1886), pp. 36–37, 90–91.

113. Mérimée, *Viajes a España* (Madrid, 1988), p. 45.

114. Lady Louisa Tenison, *Castile and Andalusia* (London, 1853), p. 211.

115. Ford, *Gatherings*, p. 337.

116. *El Respingo* (Barcelona, 1877), pp. 28–29.

117. Sobaquillo, *Las Fiestas*, p. 157.

118. Ford, *Gatherings*, p. 323.

119. Exp. 95, Leg. 11.385, Consejos, AHN.

120. Miguel López Martínez, *Observaciones sobre las corridas de toros* (Madrid, 1878), p. 31; *El Imparcial*, 9 June 1884.

121. Sobaquillo, *Las Fiestas*, pp. 156–157. I have translated as "fatherland" the Spanish expression "madre patria."

122. Cited in Kimmel, *Manhood*, pp. 421–422, n. 60.

123. Adolfo de Castro, *Combates de toros en España y Francia* (Madrid, 1889), pp. 101–102.

124. Nicolás Mariscal, *Epístola antitaurómaca* (Madrid, 1902), pp. 33–4, 38.

125. Salaverría, *Vieja España*, pp. 103–104.

126. *Diario de Sesiones de las Cortes,* 1922–1923, pp. 1239–1246.

127. *Toros: Descripción poética*, pp. 57–62.

128. *Non plus ultra* was the motto of the Catholic kings; it means "the greatest thing."

129. *Toros: Descripción poética*, pp. 62–63.

Notes to Chapter Five

1. Cited in J. Pereda, *Los toros ante la Iglesia y la moral* (Barcelona, 1990), pp. 41–43.

2. Ibid., pp. 43–51.

3. Ruiz Morales, *Documentos*, p. 43.

4. Cited in ibid., vol. 2, pp. 128–130.

5. Pedro de Campomanes, *Disurso sobre la educación popular* (Madrid, 1775), pp. 104, 152–154.

6. Exp. 9, Legajo 11.414, Consejos, AHN. The full text of the bishop's request and the Crown's reply are in P. Antón Solé, *Prohibición*, pp. 108–111.

7. Cited in Cossío, *Los toros*, vol. 2, pp. 131–132.

8. José Cadalso, *Cartas marruecas* (Barcelona, 1984), pp. 254–255.

9. Gaspar Melchor de Jovellanos, *Memoria sobre los espectáculos y diversiones públicos* (Madrid, 1977), pp. 94–98.

10. L. de Arroyal, *Pan y toros* (Madrid, 1974), pp. 18–24.

11. Ibid., p. 27.

12. José Vargas Ponce, *Disertación sobre las corridas de toros* (Madrid, 1961), pp. 140–141, 185.

13. Ibid., p. 203.

14. Ibid., pp. 214–216.

15. Nicolás Fernández de Moratín, *Obras* (Madrid, 1944), p. 141.

16. Jean-Jacques Rousseau, *The Government of Poland* (New York, 1972), pp. 14–15.

17. Antonio Capmany, *Apologiá de las fiestas de toros* (Madrid, 1815).

18. Exp. 2, Leg. 11.414, Consejos, AHN.

19. Ibid., Exp. 1.

20. MS 10621, ff. Biblioteca Nacional.

21. Ibid., pp. 15–16.

22. Ibid., fol. 23–23b.

23. Ibid., fol. 25–26; 43–44b.

24. Ibid, fol. 45.

25. Exp. 8, Leg. 11.414, Consejos, AHN.

26. Ibid.

27. Leg. 321–4369–23, Archivo, Real Chancillería de Granada.

28. Leg. 321–4369–59, Archivo, Real Chancillería de Granada.

29. Leg. 321–4368–20, Archivo, Real Chancillería de Granada.

30. A. Moreno Mengibar, "Una defensa de la corrida de toros," *Revista de Estudios Taurinos,* 1996, p. 213.

31. Exp. 11, Leg. 11.414, Consejos, AHN.

32. Ibid.

33. Ibid.

34. Ibid.

35. Leg. 2–165–147, Secretaría, Archivo Municipal de la Villa, Madrid.

36. Exp. 11–12, Leg. 11.412, Consejos, AHN.

37. Cited in T. R. Fernández, *Reglamentación,* p. 47.

38. Pérez de Laborda, *Historia,* p. 141.

39. See Shubert, *Social History,* pp. 104–105.

40. Montes, *Tauromaquia,* pp. 266–267.

41. Government regulation did not arise, then, as much from a coincidence of interests between bullfighters and the state "in the progressive . . . domestication of the crowd," as Antonio García Baquero argues, as from mistrust of the promoters. Antonio García Baquero, "Sevilla y la reglamentación taurina," in *Revista de Estudios Taurinos,* 1993, p. 162.

42. The text of the decree appears in Cossío, *Los toros,* vol. 1, pp. 808–810.

43. Exp. 15(1), 15(2), Leg. 11389, Consejos, AHN.

44. Ibid. The idea of the Spanish expression is "to advertise hare but sell cat."

45. Ibid.

46. Ibid.

47. Sig. 788, Sección alfabética, AMSE.

48. Ibid., Sig. 790.

49. Sánchez Arjona, *Anales,* pp. 14, 54.

50. *Reglamento para las Funciones de Toros de la Plaza de Madrid* in L. Vázquez y Rodríguez, *Tauromaquia* (Madrid, 1896), vol. 2, 1357–1362.

51. See Navas, *El Espectáculo,* pp. 179–184, for a list up to 1897.

52. Vázquez y Rodríguez, *Tauromaquia,* vol. 2, pp. 1362–1377.

53. Ibid., p. 59.

54. *El Tendido,* 5 November 1882.

55. Ibid.

56. On the social question, see Manuel Pérez Ledesma, "El miedo de los acomodados y la moral de los obreros," in P. Folguera, ed., *Otras visiones de España* (Madrid, 1996), pp. 27–64.

57. Exp. 12, Leg. 11.414, Consejos, AHN.

58. Ibid.

59. Pérez Ledesma, "El miedo," p. 28.

60. Emilio Castelar, *Ricardo* (Madrid, nd), p. 120.

61. Concepción Arenal, *El pauperismo,* vol. 1, p. 286.

62. *El Correo,* 7 June 1884.

63. *La Lidia,* 28 June 1884.

64. *La Epoca,* 8 June 1884.

65. Ibid., 9 June 1884.

66. Ibid., 10 June 1884.

67. *El Heraldo de Madrid,* 12 August 1852.

68. Ibid., 8 August 1852.

69. Castelar, *Ricardo,* p. 135.

70. A. Fernández de los Ríos, *Guía de Madrid* (Madrid, 1876), p. 597.

71. *El Heraldo,* 24 July 1852.

72. Navarrete, *División de plaza,* p. 27; F. de Antón, *Memoria,* p. 25. This debate continued well into the twentieth century. See C. Douglass, *Bulls, Bullfighting and Spanish Identities* (Tucson, 1997), pp. 99–100.

73. Cited in T. Merri Larrubia, "Migrantes en las jóvenes sociedades industriales: Integración y diferenciación social," *Historia social,* 1996, p. 81, cited in J. Romero Maura, *La Rosa del fuego* (Barcelona, 1975), p. 428.

74. *La Tramontana,* 14 August 1885, 2 April, 1886.

75. Sociedad Protectora de los Animales y las Plantas, *Boletín,* 7 May 1874.

76. Sociedad Madrileña para la Protección de los Animales, *Estatutos* (Madrid, 1879).

77. *Boletín,* 14 May 1874.

78. Ibid., 4 June 1874.

79. Fernando de Antón, *Memoria escrita contra las corridas de toros* (Cádiz, 1876). The Barcelona Society for the Protection of Animals and Plants held a similar competition in 1882. Its prize was won by Antonio Guerola, a former civil governor of Málaga. He pro-

posed a series of indirect measures, including special taxes on bullfight tickets and on bull-fighters' incomes. Antonio Guerola, *Memoria sobre las medidas que convendría adoptar para la desaparición de las corridas de toros* (Madrid, 1882).

80. Uria, *Historia social del ocio*, pp. 97–98.

81. Montes, *Tauromaquia*, p. 76.

82. Sánchez Neira, *El toreo*, p. 112; DFS de A, *Corridas*, i–xxv.

83. *El Toreo*, 22, 29 January 1894.

84. Montes, *Tauromaquia*, pp. 39–44, 46–49.

85. DFS de A, *Corridas*, i–xxv.

86. Montes, *Tauromaquia*, pp. 59–61.

87. Cited in Tablantes, *Anales*, p. 239.

88. *La Lidia*, 29 September 1884, 23 December 1888.

89. Montes, *Tauromaquia*, p. 65; Antonio Peña y Goñi, *¡Cuernos!* (Madrid, 1883), p. 367.

90. Montes, *Tauromaquia*, pp. 65–66.

91. *La Linterna Mágica*, 1 November 1849.

92. *El Toreo Chico*, 12 March 1904.

93. *Diario de Sesiones del Congreso de los Diputados*, 1922–1923, p. 1246.

94. New York *World*, 21 November 1897; M. Orriard, *Reading Football* (Chapel Hill, 1993), p. 203.

95. *Diario de Sesiones de las Cortes*, 1876–1877, pp. 945, 1036.

96. Ibid., 1876–1877, pp. 4221, 736–737, 843.

97. Ibid., 1893–1894, pp. 4808, 5609.

98. *La Coleta*, 11 November 1907, pp. 2–3.

99. *El Avanzado*, 7 March 1889.

100. Ibid., 9 February 1908. On de la Cierva, see above, chapter four.

101. *El País*, 19 August 1908.

102. Ibid., 20 August 1908.

103. *Los Toros*, 18 November 1909, *La Coleta*, 15 September 1912.

104. *DSCD*, 1910, pp. 2176–2177.

105. Ibid., 1914, pp. 1213, 1215.

106. *El Imparcial, El Heraldo de Madrid, La Correspondencia de España*, 5 October 1904.

107. *El Heraldo de Madrid*, 1 October 1904.

108. *El Imparcial*, 1 October 1904.

109. *El Imparcial*, 6 October 1904.

110. *La Correspondencia de España*, 8 October 1904.

111. *El Imparcial*, 7 October 1904.

112. *El Heraldo de Madrid*, 5 November 1904.

113. Ibid., 28, 29 October 1904.

114. *Sol y Sombra*, 27 October 1904. For the "social question," see chapter two.

115. *El Heraldo de Madrid*, 7 November 1904.

116. *El Imparcial, La Correspondencia de España,* 10 November 1904.

117. *El Imparcial, La Correspondencia de España, El Liberal,* 7 November 1904.

118. *DSCD,* 1904–1905, pp. 862, 1113.

119. *Sol y Sombra,* 2 March 1905.

120. Ibid., 16 March, 13 April 1905.

121. See E. Inman Fox, "'Electra' de Perez Galdos," in Fox, *Ideología y política en las letras de fin del siglo* (Madrid, 1988).

122. *El Socialista,* 9 September, 4 November 1904.

123. Ibid., 11 November 1904.

124. Ibid., 30 December 1904.

125. Ibid., 10 March 1905.

Notes to Chapter Six

1. For a listing of all such events, see Conde de Navas, *El Espectáculo más nacional* (Madrid, 1899).

2. Report to the count of Floridablanca, Leg. 675, 1789, Archivo del Palacio Real (PR).

3. Greg Dening, *Performances* (Chicago, 1996), p. 281, Jürgen Habermas, *Structural Transformation of the Public Sphere* (Cambridge, 1989), pp. 6–8.

4. Edward Clarke, *Letters Concerning the Spanish Nation* (London, 1763), p. 111.

5. Cited in C. Kany, *Life and Manners,* pp. 102–103.

6. *Times* of London, 24 October 1846.

7. *Semanario Pintoresco Español,* 1 November 1846.

8. Clarke, *Letters,* p. 109.

9. Ibid., p. 110.

10. Leg. 674, 1746, PR.

11. Leg. 676, 1833, PR.

12. Ibid.

13. Ibid.

14. Ibid.

15. Ibid.

16. Ibid.

17. Ibid.

18. Ibid., Leg. 676.

19. Ibid.

20. A handbook designed for visitors to the capital that listed all the important office holders and government officials.

21. *El Imparcial,* 19 October 1846.

22. Manuel Azcutia, *Funciones reales* (Madrid, 1846), p. 45.

23. *El Imparcial,* 19 October 1846.

24. *Prevenciones y reglas . . . 1789,* pp. 41–42; Leg. 675, 1803, PR.

25. Leg. 1–123–59, Secretaría, Archivo Municipal de la Villa.

26. Leg. 676, 1789, PR.

27. *El Imparcial,* 19 October 1846. The Constitution of 1845 enfranchised less than 1 percent of the population, all men, of course.

28. *El Imparcial,* 19 October 1846. The correspondent of the *Times* of London described the constables in this way: "The rigidness of etiquette melted away like frostwork before the sun the moment the animal appeared. The alguazils, who were stationed in front of Her Majesty's box with their faces turned towards her, forgot their respect, scampered away." 24 October 1846.

29. Leg. 676, PR. Emphasis added.

30. *Semanario Pintoresco Español,* 1 November 1846. Also *El Imparcial,* 17 October 1846, 3 December 1879.

31. *Semanario Pintoresco Español,* 15 November 1846, pp. 362–363; J. Santa Coloma, *Fiestas reales de Toros en celebridad del casamiento* (Madrid, 1878), pp. 51–52. The author notes in passing that Morales had done well in the practice sessions.

32. Cited in Guillaume Alonso, *La Tauromaquia y su génesis* (Bilbao, 1994), p. 85.

33. V. Mínguez Cornelles, *Los reyes distantes* (Castelló, 1995).

34. N. Rangel, *Historia del toreo en México: Epoca colonial* (Mexico City, 1924).

35. J. P. Viqueira Albán, *¿Relajados o reprimidos? Diversiones públicas y vida social en la ciudad de México durante el Siglo de las Luces* (Mexico City, 1987), p. 34.

36. F. de Arrese y Layesca, *Descripción de las Reales Fiestas que . . . Celebró la Muy Noble Ciudad de Lima, Capital del Perú* (Lima, 1790), pp. 98–99.

37. Viqueira Albán, *¿Relajados o reprimidos?,* p. 33. This was not limited to the capital: In Chihuahua, members of the town council and other local elites used bullfights to "bolster their own position and reinforce hierarchical values." C. Martin, "Public Celebrations, Popular Culture and Labour Discipline: Eighteenth Century Chihuahua," in W. Beezley et al., eds., *Rituals of Rule, Rituals of Resistance* (Wilmington, 1994), p. 106.

38. Cited in ibid., p. 38.

39. Ibid., p. 39.

40. Cited in ibid., p. 51.

41. Rangel, *Historia del toreo,* pp. 372–373; de María y Campos, *Ponciano,* p. 45; A. Garland, *Lima y el toreo* (Lima, 1948), pp. 39–40.

42. Ciria y Nasarre, *Los toros de Bonaparte,* p. 450.

43. J. Alenda y Mira, *Relaciones de solemnidades y fiestas públicas de España* (Madrid, 1903), p. 218.

44. Leg. 2–412–38, Secretaría, AMV.

45. Cited in *La Lidia,* 11 August 1884. Black was the color of the liberals; white of the royalists.

46. de María y Campos, *Ponciano*, p. 181.

47. Leg. 675, 1828, PR.

48. Noticias de corridas, MS 9505, fol. 28, Biblioteca Nacional.

49. Toro Buiza, *Sevilla en la historia del toreo* (Seville, 1947). In 1841 the city of Seville had held a bullfight to mark the visit of Espartero's wife. Sánchez Arjona, *Anales*, p. 18.

50. Leg. 4–106–129, Secretaría, Archivo Municipal de la Villa.

51. *Boletín de Loterías y de Toros,* 8 June 1869; *El Imparcial,* 8 June 1869.

52. Leg. 676, PR. Emphasis in the original.

53. A. Pineda y Cevallos Escalera, *Casamientos regios de la Casa de Borbón en España* (Madrid, 1884), pp. 376–378.

54. Sánchez Neira, *El toreo*, pp. 238–263.

55. Ibid.

56. Leg. 676, PR.

57. Ibid.

58. Ibid.

59. Sánchez de Neira, *El toreo*, vol. 2, pp. 391–392, 233, 275, 332–333. Emphasis added.

60. Leg. 676, PR. Leading matadors (first espadas) each earned 3,000 reales; second matadors, 1,800; banderilleros, 1,200; and picadors, 2,400. The chulos, the bullfighters' assistants, each earned 15 reales per day for a month prior to the bullfight. This scale was retained in 1846.

61. Ibid.

62. Ibid.

63. Ford, *Gatherings,* pp. 312–314. This claim did not originate with Ford. Henry Swinburne claimed that the organizers of the bullfight held to celebrate the arrival of Charles III in Barcelona in 1759 had had problems in finding enough caballeros "till this man, who was a poor starving officer, presented himself, though utterly ignorant both of bullfighting and of horsemanship. By dint of resolution and the particular favour of fortune, he kept his seat and performed his part, much to the public satisfaction, that he was rewarded with a pension." *Travels Through Spain* (London, 1835), p. 19.

64. Leg. 676, PR.

65. Leg. 4–86–8, Secretaría, AMV; *Historia de la plaza de toros de Madrid*, p. 51.

66. Ibid., p. 50.

67. Ibid.

68. *El Imparcial,* 2 December 1879. The poem is written in a bullfighter's slang, which I make no attempt to reproduce in the translation.

69. P. Nora, "Between Memory and History: Les lieux de mémoire," *Representations,* 1989, pp. 7–25.

70. Ford, *Gatherings,* p. 312.

71. *El Imparcial,* 19 October 1846.

72. Sánchez Neira, *El toreo,* p. 257; Cevallos Escalera, *Casamientos,* p. 544.

73. Cited in Ciria y Nasarre, *Los toros de Bonaparte,* p. 103.

74. Leg. 674, PR.

75. Leg. 675, PR.

76. Ibid.

77. *Prevenciones y reglas . . . 1789.*

78. Leg. 11.408, Exp. 17, AHN.

79. Leg. 11.389, Exp. 83, AHN.

80. Leg. 11.386, Exp. 98, AHN.

81. Ibid.

82. Leg. 4–86–18, Secretaría, AMV.

83. R62284, Biblioteca Nacional.

84. See *Estampas de la Guerra de la Independencia* (Madrid, 1996), the catalog of an exhibition held at the Museo Municipal de Madrid.

85. Ibid., p. 253.

86. Ibid., p. 247.

87. Ibid., p. 199.

88. On 1898 see S. Balfour, "The Lion and the Pig: Nationalism and National Identity in Fin de Siecle Spain," in C. Mar-Molinero and A. Smith, eds., *Nationalism and the Nation in the Iberian Peninsula* (New York, 1996).

89. A. Pestaña, *Trayectoria sindicalista* (Madrid, 1974), p. 89.

90. V. Caballero y Valero, *Homenaje al heroismo* (Cádiz, 1866), pp. 68–72.

91. Pío Baroja, *Obras completas,* vol. 7, p. 654.

92. *El Diario Español,* 13 May 1898; *La Ilustración Española y Americana,* 15 May 1898. The sale of flowers raised 3,035 pesetas. Other incidental amounts were raised through the sale of the meat of the dead bulls, of the bulls' heads (which three days after the bullfight were "being dried out"), the sale of banderillas and bullfighters' sashes, programs, and posters. *El Imparcial,* 14 May 1898.

93. *El Imparcial,* 14 May 1898.

94. *La Epoca,* 11 May 1898.

95. *El Enano,* 1 May 1898; Sánchez Arjona, *Anales,* pp. 56–57. Sawdust was used to produce a patriotic design in Valencia as well. *El Enano,* 10 April 1898.

96. *El Imparcial,* 13 May 1898.

97. This is a reference to the popular uprising against the French occupation on 2 May 1808, which was immortalized by Goya.

98. Serrano García-Vao, *El año,* pp. 76–84. In Sevilla Mazzantini had driven the crowd to "paroxyms of bellicosity" by shouting "Viva España" at the very moment he plunged his sword into the bull.

99. L. Pérez Jr., "Between Baseball and Bullfighting: The Quest for Nationality in Cuba, 1868–1898," *Journal of American History,* 1994, pp. 505, 509, 511–516. In 1905 the

Cuban Senate rejected a bill that proposed legalizing the bullfight. Diehard fans managed to hold clandestine corridas in the countryside. Angel Carmona, *Temperamento*.

100. W. Beezley, *Judas at the Jockey Club and Other Episodes of Porfirian Mexico* (Lincoln, 1987), pp. 14–17.

101. A. de María y Campos, *Ponciano*, pp. 125–126, 134–135; M. Horta, *Ponciano Díaz* (Mexico City, 1943), pp. 118–120; *Mexican Herald*, 1 March 1897. *Gachupín* is a pejorative name Mexicans have for Spaniards.

102. de María y Campos, *Ponciano*, pp. 174–175.

103. Horta, *Ponciano Díaz*, p. 178; Cited in E. Krauze, *Mexico: Biography of Power* (New York, 1997), p. 279.

104. *La Correspondencia Militar*, 27 September 1921; *El Sol*, 27 September 1921. As in 1898, the bullfighters fought for free, and the breeders donated the bulls. In addition, the tram company donated to the Red Cross the proceeds of that day's service to the bullring.

105. *La Correspondencia Militar*, 27 September 1921; *La Ilustración Española y Americana*, 30 September 1921; *ABC*, 25 September 1921.

106. Ariño Villaroya, *Calendari festiu*, p. 183.

107. Ronald to Foreign Office, 25 June 1953, FO 371/107674, Public Record Office (London).

Notes to the Epilogue

1. F. Narbona, *Manolete: 50 años de alternativa* (Madrid, 1989), pp. 309–321.

2. *New York Times*, 30 August 1947.

3. *La Jornada* (Mexico City), 13 September 1947.

4. Cited in Fernández, *Reglamentación*, p. 47.

A. Archives

Archivo de Protocolos, Madrid
Archivo del Palacio Real, Madrid
Archivo Histórico Nacional, Madrid
Archivo Municipal de la Villa, Madrid
Centro de Archivos de la Comunidad de Madrid
Archivo de la Real Cancillería, Granada
Archivo Municipal, Alcalá de Henares
Archivo de la Real Maestranza, Seville
Archivo Municipal, Seville

B. Published Sources

I. Newspapers and Periodicals

La Correspondencia de España
El Diario Español
Diario Oficial de Avisos de Madrid
El Enano
La Epoca
La Ilustración Española y Americana
El Imparcial
El Liberal
La Lidia
El Museo Universal
Respetable Público
Semanario Pintoresco Español
El Toreo
La Coleta

II. Books, Pamphlets, and Articles

Abenamar. *Filosofía de los toros.* Madrid, 1842.
Alberti, Rafael. *The Lost Grove.* Berkeley, 1975.
Alenda y Mira, J. *Relaciones de solemnidades y fiestas públicas de España.* Madrid, 1903.
Alvarez de Miranda, A. *Ritos y juegos del toro.* Madrid, 1962.
Apuntes necrológicos biográficos de los espadas . . . muertos desde 1771 Madrid, 1897.
Arauz de Robles, Santiago. *Socioiogía del toreo.* Madrid, 1978.

Ariño Villarroya, A. *El calendari festiu a la València contemporània, 1750–1936*. Valencia, 1993.

Arrese y Layesca, F. *Descripción de las fiestas reales*. Lima, 1790.

Arroyal, León de *Pan y toros*. Madrid, 1812.

Arte y tauromaquia. Madrid, 1983.

Azcutia, Manuel. *Funciones reales*. Madrid, 1846.

Balfour, S. *The End of the Spanish Empire, 1898–1923*. Oxford, 1997.

Baraty, E. "Comment se construit un mythe," *Revue d'histoire moderne et contemporaine*, 1997, 307–330.

Belmonte, J. *Juan Belmonte, Killer of Bulls*. New York, 1937.

Benavente, J. *Memorias*. Madrid, 1958.

Bilbao, J. *Rafael Guerra "Guerrita": Resúmen estadística de todos los hechos de su vida taurina*. Madrid, 1902.

Blanchard, F. *Fiestas reales de toros en 1833, colección de láminas*. Madrid, 1833.

Blanco White, José. *Letters from Spain*. London, 1822.

Bleu, F. *Antes y después del Guerra*. Madrid, 1983.

Boada, E. and Cebolla, F. *Las señoritas toreras*. Madrid, 1976.

Caballero y Valero, V. *Homenaje al heroismo*. Cádiz, 1866.

Campomanes, Pedro de. *Discurso sobre la educación popular*. Madrid, 1775.

Capmany, A. *Apologiá de las fiestas públicas de toros*. Madrid, 1815.

Carmena y Millán, L. *Bibliografía de la tauromaquia*. Madrid, 1883.

———. *Catálogo de la biblioteca taurina de Luis Carmena y Millán*. Madrid, 1903.

———. *El periodismo taurino: Homenaje a Menéndez y Pelayo*. Madrid, 1899.

———. *Tauromaquia: Apuntes bibliográficos*. Madrid, 1888.

Carmona González, A. *Temperamento*. Madrid, nd. *Directorio taurino y anécdotas con . . . mucho tomate*. Madrid, 1945.

Carralero y Burgos, J. *Los toros de la muerte*. Madrid, 1909.

Castañedo, A. *Torerías de la tierra*. Almería, 1911.

Cavia, M. de. *División de plaza*. Madrid, 1887.

———. *Las fiestas de toros defendidas*. Madrid, 1888.

Ciria y Nasarre, H. *Los toros de Bonaparte*. Madrid, 1903.

Coronado, C. *Poesías completas*. Madrid, 1884.

Corrales Mateos, J. *Los toros españoles*. Madrid, 1856.

Cortes, J. *Historia de la plaza de toros de Vista Alegre*. Bilbao, 1895.

Cuartero y Huerta, B. "Orígenes de la archicofradía sacramental de S. Isidro: Introducción a sus corridas de toros en los siglos XVIII y XIX." *Anales del Instituto de Estudios Madrileños* (1967): 83–97.

Defensa de las corridas de toros y defensa del toreo, refutación. Valencia, 1846.

de la Loma, J. *Desde la barrera*. Madrid, 1910.

Del Amo, B. *Matadores de toros*. Madrid, 1903.

Delgado Ruiz, M. *De la muerte de un Dios.* Barcelona, 1986.

de Sena, E. *Fiestas de Salamanca en fotografías de Venancio Gombau.* Salamanca, 1993.

Díaz Canabate, A. *Los toros.* Madrid, 1980.

Díaz y Pérez, N. *Reseña histórica de las fiestas reales celebrados en Badajoz (1287–1879),* Madrid, 1899.

———. *Reseña histórica de las fiestas reales.* Madrid, 1899.

Díaz-Y Recaséns, G., and G. Vázquez Consuegra. "Plazas de toros." In G. Díaz-Y Recasens, ed., *Plazas de toros.* Seville, 1995.

Divisas y coletas. Madrid, 1908.

Domecq y Díaz, A. *El Toro Bravo.* Madrid, 1986.

Fiestas reales con que Sevilla solmeniza el natalicio del Principe D. Alfonso. Seville, 1858.

Fiestas públicas en Cádiz con motivo del viaje de SM. Cádiz, 1862.

Flores Guevara, P. *Guijuelo: Ochenta y cuatro años de historia del toreo.* Guijuelo, 1993.

Font y Moreno, E. *Los corridas de toros ante la moral y la civilización.* Barcelona, 1880.

Ford, R. *Gatherings in Spain.* London, nd.

Francos Rodríguez, J. *En tiempos de Alfonso XII.* 4 vols. Madrid, nd.

García Baquero, A. P. Romero de Solís, I. Vázquez Parlade. *Sevilla y la fiesta de toros.* Seville, 1980.

Gil, B. *Muertes de toreros según el romancero popular.* Madrid, 1964.

———. *Cancionero taurino (popular y profesional).* 3 vols. Madrid, 1964.

Gómez Quintana, I. *Apuntes históricos acerca de la fiesta de toros en España.* Córdoba, 1897.

———. *Manual del buen aficionado.* Córdoba, 1897.

González Troyano, A. *El torero, héroe literario.* Madrid, 1988.

Govea y Agreda. *Fiestas reales con que se celebró la venida de Su Augusta Reyna y Señora.* Seville, 1846.

Los grandes sucesos de la vida tauromaca de Lagartijo, Madrid, nd.

'Guerola, A. *Memoria sobre las medidas que convendría adoptar para la desaparición de las corridas de toros.* Madrid, 1882.

Herranz Estoduto, A. *Orígenes de la plaza de toros de Zaragoza 1764–1818.* Zaragoza, (1978).

Historia de las principales ganaderías de España, por dos aficionados. Jerez, 1876.

Horta, M. *Ponciano Díaz: Silueta de un torero de ayer.* Mexico City, 1943.

Isla, J. F. de. *Descripción de la máscara . . .* Madrid, 1787.

Jalón, C. *Memorias de "Clarito."* Madrid, 1972.

López Calvo, M. *Historia de la plaza de toros de Madrid.* Madrid, 1883.

López Mártinez, M. *Observaciones sobre las corridas de toros y contra la supresión oficial de las mismas.* Madrid, 1878.

MacClancy J., ed. *Sport, Ethnicity and Identity.* Oxford, 1996.

Madariaga, S. *Essays with a Purpose.* London, 1954.

Madrid en la mano, o el amigo del forastero. Madrid, 1850.

Mangan, J. A. ed. *Tribal Identities: Nationalism, Europe, Sport.* London, 1996.

María y Campos, A. de. *Imagen del Mexicano en los toros*. Mexico City, 1953.

———. *Ponciano, el torero del bigote*. Mexico City, 1943.

Mariscal, N. *Epístola antitaurómaca*. Madrid, 1902.

Marshall, A. G. "Is a Bull Female?" *American Ethnologist*, 1985: 541–542.

Martínez Novillo, A. "Los toros en la Guerra de Sucesión: los inicios de la tauromaquia profesional," *Revista de Estudios Taurinos* (1996): 223–234.

Martínez Rueda, M. "Elogio de las corridas de toros," *Quarterly Review* (October 1838), pp. 385–424.

Martínez Shaw, M. "Vargas Ponce y el antitaurinismo de la Ilustración." In *Taurología*. Autumn 1990, pp. 84–94.

Mérimée, Propser. *Viajes a España*. Madrid, 1988.

Millán, P. *Carteles de oro*. Madrid, 1899.

———. *Los novillos*. Madrid, 1892.

———. *Los toros en Madrid*. Madrid, 1900.

Montes, F. *Tauromaquia*. Madrid, 1836.

Moreno Garbayo, N. *Catálogo de los documentos referentes a diversiones públicas conservadas en el Archivo Histórico nacional de Madrid*. Madrid, 1957.

Moreno Mengibar, A. "Una defensa de la corrida de toros," *Revista de Estudios Taurinos*, (1996).

Navarrete, J. *División de plaza: Las fiestas de toros impugnadas*. Madrid, 1885.

Navarro y Murillo, M. *Contra las corridas*. Madrid, 1881.

Nieto Manjón, L. *"La Lidia," modelo de periodismo*. Madrid, 1993.

Noel, E. *Diario íntimo*. Madrid, 1962.

Oriard, M. *Reading Football*. Chapel Hill, 1993.

Ortiz Blasco, M. *Tauromaquia A–Z*. Madrid, 1991.

Palacio Atard, V. *Los españoles de la ilustración*. Madrid, 1964.

Peña y Goñi, A. *Guerrita*. Madrid, 1894.

———. *Lagartijo y Frascuelo*. Madrid, 1887.

Pérez de Laborda Villanueva, V. *Historia de una ganadería navarra de toros bravos en el siglo XIX*. Tudela, 1982.

Pitt-Rivers, J. "El sacrificio del toro." *Revista de Occidente* (1984): 27–47.

———. "The Spanish Bullfight and Kindred Activities." *Anthropology Today* (1993).

Pineda y Cevallos Escalera, A. *Casamientos regios de la Casa de Borbon en España 1701–1879*. Madrid, 1881.

Pink, Sarah, *Women and Bullfighting* (Oxford, 1997).

Pontes, F. *Reseña general de las corridas de toros*. Madrid, 1851.

Price, L. *Tauromoachia, or the Bullfights*. London, 1852.

Raitz, K, ed. *Theatres of Sport*. Baltimore, 1995.

Redondo, L. *Guerrita, su tiempo y su retirada*. Madrid, 1899.

Relación de las demostraciones de acción de gracias que celebró la Universidad de Salamanca por el deseado y feliz nacimineto del Serenísimo Príncipe Luis I. Salamanca, 1707.

Relación de las funciones con que solemnizó la libertad de Fernando VII Sigüenza en los días 29, 30 y 31 de mayo, 1815. Madrid, 1815.

Relación de las funciones que hizo el MIA Villa de Naza con motivo de la publicación de la Constitución política de la Monarquía española. La Coruña, 1812.

Relación de los festejos con que Bilbao ha celebrado el recibo de la Bandera, regalo de SM a la Guardia Nacional. Madrid, 1835.

Relación de los festejos con que han sido obsequiados los Reyes y Señores D. Fernando VII y Da. María Josefa Amalia en Vizcaya. Bilbao, 1828.

El Respingo. Barcelona, 1877.

Retana, W. *Fiestas de toros en Filipinas.* Madrid, 1896.

Rivas y García, J. *Informe sobre la abolición de las corridas de toros.* Cádiz, 1877.

Rojas y Solís, R. de. *Anales de la plaza de toros de Sevilla, 1730–1835.* Seville, 1907.

Ruiz Morales, D. *Documentos históricos taurinos.* Madrid, 1971.

Salaverría, J. M. *Vieja España.* Madrid, 1907.

Sánchez de Neira, J. *El toreo; gran diccionario tauromáquico.* 2 vols. Madrid, 1879.

Sánchez Lozano, J. *Manual de tauromaquia.* Seville, 1882.

Sánchez Vigil, J. M., and M. Durán Blázquez. *Luis Mazzantini: El señorito loco.* Madrid, 1993.

Santa Coloma, J. *Fiestas reales de toros en celebridad del casamiento.* Madrid, 1878.

Sanz Egana, C. *Historia y bravura del toro de lidia.* Madrid, 1958.

Serrano García-Vao, M. *El año taurino: Fiestas taurinas celebradas en la plaza de toros de Madrid en 1898.* Madrid, 1898.

Sobaquillo, *Las fiestas de toros defendidas.* Madrid, 1886.

Solé, A. "Prohibición de las corridas de toros en días festivos y los Obispos de Cádiz." *Archivo Hispalense* (1971).

Solís Sánchez-Arjona, A. de. *Anales de la plaza de toros de Sevilla, 1836–1934,* Seville, 1942.

Tapia, D. *Historia del toreo.* Madrid, 1992.

La tauromaquia en Colmenar Viejo. Colmenar Viejo, 1994.

La tertulia, o el pro y el contra de las fiestas de toros. Madrid, 1835.

Thebussem, Doctor. [pseud.] *Un triste capeo.* Madrid, 1892.

Tierno Galván, E. *Desde el espectáculo a la trivilización.* Madrid, 1961.

Tijera, J. de la. *Las fiestas de toros.* Barcelona, 1927.

Toro Buiza, L. *Sevilla en la historia del toreo.* Seville, 1947.

Toros: Descripción poética. Madrid, 1846.

Uhagón, F. de. *La iglesia y los toros.* Madrid, 1888.

Uria, J. *Historia social del ocio en Asturias.* Oviedo, 1997.

Vargas y Ponce, J. "Disertación sobre las corridas de toros." In Real Academia de la Historica, *Archivo Documental Español,* vol. 18. Madrid, 1961.

Vázquez y Rodríguez, L. *Crónica de los festejos reales.* Madrid, 1880.

———. *Curiosidades tauromacas.* Madrid, 1881.

———. *La tauromaquia.* Madrid, 1896.

Velarde, J. *Toros y chimborazos*. Madrid, 1886.

Velázquez y Sánchez, J. *Don Clarencio: Año tauromáquico*. Seville, 1850.

Vidart, L. *Las corridas de toros y otras diversiones*. Madrid, 1887.

Walton, J. K. and J. Smith. "The First Century of Beach Tourism in Spain: San Sebastián and the *Playas del Norte* from the 1880's to the 1930's." In *Tourism in Spain: Critical Issues*, edited by M. Barke, J. Towner, and M. T. Newton. Wallingford, 1996.

III. Travelers' Accounts

Bates, K. L. *Spanish Highways and Byways*. New York, 1900.

Bazin, R. *Terre d'Espagne*. Paris, 1895.

Blackburn, H. *Travelling in Spain in the Present Day*. London, 1886.

Boileau, L. *Voyage pratique d'un touriste en Espagne*. Paris, nd.

Clark, William George. *Gazpacho, or Summer Months in Spain*. London, 1850.

Clayton, John William. *The Sunny South*. London, 1869.

Darío, Rubén. *España Contemporánea*. Paris, 1900.

De Amicis, Edmondo. *Spain and the Spaniards*. Philadelphia, 1895.

Dunbar, Sophia. *A Family Tour Round the Coasts of Spain and Portugal*. London, 1862.

Franck, Harry Anderson. *Four Months Afoot in Spain*. Garden City, 1926.

García Mercadal, J. *Viajes de extranjeros por España y Portugal*. Madrid, 1962.

Gautier, Théophile. *Wanderings in Spain*. London, 1853.

Hartley, C. Gasquoine. *Things Seen in Spain*. London, 1911.

Herbert, Mary Elizabeth. *Impressions of Spain in 1866*. London, 1867.

Hutton, Edward. *The Cities of Spain*. New York, 1924.

Imbert, P. L. *L'Espagne: Splendeurs et misères*. Paris, 1876.

Lomas, John. *Sketches in Spain*. Edinburgh, 1884.

Macbeth, Madge. *Over the Gangplank to Spain*. Ottawa, 1931.

Mackenzie, Alexander S. *Spain Revisited*. London, 1836.

Marden, Philip. *Travels in Spain*. Boston, 1909.

Paris, Pierre. *L'Espagne de 1895 et 1897*. Paris, 1979.

Quin, Michael J. *A Visit to Spain*. London, 1824.

Revelations of Spain in 1845. London, 1845.

Roberts, Richard. *An Autumn Tour in Spain in the Year 1859*. London, 1860.

Roscoe, Thomas. *The Tourist in Spain*. London, 1837.

Rose, Hugh James. *Untrodden Spain and Her Black Country*. London, 1875.

Scott, C. Rochfort. *Excursions in the Mountains of Ronda and Granada*. London, 1838.

Shaw, Rafael. *Spain from Within*. London, 1910.

Spain Revisited. London, 1836.

Tenison, L. *Castile and Andalusia*. London, 1853.

Thompson, J. Enoch. *Seven Weeks in Sunny Spain*. Toronto, 1923.

Twiss, R. *Travels through Portugal and Spain in 1772 and 1773*. London, 1775.

INDEX